## Praise for Betwixt and Be

"Powerful and poetic while remaining grounded in the timeless wisdom of the Witch, *Betwixt and Between* opens the sacred gates to the often misunderstood Anderson Faery Tradition. Storm Faerywolf deftly shares powerful teachings and techniques for those who would seek to know the way of Faery, helping Witches on any path find their way deeper into the mysteries."

—Christopher Penczak, author of the
Temple of Witchcraft series

"There are many paths that witches may walk, and they are guided by as many lights as there are stars in the sky. In *Betwixt and Between* by Storm Faerywolf, the light of one of the traditions born of Victor and Cora Anderson's teachings is presented as a flame, a beacon, that will call home those whose souls that long to become the enchantment of the Earth. The teachings and the techniques in the book are also seeds and portals that can grow and broaden the practice of any magical practitioner."

—Ivo Dominguez Jr., author of
*Spirit Speak* and *Casting Sacred Space*

"This daring work will lead you astray into wildness and then back to your self again. Faerywolf's mastery of the Craft is fully present. If you have the courage to claim your full nature, *Betwixt and Between* will give you the tools."

—David Salisbury, author of
*A Mystic Guide to Cleansing & Clearing*

"*Betwixt and Between* is an elegant glimpse into an important facet of American Paganism. Faerywolf offers not only a history of Faery Craft, but also basic fundamentals of good Witchcraft. Full of beautiful exercises and simple practices, Faerywolf leads the reader through their Craft journey as deftly as if he were in the room. An excellent addition to every practitioner's bookshelf!"

—Courtney Weber, author of
*Brigid: History, Mystery, and Magick of the Celtic Goddess*
and *Tarot for One: The Art of Reading for Yourself*

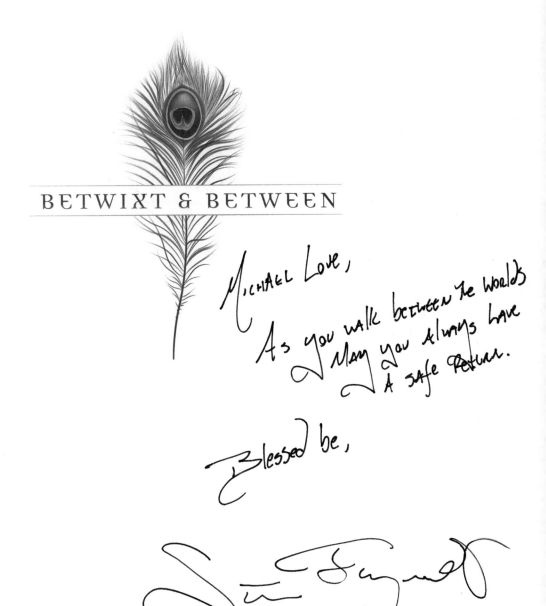

# BETWIXT & BETWEEN

Michael Love,

As you walk between the worlds

May you always have

a safe return.

Blessed be,

## About the Author

Storm Faerywolf (San Francisco Bay Area) is a professional author, poet, teacher, warlock, and co-owner of *The Mystic Dream*, a spiritual book and supply store, where he teaches and offers spiritual services to the public.

He is an initiate of the Faery tradition with more than thirty years of experience practicing Witchcraft, and has been teaching both privately and publicly for more than twenty years. He holds the Black Wand of a Faery Master, is the founder of *BlueRose*, a school and lineage of the tradition, and offers training both in-person as well as online. He has penned numerous articles and books on the esoteric arts and travels internationally giving lectures and offering classes on Witchcraft, folk magic, and spiritual practice.

For more information about his classes, services, books, CDs, or art, visit his website at faerywolf.com.

EXPLORING THE FAERY TRADITION OF WITCHCRAFT

# BETWIXT & BETWEEN

Foreword by Orion Foxwood

## STORM FAERYWOLF

Llewellyn Publications
Woodbury, Minnesota

First Edition
First Printing, 2017

Cover art by Shutterstock.com/58320385/©Excellent backgrounds
                    iStockphoto.com/20381305/©JulietArts
Cover design by Kevin R. Brown
Interior illustrations by the author and Llewellyn Art Department
Part page art by iStockphoto.com/20381305/©JulietArts
Vitruvian Man on page 89 from Dover: Magic and Mystical Symbols

Llewellyn Publications is a registered trademark of Llewellyn Worldwide Ltd.

**Library of Congress Cataloging-in-Publication Data (Pending)**
ISBN: 978-0-7387-5015-6

Llewellyn Worldwide Ltd. does not participate in, endorse, or have any authority or responsibility concerning private business transactions between our authors and the public.
    All mail addressed to the author is forwarded, but the publisher cannot, unless specifically instructed by the author, give out an address or phone number.
    Any Internet references contained in this work are current at publication time, but the publisher cannot guarantee that a specific location will continue to be maintained. Please refer to the publisher's website for links to authors' websites and other sources.

Llewellyn Publications
A Division of Llewellyn Worldwide Ltd.
2143 Wooddale Drive
Woodbury, MN 55125-2989
www.llewellyn.com

Printed in the United States of America

*This book is dedicated to the loving memory of Victor and Cora Anderson, Grandmasters of our tradition, as well as the late Gwydion Pendderwen. What is remembered lives.*

# Acknowledgments

This book would not have been possible without the love and support of many fine Witches and Warlocks. My heartfelt gratitude goes out to each and every one of you who—in your own ways—have helped make this book a reality.

First, to my husband, brother-of-the-art, and coconspirator, Chas Bogan, who has always stood by me with sound advice, inspiration, and the occasional cocktail. Thank you for being my touchstone and bringing me back to earth when necessary. Your love and encouragement have sustained me in my darkest times and given me the strength to continue in the face of adversity.

To my beloved Devin Hunter, who set the wheels in motion for this book to become something more than simply a collection of articles and handouts for my private students. I am inspired by your energy, your enthusiasm, and your tender heart. Thank you for sharing your Craft and your love with me.

To my Faery teacher and initiator, Mitchell, trusted friend and guide on this long and winding path. Thank you for your deep insight and your unwavering support. They mean more to me than you know.

To Anaar, you may be the Grandmaster of our tradition and my sister-of-the-art, but you will always first and foremost be my friend. Thank you for your insights, encouragement, and the many hours spent talking about life, art, and the Craft. Your window into the lives of Victor and Cora Anderson has provided for me a much-needed grounding in the old ways of our tradition. IO Evohe! Blessed be.

To my Faery sisters Karina, M, Thorn, and VeeDub, thank you for the many conversations about your perspectives on our wildly diverse tradition, and for the wild black-hearted laughter that always ensued.

To Soulfire for the many hours of deep conversations about the Craft and a more intimate look into the work and lives of the Andersons. Thank you for keeping their words in print for future generations of Witches.

To my good friend Christopher Penczak, who has always been a loving voice of grounding and support. Your friendship means a lot to me. Thank you for encouraging me to write this book and to stay true to my vision of the Craft.

To Orion Foxwood, my brother from another Faery mother, whose beautiful and encouraging words have given me much in the way of support and inspiration.

To my initiates, Puck DeCoyote, Christopher Angelo, Lance Moore, Jared Morgan, Night Shade, Heather Aurora Rose, Lynx, Christopher Blackthorn, Aaron "Sphinx"

Capps, and Shelley Circe Griswold, as well as to all of my other students who have helped me develop this work both in the classroom and in the magic circle. Without you all this would not have been possible.

My deep gratitude to all of you for assisting me in tending this sacred fire we call the Faery tradition.

### The Sacred Fire

Like a fire so it shines
Bright against the empty dark
Dividing into perfect two
And with light, so then color
A splendid texture rich with hue.
This flame it burns against the cold
Against the snapping madness of the unknown
It warms the blood and stills the mind
And calls the trance upon our kind.
A dance... around the fire
Sweat slick thick upon my skin
I take a torch and place it in.
Taking fire from the gods
I hold aloft the sacred flame
A lantern in the velvet night
And so I learn the ancient dark terrain.
Triple Will my compass true
My life a vessel for Your power
Descend with heart of coal aflame
And let me come to know this flower.
High above it blooms so bright
Like a beacon in the night
To hold at bay all shade and fright
And grant the power of the sight.
Beyond the Outer Darkness comes
The wraith, like curled gray smoke appears
Into the mirror of midnight
I scry what lies beyond our fears.
And now I dance again around
This growing fire of which we tend
That seeds a hundred little flames
As next they come with torch in hand.
And soon one day they dance away,

*With lanterns set against the night*
*To carry then their precious flame*
*To share their sacred light.*
*And though they've come, and though they've gone*
*A hundred times upon and more*
*And though they've lit their darkened homes*
*Still we tend this sacred fire.*

# Contents

# Exercises, Figures, Myths, Rituals, Journaling, and Recipes

# FOREWORD
## BY ORION FOXWOOD

*Stand I at the crossroads at the place between night and day.*
*And, with my witch's finger, open I the Faery way.*
*And stand I at the crossroads at the place between life and death.*
*And bless I all who read this book,*
*With my witch's breath!*

Congratulations, dear reader! If you have concern for the ecological well-being of earth and her inhabitants (inclusive but not exclusive to humanity) and you feel a drive from within your blood to become a Witch, a seer, a reckoner of the old magic … and should you wish to become an agent of effective and positive change, then you are clearly moving in the right direction. *Betwixt and Between* by Storm Faerywolf is a poignant and potent literary force for change. As such, it is an applicable resource for claiming sovereignty over your power and wielding it consciously and clearly. But change begins at home and that is first and foremost within the individual Witch, and occult power is a hard-won treasure that requires a certain level of self-mastery. For all great magical work starts within, leading our awareness to the very core of our being, which is essential spirit, or pure energetic consciousness. From this "original pulse" comes the great animator of our lives and the life in everything.

Storm guides the reader through an enquiry on what affects the expression of this force—our thoughts, feelings, beliefs, habits, etc. In my view as a Faery seer, one should not engage in an intimate exchange with the Faery realm and its inhabitants without having some intimacy with our own inner life. For Faery is the underbelly, the foundation, the preform bedrock of all life on earth. Within it are great treasures of wisdom, magic, and integrative knowing; all essential for encountering and translating the ever-arriving transpersonal directive of the stars. Knowing this is why I am happy to provide this foreword as a gate-opener into this book and the insight, inspiration, and techniques it offers.

At this time in the evolution of humanity, when our complex outer lives require us to extend ourselves for increased productivity, efficiency, and effectiveness, the cost for this is the well-being of our inner lives all the way to the source of our life pulse, our core. Our outer senses and cognitive skills seem to increase while presence, intimacy, and inner visionary guidance continue to diminish and be offered up as payment for technology. In short, for the well-being of the life of our world and the survival of our species, we are being called inward to "re-source" ourselves and anchor to the same pulse that all of earth beats with. In doing this, a sense of homecoming, self-worth, purpose, and familial unity will rise from within and heal the core-wound within … the illusion of isolation.

If enough humans hear this call, we will be unified in a cocreative life with our world, which in turn will inspire choices that are considerate of the life force and all the forms that flow from it. This is the healing power we must seek, and it lives within us, waiting to be excavated so it may nourish our hungry minds with its nonconflicted state of wonderment, peace, insight, presence, contentment, and purpose. Touching it, we touch the source centered in the substance of our own body. But, contrary to many philosophies, this inner change does not get fully activated by flowering our awareness in our thoughts and feelings. That same awareness must marry itself to a deeper part of us that is stellar. It is a spark from the original starlight of our world, which in my Faery Seership tradition is called "the Dreamer." This pulse is our life force and this is also what the deep Faery beings—the angels in the land—are comprised of. Thus, they are our original ancestors and we (both human and Faery) draw life from this same source.

There are several reasons why I feel this book is valuable. The most important one is that *it heeds the call of the ancestors of not only humanity but all earth life.* This call is even older than our indigenous ancestors, though they were guided by it. It's the call of our life force and of the beings that dwell in that state. These Faery or "shining ones" mediate the animating power from the under-realms to all surface world life.

Another reason is that *it is filled with solid guidance on the development of the subtle and energetic senses as a means to perceive a range of life on earth that is too often denied to modern humans.* This "range" was a common presence in the life of our ancestors and they knew that our relationship with it would support life and shape our destinies. To help us, the wisdom keepers of old in partnership with the Faery developed rituals, wisdom teachings, prohibitions, and prayers. These were the glue that held humanity in a cocreative tribal relationship with life and its life-forms. It kept us anchored in the truth that all life arrives from one source and we are intertwined in a web of interconnectedness and interdependency. But sadly we have annihilated or alienated most of the indigenous tribes that had this wisdom, which they gained when we lived closer to the core, our inner spirit, the life force, the soul of the world. That was when we revered all life as our relations.

Humanity has been lulled to sleep or perhaps dormancy on that level of awareness by a type of consensus forgetfulness. I call this "the spell of forgetfulness" and though described as a spell, it is not a spell cast by a Witch. No, this spell (intentional or not) was cast by a shift in attention wherein humanity drifted away from a living awareness of life's invisible rhythms, tides, subtleties, and, sadly, the ancient beings that dwell there. This attention was once like a romance, keeping us intimate, cocreative, and in sacred relationship with nature and her shared destiny. We have forgotten that we intertwined with her, for indeed we are the human part of her. This "drift" was not sudden, nor was it overt. It was slow, consistent, and eroding, and it found its way into our religions, sciences, cultures, and overall paradigms. It rooted itself in an illusion of isolation that has convinced much of humanity that it is somehow distant from this living holism often referred to as "nature," as if exiled or abandoned. Yet nothing could be further from the truth.

In my opinion, this illusion of isolation and its outgrowth of chronic fear, fury, and shame and the decisions, behaviors, and loss of life force related to it comprise the body of the true adversarial devil. You know, the mythical one that tempts us to stray from our inner guidance, which incidentally knows what the life force knows. This devilish force sprang from the human imagination and cages us, preventing us from encountering the fullness of life and modes of that life's expression: the myriad of "life-forms" that include the visible, the invisible, and the gray places in-between, or as we say in the Faery Tradition, *Betwixt and Between*. There are those forces of life and conscious beings that are invisible (or sometimes visible in a fleeting way) and that live in the spaces between our senses, in the "tweeny time" between dusk and dawn where neither light nor darkness claim their stay. These spirits have been known in many ancient traditions over thousands of miles and many centuries. They include such beings as fairies, elves, sprites, mermaids, and even the human ancestral spirits that populate the pulse of life, inspiring the life-guided interior imagination and the expressions of the external landscape.

The material shared by Storm Faerywolf instructs us to engage the flow of the life force and inventory the forces that act upon and shape it from our interior, then engage the subtle senses and energetic states of being in a fascinating and fresh way. Do this type of work consistently and over time you will feel the healing of the illusion of isolation, an increase in power over your destiny, and knowledge that arrives from some vast source, and you will shine brightly with the life force and attract the attention of the angels in the earth, the Faery. And I assure you, a sacred relationship with these incredible beings imparts to the human counterpart such abilities as wisdom, power, inspiration, knowledge of things unknown, prophesy, and healing, to name a few. I should know, I have been married (the traditional name for the symbiosis) to one named Brigh for many years, and the material I wrote for my book *The Tree of Enchantment* and the teachings I share to apprentices in the House of Brigh Faery Seership Institute are the children born of that relationship. In these days and times, these partnerships require humanity to engage life in a different way that inspires the vital pulse of the sacred land to bring forth Eden. Who knows what incredible gifts wait inside you for your senses to be ignited, so that you can weave the magic of the Witch and his/her familiar-spirit? But, as Storm points out, "we must recognize this inherent holiness; our own authority as caretakers of the divine spark of life that we each contain within ourselves."

As an Elder in Traditional Witchcraft, there are certain attitudes in a Witch that I find admirable and of the old ways as I know them, and one of the major ones was role-modeled in the tone of this book. Storm fulfills his oath-bound commitment and respect for his initiatory tradition of Faery/Feri, honoring the folkloric roots of Faery while expressing a stream of teaching that is also as fresh, ever-changing, alive, and vibrant as nature. His development of contemporary processes and techniques to bring the subtle senses out of dormancy and into current and living awareness is commendable. My work in Faery seership makes that center stage because we must unearth these ancient sensory pathways (the roots) and raise them up to the base of humanity's top-heavy perceptual field. In doing so, *Betwixt and Between* supports the resacralizing of the underworld.

Storm also encourages a direct and interactive relationship with the life force that begins from within and flows out to meet the life that flows through everything. The foundation to this is building an integrative understanding and application of the Three Souls, or what Faery seership calls "the walkers." These souls are what allow humanity to work magic as well as to journey, commune, mediate, and translate across the realms of existence. This is clearly a common insight shared across our traditions and there are others, but I leave those to you, the readers and students of Faery, to discover with delight. This is one of those beautiful crossroads where we can meet and celebrate, share and mediate a vision to unify the realms. This is so valuable in the healing of our species of its illusions of isolation and, thusly, healing our beautiful world.

In my experience, not all Feri initiates work with the Faery, yet many do. However, there has not been (to date) a resource that illustrates the mutuality in both paradigms. In those places of unity of spirit, wonderment arrives. Perhaps this is, as Storm points out, one of the states of being that Faery offers … core innocence, or the Feri "Black Heart of Innocence" or Faery seership's "Hidden Heart of Blue Flame." This is the untainted, unstained starlight core of our being that the Faery beings inspire when they touch us and our blood remembers. It is wild, ever-renewing, powerful, fierce, and creative, and it is the giver of true freedom.

Now, the gate is open … read the book … engage Faery. Welcome home to a world of enchantment. I leave you these words shared with me by Brigh, my Faery wife, my Queen … the soul of my Faery work:

*There is a place where matter, mind, and magic meet.*
*Meet me in that place, and let's make the magic that made the world!*

# INTRODUCTION

*Anything I can tell you, I would be glad to share with you, because the secrets of the craft are like the secrets of science. How in the world can you learn if you don't ask, if you don't try to learn? Everybody has a right to know how they are made and how these things work. It's just that the people who belong to the craft, if they're really following the right way, are like scientists or doctors. And they should have the responsibility and the dignity of all of that. But the knowledge shouldn't be withheld from people, and we shouldn't say, "We are the only ones who have the right for it." Everyone has a right to know.*

—Victor H. Anderson (1917–2001),
Grandmaster of the Faery Tradition
From *Heart of the Initiate: Feri Lessons*

At the time of this writing, I have been a practitioner of the Faery Tradition for more than twenty years. During this time, I have received the sacred rite of initiation into our priesthood and have continued to work diligently to better understand the complexity of this wild path by exploring the varied practices from the disparate lines of our shared tradition. In 2007 I was ritually passed the Black Wand, an honorific bestowed upon me by one of the founders of the tradition. Shortly afterward, an initiate from another lineage again gave me this same wand, only in a slightly different form. Though the lineage into which I had been trained and initiated had abandoned the use of the wands prior to my training, after being given this title I chose to adopt the practice into my own as a means to better honor and explore the teachings of the founders. These rites marked me as a Master of the tradition and—in those lines of Faery that recognize the practice—have ritually empowered me to found my own lineage of the tradition, which I have named *BlueRose*.

Part of my life's calling has always been to be a visible practitioner of the Craft. Toward this end I have given lectures, taught classes, organized and participated in public rituals, and performed political actions to help raise awareness of the Craft and for religious freedom. I currently make my living as a professional Warlock[1] offering classes and private spiritual and magical services to the public through my shop *The Mystic Dream* in Walnut Creek, California. Here, positioned on the "front lines," I am able to make myself available to those who are in need the most and not just the few who are in my own covens and circles. The Craft is a means to help ourselves evolve, to be certain, but it is also traditionally about *service*. The cunning man, the wise woman, the root worker, and the Faery doctor all stand as historical examples of how the magical arts have been offered as a service to those in need, and I am proud to be part of this continuing tradition in the modern day.

My work with Faery has been, and continues to be, about cultivating a practical and personal connection with the spirits and powers of the hidden kingdom so as to do justice to the spirit of the tradition that we hold dear. The practices outlined here are based on the traditional material that I received and have evolved over time into what I teach in my private classes to students all over the world. While certain elements have been changed to respect the privacy and creative work of other initiates and practitioners, the essence of that presented here represents a viable vehicle of an "outer court" version of the Faery Tradition. Before his death in 2001, Victor Anderson was outspoken in his belief that the tools of our tradition should be made more widely available, even stating that he felt that they should be taught in colleges.[2] This, along with my own gnosis, has led me to a place in which I am called to present some of the tools and lore of Faery in order to encourage others who may also hear the call to better follow the path of their heart.

When I first heard that call, I knew that I had found home. If these tools can help just one person deepen their magical work and lead them closer to their spiritual home,

---

1. Contrary to popular belief in Neopagan circles, Warlock does not mean "oath-breaker." This was an etymological fallacy perpetuated by Gerald Gardner and adopted by well-meaning though ill-informed Pagan practitioners ever since. For some of my views on reclaiming the word as a positive term for male Witches, read my article "Crafting the Warlock: A Conjuring of the Male Mysteries in Modern Witchcraft," accessed May 12, 2015, http://faerywolf.com/warlock/.

2. From private conversations with Anaar and other direct initiates of Victor Anderson.

then I will have done my job. It is my fervent hope and prayer that others may use the material presented here as a means to better guide them through the changing landscape that is Faery; to provide them the means to create a magical practice that is traditional, effective, powerful, as well as beautiful; and to also better help those few who likewise hear the calling.

The work presented here captures what I have been developing and teaching my own students for the past twenty years. Many of the exercises, spells, and incantations are exactly what I teach as part of the Faery oral tradition as expressed in BlueRose. While this book could never present a definitive guide for all of Faery Tradition (for there are as many ways of practicing and teaching as there are initiates) it does reflect a viable way of transmitting the Faery tools appropriate for use by the uninitiated.

The Faery Tradition itself is a path of both great beauty and power. It is a unique strain of the Craft, having entirely separate origins that predate Gardner's Wicca. It is also—in its present form—a wholly American phenomenon. Its "mecca" lies on the West Coast of the United States, but its origins and influences span across both globe and eon. It is less concerned with dogma than it is results and more concerned with magical power than it is an agricultural fertility cycle.

The main power that Faery offers is an initiatic current of magical energy and consciousness—the "Faery Power." This Power is ritually passed from initiate to student in an unbroken chain of initiatory connection that spans back through the founders to ancient beings of great power. This experience marks the new initiate as a priest[3] of our tradition, as well as transforming them into a racial descendant of "the little people," the Faery race. This can only be passed in a secret rite, which adopts the student into the family tradition.

This process has been, at times, problematic. The power that we share is amoral; it can be used to bless or to bane in equal measure. Like all powers, it manifests in multiple ways, as light as well as dark. The path of the Faery Tradition is a constant balance between the two, a precarious journey across a bridge of swords that can leave the initiate scarred and bloodied if they are not extremely careful.

But there is another power that Faery offers. A body of material has evolved around the initiatic priesthood which *on its own* offers the practitioner much in the way of development, both spiritual as well as magical. This book will provide you the tools necessary

---

3. I am using the term *priest* in this book in the non-gendered sense to mean "one who priests"—one who enacts the quality of mediating divine presence. Some lines of our tradition use this term exclusively, while others use *priestess* as a specifically female-oriented term. There is no universal usage within Faery.

to begin your own Faery-style magical practice. It will introduce you to our foundational prayers, rites, and certain spirit contacts with which our tradition works and presents them in a way that I hope encourages personal experimentation and creative exploration, two qualities that I think are essential for a Faery practitioner.

This is not, however, your average beginner's book on the Craft, as it assumes some prior working knowledge of magic and the occult. While a beginner could certainly benefit from the exercises and philosophies in this book if they are diligent in their implementation, this work is intended for an intermediate audience, someone who has already explored certain basics of the Craft and now is looking for something more than the current public model of modern Witchcraft generally allows for. For some, Faery will fit this need, as it offers much in the way of personal development and power for those who will work with the tools wholeheartedly.

To be clear, this book will *not* make you a Faery initiate. To be an initiate of Faery is to be ritually adopted into the family tradition. Only another Faery initiate can do this, in a secret rite that passes the Faery Power unique to our tradition. Nor does this book reveal any secret that I was sworn to keep, though it does reveal much in the way of secrets, for those who have the ear to hear or the eye to see.

This book offers some powerful tools, philosophies, rituals, and lore to help inspire your own magical work and provide you with a workable BlueRose Faery-style Witchcraft practice. Though it will take longer without the guidance of an initiate and the Power, if you are persistent in your work you will develop the skills necessary to do this magic effectively on your own. The alliances that you make with the hidden realms will be yours alone, and if you work diligently you may find that your magic is stronger, your life force is more aligned, and you are standing in your power.

But be warned! Faery is not a fair-weather practice. We must be prepared to examine our deepest fears and insecurities if we are to attempt to travel the astral worlds and return unscathed. Faery promises power to those who dare to wield it but in so doing it changes us forever. We become more of who we are. This is the real danger of Faery…we discover—absolutely—who we really are. This doesn't happen overnight. It is a process. And it can be slow and it can be hard…it can stretch your sanity to the breaking point, for in fact that's exactly the goal. We break our senses wide open and then we can see. And then can we join the Faery dance. But only if we see, so only if we break.

Faery is not for everyone. The late Grandmaster of our tradition, Victor Anderson, whose encouraging quote opens this introduction, asserted the elite nature of our Craft when he said, "But can everyone handle it? Can everyone know? Can everyone be a doctor or a musician? No."[4]

If you are not prepared to be painfully honest with yourself and disciplined enough to actually do the work, then you would be better to not bother with it. Just forget about us and move on … we can be just another strange and interesting footnote in the history of the Craft and your life will remain unchallenged and unchanged. But if you hear the call and dare to use these tools to look inside yourself, you may find a universe of wonders and holy terrors staring back, and you will have found your true power. Will you stay the course and learn to live beyond your fears? Will you stare into the abyss and survive intact? Will you be one of the few who, surviving the encounter with Faery, returns with the gifts of enchantment?

Will you claim your power?

---

4. Victor Anderson, *Heart of the Initiate: Feri Lessons,* used by permission, © 2010 Victoria Daniell.

# PART ONE:
## PREPARING FOR THE JOURNEY

We begin our journey into Faery in the old way: by delving into the deep well of the bardic and allowing phrase and symbol to wash over us like soothing waters, lulling us into the state of enchantment. Here we engage the poetic truths that are at the heart of our tradition and hold them as equals to those truths we recognize as being rational. Here we embrace the paradox: that two very different ways of viewing the world can both be true. Here both poetry and prose combine to reveal a deeper truth—the origins of the universe and the birth of the gods.

## A Faery Creation Myth

In the time before time, all was empty, still, and dark and s/he who is the Nameless Name, God Herself, floated alone in the endless darkness of the Void. She turned to look into the curved black mirror of space and saw her own reflection smiling back. Moved by the image of radiant beauty before her, God Herself knew love and moved closer that they might embrace.

From the mirror she did come forth, and with the first kiss love ignited into deep desire. As their bodies touched and writhed together, passions swelling to a crescendo of holy lust, God Herself gave in to the waves of pleasure and with her orgasm gave birth to stars and planets ... to nebulae and *life* ... all that is ... all that was ... and all that ever will be.

In sheer joy of being alive, the reflection changed into a laughing child. She was Nimüe, the Flower Maiden, innocent and wild with snow-white skin and star-filled eyes. Her red hair woven with writhing snakes and a new crescent moon upon her brow, she flashed a toothy grin and giggled, the sound of her laughter bringing delight to all the worlds.

Together they rested, and in her dream God Herself had a vision of two bright spirits, shining like stars in the stillness of night. They were circling ... one around the other ... two lights in the empty dark ... the serpent and the dove ... twin flames ... fighting against one another, then embracing in fiery passion ... two flames now flowing into one. Then in the span of a single breath she took them into her womb and perfected them into God.

When she awoke, her body had become the fertile earth, her blood the rivers, and her womb the teeming seas. The full moon on her crown, she found her belly had grown to fullness and her black hair hung down like a veil against the backdrop of her silver-white skin. Her breasts now heavy with milk, she had become Mari, the Mother, and, standing upon both land and sea, she gave birth to her son, the ever-young Blue God, the Dian y Glas.

Proudly naked, clad by stars, with peacock feathers in his hair, a swollen phallus, and a green snake coiled around his neck, he was her son, her lover, her other half. He was the highest spirit, the Morningstar, and his beauty shined brighter than all the stars in heaven. To lay eyes upon him was to fall in love. He began to play his silver flute … and all who heard his Faery music became enchanted and joined his dance.

As he danced farther away from the Mother, he began to change … growing older … stronger … becoming Krom, the Summer King. His head was that of a stag, his muscular golden skin glistening in the light of the day, and a garland of flowers around his neck. His hardened sex upraised, he radiated as the golden sun and shined his love upon the earth.

He danced … moving now back to the Goddess, and he grew older … darker. He gathered the darkness around himself like a cloak, and when he opened his great bat wings he had become the Arddu, the Lord of Sex and Death. With the head of a goat, a torch of fire between his horns, and a red jewel upon his brow, his breath was the coldness of winter and his was knowledge of what comes after life.

As he began to move closer to the Goddess, she revealed her aged face and opened her night-black robes to receive him. For she had now become Ana, the Crone. Crowned with a coven of blue stars, the raven at her side, she guided him to her to meet with her silver scythe of oblivion as his light returned to her darkness, as all things return to that from which they came.

*Holy Mother,*
*In you we live, move, and have our being.*
*From you all things emerge.*
*And unto you,*
*All things return.*

# CHAPTER I
# THE ORIGINS
# OF THE FAERY TRADITION

*Faeries, come take me out of this dull world,*
*For I would ride with you upon the wind,*
*Run on the top of the dishevelled tide,*
*And dance upon the mountains like a flame.*
—WILLIAM BUTLER YEATS, *THE LAND OF HEART'S DESIRE*

The true face of Faery is not what one might think. When encountering the term *Faery,* some might be inclined to draw from images in popular culture, imagining fanciful sprites or cute, enchanting pixies in an array of bright and pleasing colors dancing from flower to flower, a perfect stage set for the delight of children everywhere. While this description might even be true for a small portion of those beings that European folk tradition describes as Faery, it fails to convey the depth and even danger that Faery might pose. Far from being diminutive beings of whimsy and delight, the Fae are a mighty spiritual race of beings that are inextricably intertwined with the hidden workings of nature and the very origins of Witchcraft. The vast majority of reported encounters with the Fae would paint a much more intense and oftentimes darker picture involving themes such as abduction, imprisonment, madness, and even death.

The word *Fairy* comes from older terms meaning "enchantment, magic, Witchcraft, sorcery," as well as "fate,"[5] making it clear that Faery is more than just a particular place,

---

5. Douglas Harper, "Fairy," the Online Etymology Dictionary, accessed May 11, 2015.
   http://www.etymonline.com/index.php?term=fairy&allowed_in_frame=0.

species, people, or culture, and it draws from something much more primal: the origins of magic itself.

Faery is also the name given to a particular form of American Traditional Witchcraft. Since we are a tradition that is mainly taught orally, sometimes the name is also rendered in any number of variations such as "Faerie," "Fairy," or "Feri," this last being the late founders' attempt at differentiating our tradition from the myriad of others that also bear the same or similar name. While I have used all of these spellings in my own work, I tend toward "Faery," as it was the preferred spelling at the time of my introduction to the tradition and it better reflects the poetic connection with the folkloric Faery traditions from which I draw continual inspiration.

The philosophical core of the tradition exists somewhere in between science, spirit, and poetry, bridging these worlds together through the states of magical ecstasy that are a hallmark of the tradition. Culturally separate from British Wicca, Faery is a Witchcraft unique in its customs and practices, and yet it borrows heavily from whatever other magical practices it encounters, strengthening the practitioner and improving the effectiveness of the magic being done. With this in mind, it should be no surprise to encounter in our circles beings and practices originating from Ireland or Wales alongside those of Middle Eastern, Basque, Polynesian, and African origins. A popular saying in our tradition is "All gods are Feri gods,"[6] a statement that speaks to the diverse and deep eclecticism that is at the heart Faery Witchcraft. Much as in the Cunning and Conjure traditions from which our practices also derive, we will use "whatever works" to assist those who come to us in need, always striving to find better ways to achieve the results that we are looking for. This basic value helps us to recognize the inherent magic and spirit within *all* cultures and to strive to work with them respectfully and in concert with our own guiding divinity.

One aspect of our tradition that is sometimes difficult for outsiders to understand is our practice of using art and stories as a means to inspire poetic gnosis. This is the concept of the hidden kingdom and the deeply held spiritual belief that artists, writers, poets, musicians, ritualists, and similar have access to the Fae: the invisible processes of magic and spirit that exist behind what we know of as everyday reality.

---

6. Often misattributed to Victor Anderson, this actually comes from my article, "The Gods of Infinity: The Lemniscate and its Presence in F(a)eri(e) Magick" ©2010. http://faerywolf.com/the-gods-of-infinity -the-lemniscate-and-its-presence-in-faerie-magick/. It is based on a conversation with Victor in which he asserted that Faery did not have its own pantheon but instead worships "all" the gods.

This fuels the very Faery spiritual quest of searching for threads of Faery everywhere: art, literature, myths, visions…they are all equal in the eyes of the Fae. History and fanciful tale alike are both able to convey a deep spiritual message in equal measure, we need only the eyes by which to see.

Though the name of our tradition might suggest otherwise, not all initiates or practitioners work directly with the Fae or their realm. Drawing from the Irish tradition of the Faery doctor, what we share is a talent and a skill in contacting the spirit world and using the information gleaned there for practical results in this one. Refined, this is the art of spiritual travel—of projecting our consciousness into other realms and places that enable us to more clearly interact with spirits, otherwise becoming enchanted with what we have come to call the Faery Power, a current of magical power that characterizes the initiatory lineage of the Faery Tradition.

This power is amoral in nature. It can bless or blight in equal measure, and, indeed, in our tradition there is no religious prohibition against cursing one's enemy as one would find in the Wiccan permutations of Witchcraft. No "harm none" and no "Rule of Three" are to be found in the core tradition. Ours is a path that is neither black nor white. The lack of a definite moral code within the tradition has been well noted by various initiates and teachers, both public and private. While no universal moral code is taught, the practices and lore of the tradition leads one to develop his or her own examined code of ethics, making this practice dangerous, especially in the sense of identifying and challenging the underlying beliefs we may have about ourselves, which if left unexamined could provide the opportunity for our downfall.

Another distinguishing factor between our tradition and that normally found in modern Craft is that ours is not based on a theological idea of a binary gender. Therefore in Faery there is no special consideration for gender roles, no rules of prohibition or exaltation due to one's gender or perception thereof. Where in Traditional Wicca only the high priestess can embody the Goddess, in Faery we see the Goddess as inherent in all beings…sexualities and genders and races and cultures are all herself, exploding kaleidoscopic into existence. The fertility aspect—so important in the magic of the Wicca—plays little role in the rituals of Faery. Ours are about *ecstasy,* achieving states of nonordinary consciousness in which we are able to touch the gods and spirits with whom we are familiar. Because of this, a high emphasis on creativity and spontaneity is encouraged over highly scripted rituals, though both exist side by side in the Faery liturgical record.

Ours is not a path that is strictly an intellectual exercise. *Faery* is also related to "feral," reminding us of the wildness that is our natural birthright. This wild nature is a well from which we may draw the enchanted waters of our own soul's magic. We engage the primal powers of earth and body, of stone and star. We seek a state of wild enchantment by which we can touch the Old Powers of the Craft, which are at their core ecstatic and sensual, and what we of the tradition call the Black Heart of Innocence.

Though quite small in terms of numbers, the Faery Tradition has served to help inform the larger Witchcraft culture through the varied works of its initiates, who each use the tools and lore of the tradition to evolve their own magical practices. Initiates, including Starhawk and Gwydion Pendderwen, helped to shape the Neopagan movement by teaching as well as publishing books and musical albums devoted to the lore and mysteries of the Craft as they saw it, inspiring many others to seek out our tradition and even to be initiated into our priesthood. These initiates have in turn created their own books, classes, poetry, and art expressing the mysteries. The result is a growing body of work that is diverse and ever-changing, as well as a culture that keeps the core teachings alive while engaging the tradition in a spirit of exploration and experimentation. True to the tone of Traditional Witchcraft, we strive to delve into the hidden secrets of nature, to commune with the intelligences that govern the natural world, and to continue to learn about the workings of the universe, just as our ancestors before us did.

Though the initiatory core of our tradition is universally held in secret, there is no consensus among the disparate lineages as to what constitutes other secret material. Some of us are free to share openly, while others insist on enforcing strict rules of secrecy involving any and even sometimes all aspects of the tradition. The result has been friction and controversy whenever someone has decided to share their knowledge and work where it pertains to Faery practice and lore, as inevitably anything published will reference something that someone else will consider to be secret, forming the basis for heated politics as well as the many "Witch wars" that have plagued our modern history.

My own first experiences of Faery were of a tradition that was for the most part open to anyone who wished to pursue the path and actually do the work. Public classes (often for a fee) were the norm and large numbers of students interacted with a growing network of other practitioners and initiates, as the advent of the Internet provided a new opportunity for people to connect with each other outside of their own covens and lineages. Public projects, such as an open Feri e-mail list and a publication declaring itself to be "A Zine of Feri Uprising," ushered in a new age of sharing between the many lines that had previously been estranged due to politics and infighting.

As the community continued to grow, it became apparent that those of us for whom the tradition had few secrets were expected to curtail our expression of it or suffer the insults, or worse, from those who held their particular experience of the tradition to be more true, correct, pure, or even older (a blatant and incorrect euphemism for the afore-mentioned states of being). One might be forgiven if they were to assume that the reason for these differences in levels of secrecy would be because someone along the way (either consciously or mistakenly) began revealing things that were once considered private. When looking more closely, however, one finds the error in this thinking as even one of the tradition's founders remarked, "Faery has few secrets."[7]

To me, this controversy reflects a fundamental misunderstanding of the very core of our tradition—a tradition that encourages one to cultivate one's own "divine authority" and to allow the changeable nature of Faery to be expressed through a bardic and ecstatic practice. Creativity is at the very heart of the Faery Tradition.

## The Mythic History of the Faery Tradition

According to oral tradition, our lineage is said to have originated from a race of magical beings that inhabit the earth, the hybrid offspring of humankind and the divine other-worldly beings known to us as the Guardians or Watchers. These Watchers are described in the traditions of several ancient cultures as having descended to earth from beyond the stars, bringing with them great knowledge that they used to teach the arts of civiliza-tion, science, cosmetics, warfare, mathematics, and sorcery to a humanity in its infancy. They are beings of light and power that are said to have brought magic to the world. The Book of Enoch, an apocryphal and banned book of the Bible, describes them as wicked or "fallen angels," the sons of God who took wives from the daughters of men and whose offspring were sometimes called the Nephilim.

Though the root of the word *Nephilim* means "fallen," most (but not all) anthropo-logical accounts now use the term to refer to the offspring of humanity and the angelic race and not the fallen angels themselves. There is, however, some confusion as to whom exactly the biblical texts are referring to when they use the term. Does Nephilim in the following passage refer to the sons of God (i.e., the angels) or to the men of renown?

---

7. From a private conversation with Cora Anderson circa 2006.

*The Nephilim were on the earth in those days, and also afterward, when the sons of God came in to the daughters of man and they bore children to them. These were the mighty men who were of old, the men of renown.*[8]

In the lore of the Faery Tradition, the word *Nephilim* is specifically used to describe the angelic Watchers themselves, who rebelled against a false god and brought humanity the opportunity to spiritually evolve or to become as gods ourselves.

Some modern practitioners of the Craft are uncomfortable with the term "angel" because they feel it is too Christian for their Pagan sensibilities. What they fail to understand is that the concept (and even the term) predates that religion by thousands of years. "Angel" is simply the English transliteration of the late Greek *ággelos*, which in turn was likely based on the much older Mycenaean form of the word *a-ke-ro.*[9] These terms were used to denote a type of divine messenger spirit, or an intermediary between heaven and earth.

The ancient Sumerians referenced a set of beings that fit this description that they called the Anunnaki, chthonic deities of fertility and the underworld. The name could be translated as "princely offspring" or "offspring of Anu," referring to the ancient Sumerian sky god who presided from the highest heaven and who was the father of all other gods and spirits. The stories of both the Anunnaki and the Watchers depict them as cultural exemplars, using their divine knowledge in order to guide early humans in their evolution.

The Irish Tuatha dé Danann ("people/children of the goddess Danu") is another example of this same set of divine teachers as manifested in another cultural milieu. In this mythic cycle, they arrive in ancient Ireland on a big cloud and bring their godly knowledge to fight and conquer the inhabitants there, including the primordial Fomorians, chthonic deities of chaos akin to the Greek Titans. They then establish a civilizing presence using their highly developed skills of magic and sorcery. There they rule peacefully until driven by the invading Milesians into "the hollow hills" (i.e., beneath the earth) where they became known as the *Aes sidhe* ("the people of the mound," possibly referencing ancient Celtic burial mounds), and then later as elves and faeries.

---

8. Gen. 6:4 (ESV).

9. Palaeolexicon, "The Linear B word a-ke-ro," accessed May 13, 2015. http://www.palaeolexicon.com /ShowWord.aspx?Id=16647.

*Faery* is a term used to describe a place as well as the many diverse beings who inhabit it. As a place it is neither here nor there, occupying a space of liminality, or being "in-between the worlds." As such, places where two worlds meet were said to be secret entrances into their realm, places where the veil separating our world from theirs was unusually thin and one might be able to more easily—or even mistakenly—step through. Where two roads crossed would be one such place, as would a beach (where land meets sea), the top of a mountain (where land meets sky), or the edge of a forest (where civilization meets the wild). Other places, such as caves or within a circle of mushrooms (often called a faery ring), were also traditionally considered to be potential entrances into the world of Faery. Even certain times of the day, such as at dawn or dusk (in-between day and night), and certain times of the year, such as Samhain and Beltane (the Gates of the Year) and, of course, Midsummer (which had long been associated with faeries before Shakespeare wrote the famous play) were once widely considered to be particularly powerful in terms of Fae interactions.

Certain precautions would be taken at these times and places to help prevent possible abduction by the Faery horde, such as carrying iron or wearing bells to dispel their influence. One could appease them or even gather their favor by making offerings of bread, milk, honey, and other foodstuffs.

As a people, they are as diverse as they are strange; some are inclined to interact with and even assist humanity while others are neutral or even openly hostile to human presence. The Fae inhabit what is sometimes called the otherworld, a dimension or realm of existence that intersects our own reality. Poetically said to exist beneath certain hills, mounds, and sacred sites, as well as more generally "under the earth," the Faery realm shares this description with some pre-Christian accounts of the afterlife, and certain folk traditions even asserting the identity of the Faery people as the souls of the Pagan dead.

Time in their shining realm was often said to run differently; a few minutes there could mean years in our own, while extended periods in Faery might be only moments here on earth. Folklore recalls tales of people stepping into Faeryland who return in what seems like only hours, only to find that their family and loved ones have all grown old and died in their (considerable) absence.

These Faery beings further intermarried with humans, passing down their magical bloodline in various forms into the present day. This bloodline brought with it the ability to see and interact with the hidden kingdom, the unseen spiritual reality behind what we understand as nature, enabling those who are possessed of it the opportunity to influence those processes (i.e., "to work magic"). This is the source of the Faery or Witch blood: that ancestral thread of enchantment that characterizes the lineage of Traditional Witchcraft. This is the poetic origin of Witchcraft on earth: the hidden knowledge of magic being made known to a select few by our celestial ancestors and passed down through initiatory processes by various covens, lodges, traditions, and tribal groups, each taking on the nuances of the eras and cultures in which they were practiced.

We are taught that Faery is indistinguishable from the earliest forms of human magic. Since the core tradition is not characterized as much by liturgical observance and more by energetic lineage, it is impossible to draw a time line that would show a linear progression of the enchanted lineage that has come to be called Faery Tradition. Instead we are asked to approach the issue as one might approach poetry, to allow the message to wash over us and to contemplate what in us has changed because of it. Since *Faery* is essentially "the art of magic and enchantment," then we can see Faery in *all* magical cultures and practices, and not just those that are Celtic in origin.

While we recognize the universal element of Witchcraft, our particular lineage can point to certain cultural nexus points in which this magic can most easily be seen. Since humanity first evolved in Africa, we must also look there to find the birthplace of our tradition. From there it is said to have spread out as humans migrated into Eurasia and Polynesia, the Middle East, Ireland, Wales, the British Islands (particularly the lands associated with the ancient Picts and the Lowlands of Scotland), and then finally the Americas (particularly through the Southern Appalachian region). The mythical Faery blood was passed down in certain families with others being spiritually and magically "adopted" into these families by the rite of initiation.

What we have come to call *Faery* describes any number of different beings that all share a common series of elements: they are magical, they are *strange*, and they live practically among us but most often tucked away in wild places or within (or beneath) the earth. Many are described as having an aversion to iron and most as being hostile to humankind, though some will even assist humans if offerings are made and respect is given. Often called "the Little People" worldwide (though sometimes described as being quite large!), their presence has been recorded and named by many different cultures all over the world: the Alfar or Elves of Nordic mythology, the Islamic and pre-Islamic Djinn, the Polynesian Menehuna, the Mogwai of ancient China, the Patupaiarehe of the Maori, the Yumboes of West African folktales, and the Nimerigar of the Shoshone Native

Americans are all examples of this hidden magical race acting and appearing in different ways according to the particular area of land in which they have manifested.

Much of the folklore surrounding these mysterious beings is actually focused on protecting against them, as they were most often described as being mischievous or outright dangerous to those who might happen upon them. There is, however, also much in the way of making offerings to appease them or even enlist their aid.

Witches have long been associated with the Fae. Folklorist Charles Godfrey Leland in his famous work *Aradia, or the Gospel of the Witches* describes the folk belief of the underground Witch cult as worshiping the goddess Diana, who is described as "the Queen of the Witches and Faeries." Since we have seen that Faery is ultimately less about a specific place or people and more about a general state of magic and enchantment, we can begin to see how the two became intertwined in the popular mind-set of the time. Witches were also long known to derive or augment their powers through the aid of a "familiar spirit"; a Faery being would make a powerful ally indeed, and through contracts made by traditional custom, one could work with the Fae to empower their workings. If nothing else but for the *belief* that such a contract existed, the locals of pre-modern Ireland would assume the local cunning man or wise woman was in league with the faeries, or was actually one of the Fae themselves. The lines were likely intentionally blurred, for if you believed that the old man or woman with whom you were consulting might secretly be one of the shining ones you were far more likely to be on your best behavior, lest you incur the wrath of the "good folk." It is for this nebulous association that the traditional name for a magical healer and spell worker in Ireland is a "Faery doctor," and it is from this term that the Faery Tradition derives its moniker, bringing an old tradition into a new era.

## Early Modern History

No account of the Faery Tradition would be complete without the story of the blind poet and shaman, Victor Anderson (1917–2001). He is considered by many to be the founder of the Faery Tradition of Witchcraft. In 1926, in the forests near his New Mexico home, a "small, dark woman" who claimed she was a faery initiated nine-year-old Victor into Witchcraft. As the story is told, he heard the sound of drums coming from the forest near his home and followed the sound until he found her in the middle of a circle with small brass bowls, each filled with different herbs and substances. He instinctually removed his clothes, she invited him to step into the circle, and she initiated him into the Craft.[10] During this experience, he had a vision, despite his near blindness, in which he envisioned a jungle scene with a green full moon and a star-filled sky. The woman became the Goddess, and he heard her whispering her name … "Tana … Tana … I am Tana …" He saw the God as an effeminate horned male with an erection and rays of light emanating from his brow. After a while, the vision faded and the old woman washed him "in butter, oil, and salt" and instructed him on the ritual use of the various herbs and ointments present. She told him to be patient and that "your people will find you," and that was that. The next day, he would recall the previous night's events as being almost like a dream, but he insisted until his death that it had been an actual physical occurrence.

In 1932, he moved to southern Oregon, where he found and was initiated into the Harpy Coven, a group of Witches who practiced the Craft as a sort of "devotional science." Little has been revealed to the public about their practices, save that they ate celebratory meals in a circle and prayed to a spirit of the fire that they called "the Devil" (a reference to the "deva" of the flame, which represented the "soul fire" or spark of divinity within humanity and not the Christian anti-god). After this coven broke up following World War II, Victor and his wife, Cora, moved and began teaching the Craft from their California suburban home and would go on to initiate some of the most luminary teachers of the Craft, including Starhawk and the late Gwydion Pendderwen.

Victor's teaching style was reportedly unconventional. He would often recite poetry while rocking in his chair, lulling the student into a trance with his words before abruptly demanding: "What does that mean?" forcing the student back into a rational mode of awareness. These shifts in consciousness were essential for developing the skills necessary for both traversing the astral worlds as well as returning with the ability to logically examine the often illogical experiences one had there.

Much of his knowledge was based on past-life recall (he claimed full knowledge of previously being a Voodoo priest, a Polynesian kahuna, and a Jewish rabbi, among others) or what he gleaned while astral traveling (his work with deities and spirits was extensive, to say the least). So, there was a greater flexibility in his teaching style than is

---

10. Victor stated that the woman initiated him "by full sexual rite." While there are elements to his story that suggest this was an astral experience, if we are to believe his claims that this was a physical occurrence, then this amounts to what can only be seen in modern society as the sexual abuse of a child—a disturbing piece of Witchcraft lore, to be certain.

usually seen in other traditions in which rituals or customs are strict and handed down in a linear fashion.

Cora was also a magically powerful Witch in her own right. Having been brought up in rural Alabama, she was no stranger to magical folk practices. The rich magical traditions of the American South, particularly the region named for the Appalachian Mountains, was a hotbed of folk magic. Many European settlers brought their folk beliefs with them, and they intermingled with the beliefs and practices of the indigenous Native American population as well as with the black slaves and Irish indentured servants.

Cora's style was much different than Victor's. While he reveled in the attention that his shamanic talents garnered, Cora was content to hang back and offer her simple, gentle wisdom. Hers was the magic of hearth and home, and particularly of the kitchen, where she spent time preparing food she had enchanted, much of it for healing.

Having been brought into a pre-existing tradition, Victor was adamant that he was not the founder of our tradition but was instead a "Grandmaster and Fairy Chief" and the seminal teacher of what might be considered to be his "chapter" of the Old Craft. He held the Black Wand and was a respected elder of our path, training those who came to him in his unique style that included astral travel and the contemplation of ritual poetry.

In the years that followed, both Victor and Cora continued to practice and teach their particular version of the Craft. They lived their lives, raised their son, and taught their Craft.

Another prominent figure in the early modern Faery Tradition was that of Gwydion Pendderwen, the "Faerie Shaman" (1946–1982). Born Thomas deLong, he was a friend of the Andersons' son since childhood and began training in the Craft under Victor when he was older. Gwydion was a highly respected musician and bard; his music touched the hearts of many in the suddenly exploding Pagan movement, as he sang about such themes as ancient gods and goddesses as well as spiritual environmentalism.

Working with Victor to develop the bits and pieces of lore into a coherent and workable system that could be taught, Gwydion set his poetic talents to the task and created some of the most beautiful liturgical material that our tradition has today. His own spiritual interests informed the early modern tradition and were largely centered on Welsh and Irish folklore, as well as Voodoo, which all made their way in some form into Faery ritual practice. His creative talents provided him a platform from which he spoke about Faery and the poetic processes of magic and prophecy.

Gwydion was an active conservationist, co-founding "Forever Forests," a group dedicated to healing the earth through reforestation as well as being a community builder, co-founding Nemeton as a networking group for Pagans and Witches. He purchased some land in Mendocino County, California, and renamed it "Annwfn," a reference to the Welsh underworld, which he then left to the Church of All Worlds, with whom he had long worked. His untimely death from a car accident in 1982 at the age of thirty-six was a tragic loss not just to our tradition, but also to Paganism as a whole.

In 1979, a book called *The Spiral Dance* was published, which changed the world of Faery Tradition forever. Written by Starhawk, a practicing Witch who had been initiated by Victor, this book used some Faery concepts to present her vision of Witchcraft blended with ecological activism and feminist politics. The community that surrounded her at this time continued to explore and evolve based on their shared experiences in trance and ritual. The result was what became the Reclaiming tradition.

Another figure of note in the modern history of Faery is the coven (and later lineage) Bloodrose. Named after Victor's seminal work of Craft poetry, Bloodrose combined the creative efforts of its members and positioned itself as a teaching coven, inviting interested parties to attend classes for a small fee. The work was at once groundbreaking as well as controversial; prior to Bloodrose, all people were either trained individually or in small groups, mainly small covens. Now a larger (and for pay) classroom model was emerging, and this caused some to question its validity.

Like it or not, Bloodrose made its mark. And it did so by its own merits. Where Victor taught with little structure, Bloodrose took these precious seeds of wisdom and nurtured them into a workable system. Where Victor, for example, may have asked a student to contemplate the five points of the Iron Pentacle, Bloodrose created a means to energetically *engage* it—detailing a series of meditative steps and precise visualizations designed to guide the student through specific experiences that would incrementally lead to greater amounts of power, awareness, and control.

Like Gwydion before them, Bloodrose also placed special emphasis on the stream of poetic ecstasy provided in the Celtic folktales and ballads. Studying Welsh and Irish Faery lore was required, and the group produced some striking and invocative poetry. It would also, however, be accused of changing the tradition due both to the innovations previously mentioned, as well as a tendency of some of its members to take a somewhat reconstructionist view.

While Bloodrose continued to grow (it was and remains arguably the largest lineage of our tradition in terms of numbers of initiates) it began to experience discord. Allegations of sexual impropriety with students began to surface, as did stories of spiritual manipulation and coercion. Allegations that were quickly brushed aside, despite the best efforts of some. This, along with disagreements on ritual or theological minutiae, caused a rift between the founder of Bloodrose and the Andersons—one that would never be healed. Things would continue to heat up until sometime in the early 1990s, when Bloodrose abruptly and dramatically experienced a mass exodus of students amidst the growing scandal. The coven's founder pulled back from public light but continued to quietly teach until his death in 2007.

Victor and Cora continued to train and initiate many people over the years, and from those teachings many different lines of the tradition have formed, each with their own approach to the tools and powers with which we commune. Some have placed an emphasis on activism and community work, and others practice strict secrecy. Some are focused on working with the Faery realm and its inhabitants, while others forgo such workings altogether, focusing instead on practical magic or devotional rites. What we all share in common is infinitesimally small—a "seed" that is planted at initiation and one that strives to grow into a thing of beauty and power. This power comes in many forms. The form presented in this book is just one of many possibilities, offered here in the hope that this seed will take root in fertile ground and perhaps inspire even just one person toward a better knowledge of themselves and the Craft they strive to embody.

### *Dandelion*

*Thou strange and beautiful weed!*
*That spreads aloft on wings of air*
*By chance to rest and go to seed*
*To grow with golden plumage soft and fair.*
*When you as angels' gowns have turned*
*We make a wish and set you free*
*Words take flight with tufts of white*
*To land unknown just beyond our sight.*
*Fear not the seeds that spread so wide*
*Though suburban lawns shall scorn your sprouts*
*For all the scorn in all the world*
*Shall hinder you not*
*Thou fairy seed, thou wild flower.*

# CHAPTER 2
## OPENING THE WAY—
## BEGINNING THE FAERY PATH

*I believe in everything until it's disproved.*
*So I believe in fairies, the myths, dragons.*
*It all exists, even if it's in your mind.*
*Who's to say that dreams and nightmares aren't as real as the here and now?*
—JOHN LENNON

The work that is the primary force in the Faery Tradition is shamanic in nature. It relies on our ability to effectively alter our consciousness to allow for direct communication with very real spiritual beings and powers that are normally outside our awareness. This can be a dangerous practice. When we eventually touch these powers, they cause changes within us, shining a light deep within our own shadow, and then we are suddenly better able to see what lives there. Shining this light causes these long-buried demons to spring to life; they rise up into our consciousness and we can no longer pretend that they are not there. True, we could go back to sleep, but we will always feel them tugging at our awareness. They influence our decisions, preventing us from being as happy, aligned, and powerful as we could be. They keep us trapped in old patterns of fear, doubt, shame, and worse. This type of work will make you unable to ignore them anymore.

Most people would prefer not to engage the shadow. To do so is painful and can make us feel weak, but the only true weakness is in not making the attempt to transform those blocks and impurities that plague us, even if at first we are unable to see them for exactly what they are.

We must be prepared to work with those changes and not against them, thus lessening the chances of this process being a painful or even a harmful one. Before we can effectively (and more safely) travel the worlds and touch the powers of deep enchantment we must make sure that our vessel is sound. And this too is a process of molding and tempering…of heating and shaping. Like a blacksmith forging a sword, we diligently work the practice upon ourselves as both the worker and that which is being worked. *We* are that which we are shaping.

We must become skilled at the art of trance. And this means that we must become proficient in the language of poetry and symbolism. Certain visualizations, sigils, colors, words, phrases, and the like are used by the ritualist as keys that seek to unlock specific realms or grant access to certain spirits.

Toward this end, we must first become proficient at those basic psychic-development practices of relaxation, grounding, centering, and paying proper attention to breath and posture, as well as to maintaining a disciplined routine. For those who feel that they are "too advanced" for this type of work, you are in luck: I guarantee that you are definitely *not* too advanced for a foundational practice. No matter how far we progress on the path we must always make sure that we are able to maintain a skilled discipline, otherwise it is far too easy to slip into unconscious, lazy behavior, lessening our power and negatively impacting the results of our magical work.

My recommendation for a sustainable, formal practice is to perform the practices I provide a *minimum* of four times per week, on average. Notice that I say "formal practice." In addition to the formal practice, you should also create an *informal* extension of it, which you will strive to practice daily. Perhaps even multiple times per day, depending on the exercise and the need. This informal practice will consist of doing simplified versions of the formal work while you are engaged in some other activity, such as dusting your house, taking a shower, folding laundry, walking to the bus stop, or even simply while waiting between other activities. This informal work is done internally, without the use of tools or physical actions, and is what will keep the energies raised during the formal work engaging your life on a deep level. This ensures that our entire lives become part of our spiritual practice, and not just those times that we sit in front of our altars and light our candles.

While it is certainly important to establish a discipline, it is *not* always necessary to completely overhaul our lives in order to make it happen. It need not happen overnight. We can take little steps to start the creation of such a routine and gradually build our spiritual practice from the ground up. We can, however, expect the results of our magic to be equal in measure to the time and effort that we have put into its practice.

One of the main skills necessary to make this happen, however, is not something that most people would consider to be magical or spiritual, and as such it rarely gets the attention it deserves: *time management*. When I have brought this up in classes over the years I am often met with glassy-eyed stares of disappointed disbelief, as surely the *real* answer to the success of establishing and maintaining a magical practice couldn't possibly lie in something so *mundane*. This assumes first that the mundane offers nothing to the magical, and second that there is a substantive difference between the two, or that they are mutually exclusive, thus revealing what is often a major stumbling block for most people. This is also why most people fail at deepening their magic: assumptions make for poor guides.

We need to make a commitment to our practice and this means scheduling the time and treating that time as sacred. It is no less important than exercise, eating properly, or any of the numerous other self-investments that are all too often ignored and neglected. This casual neglect in turn diminishes a Witch's personal power. A Witch needs to practice a fierce compassion *first for ourselves*, making sure that our needs are taken care of before attending to those of others. It's just like what the flight attendant says each time we board a plane: "If the oxygen masks are released, secure yours first before assisting those around you."

In addition to the exercises given (which are to be adopted into your formal practice and performed for the recommended minimum of four times per week) you should also be keeping a journal of your experiences. This is an essential part of the work, as it allows for the different layers of our consciousness to continue interacting with what we have experienced in the trance worlds. The act of writing helps move energies between different areas of the brain, each possessing their own drives and methodologies. Writing allows the nuances of the trance experience to further work its magic upon us in ways we might not otherwise imagine.

## A Traditional Faery Altar

Your altar is where you will be focusing much (though not all) of your spiritual work. Traditionally, the altar is placed in the north, the place of magnetic power in the Northern Hemisphere. Practitioners in the Southern Hemisphere may wish to align their altars to the south to better honor the power of the land on which they actually live.

We will add to it over time (and even create other altars for specific purposes) but for now all you will need is a space where you can be undisturbed, a surface on which you can place your tools as you obtain them (wand, blade, chalice, cube, mirror, and cauldron), a black altar cloth, images of goddesses and gods with whom you have a working relationship, a bell, a bowl of salt, a bowl of water, an incense burner, an ash pot (for burnt matches, etc.), and three candles: blue, red, and a single black candle to represent the Star God/dess, the primary deity in Faery Witchcraft. To this you may wish to add whatever other objects of power and inspiration you desire. A basic central arrangement around which you may build is shown in figure 1.

*Figure 1: A Faery Altar*

There are some other objects that you may wish to place upon the altar. It is traditional for a coven of gay men to include an image of a gray dove upon their altars, while a lesbian coven uses the image of a gray wolf. This gives rise to their names within our tradition: a gray dove coven or a gray wolf (or gray hound) coven. These animals are to-temic presences of the Divine Twins, and they can be thought of as holding that specific energetic presence in these circles. This reminds us that while we can gather together of like minds and experiences, we still share the world with others, and so we should strive to learn from these other perspectives.

A good Faery altar should be somewhat indistinguishable from an art installation; it should delight, inspire, and, above all else, be *beautiful*. Art is a primary tool and practice in the Faery Tradition. Faery Grandmaster Anaar, an accomplished dancer and artist in her own right, has stated that Feri is a "religion of art."[11] Through the lens of art we seek to better understand the Goddess and her continually unfolding creative power.

The Star Goddess is black to represent the blackness of the empty Void from which all things originated. According to our custom, her candle is also supposed to be the largest that we can find, but in a pinch even just a black taper or votive candle will do. You may decide you wish to dress it with herbs and oils, but for now just the candle itself will suf-fice. While we will be doing meditative and energetic work leading up to it, the lighting of the Star Goddess candle is the very first act that we do in a Faery ritual working. This represents the first light that divided the primal dark, and as such each time we light her candle we are tapping into the creation of the universe itself. This makes our ritual circle a true microcosm of the universe. We are participating in the powers of universal creation and destruction each time we perform our rites.

The blue and red candles represent the Divine Twins, a central concept of our tra-dition. Bloodrose defined these candles as representing simply "the Goddess" and "the God" and used them to invoke a litany of deities aligned to the Old Craft as taught by Victor. But this is only one way amongst many in which to view these variable powers. Though they often manifest as opposites, they are not exclusively so, as each can fulfill the role and function of the other. In her book *Fifty Years in the Feri Tradition*, Grand-master Cora Anderson speaks of how the Twins can flow together as easily as two candle flames flowing into one.

In BlueRose we first connect to these Twins in the forms of the Scarlet Serpent (a pri-mal, embodied presence of earth and fire) and the Azure Dove (a refined, transcendent

---

11. Anaar (April Niino), *The White Wand: Ruminations, Meditations, Reflections Toward a Feri Aesthetic.* Privately printed. Pg. 51. (Available for free as a PDF download: http://whitewand.com/The%20 White%20Wand.pdf).

one of water and air). When these powers come together, they merge and become our beloved Blue God, who traditionally displays both avian and serpentine symbolism in his iconography. He is thus embodied transcendence, a state of being that we as Faery practitioners strive to cultivate within ourselves, in part by identifying with the Blue God, who is the brother, son, lover, and other half of the "clitoral-phallic presence of God Herself,"[12] aka the Star Goddess.

## Opening the Way

The concepts and exercises given in this section comprise the beginning of what we in BlueRose call Opening the Way—the collective name given to the foundational practices upon which we will continue to build. In the group of exercises given below, three of them are parts of Opening the Way. As new exercises (and alterations to existing ones) are made available, you should augment your overall practice to include the newer material.

The beginning of the training in Faery Tradition must begin with the breath. In many cultures, the word for breath and spirit are the same. This reflects the primal importance of the breath and how we might focus it for the purposes of altering our spiritual awareness. Though many different techniques may be used to achieve the same results, one of the simplest is the four-fold breath.

This first exercise is so simple that many do not even consider it, believing that something so unassuming could not possibly be powerful. This would be a terrible mistake, as this exercise forms the energetic foundation for everything else that we will encounter in our work between the worlds. Take your time with it, *especially* if it feels "boring." If you find yourself getting anxious, shift your awareness to that of observing the sense of anxiety, boredom, frustration, etc. When you can do this effectively for at least five minutes in a sitting, then you will be ready to move on to the next exercise.

### Opening the Way 1: The Four-Fold Breath Exercise

Begin by sitting comfortably with your spine straight. Relax and exhale fully, feeling your muscles pushing out all of the air from your lungs. Now, breathe in deeply through your nose to the count of four and allow your breath to seemingly flow into your lower belly as you silently focus on a space about three-fingers width be-

---

12. Oral tradition, Victor Anderson.

neath your navel. Hold your breath for the count of four ... and then exhale to the count of four, then holding again for four counts. Repeat this process for at least a few minutes. If your mind drifts during this time, simply and gently bring it back to the present moment ... just observe your breath moving in and out.

## *Opening the Way 2: Grounding Exercise*

Another beginning exercise that we often encounter is that of grounding. This is a process of energetically aligning our consciousness and of mentally and spiritually connecting our energy body to the energy body of the earth. Much like a large appliance has a grounding wire to ensure that power surges will not damage the mechanism, when we establish a grounding cord into the earth we too are better prepared to encounter surges of energy that might otherwise cause us distress or even some form of harm. While there are many different techniques available to do this, my favorite is to use the time-honored imagery of the tree, with roots deep in the earth and branches high up in the heavens.

Begin by sitting properly as in the four-fold breath exercise and engaging the four-fold breath. When you are feeling relaxed and open, softly focus your awareness on that space beneath your navel and imagine a red ball of light beginning to form there. Imagine breathing in and out of this ball, each breath giving it life force and increasing its light and substance. After several moments to a few minutes, imagine that this ball sprouts a cord of red light that stretches down through your perineum, seeking downward like the taproot of a great tree. Take your time as you imagine this cord effortlessly flowing down through the layers of the earth until it finds the iron center ... the molten outer core ... and then the crystalline inner core of the earth. Once there, take a few moments to simply observe how you are feeling, and then imagine that you can "breathe up" the red power of this core into your roots, breathing this light slowly, all the way up, until you feel it enter through your perineum and slowly fill your body with every breath.

Now, imagine that this light sprouts out through your shoulders and your crown in the form of branches that stretch upward into the starry heavens. Take some time to contemplate the iron in the centers of the very oldest of those stars and how this light shines down to you ... an electric blue cosmic light ... into your crown, as you slowly breathe. Imagine it filling you and flowing out through your roots and into the earth below. Observe how you feel in this state and maintain this awareness for a couple of minutes, at least until you have mastered the exercise, at which point maintaining awareness of this sensation for just a few moments will do.

## The Origin Exercise

The Origin exercise is usually given to beginning students on our path. Its core comes to Faery Tradition by way of Arica training, a modern tradition of spiritual self-development. It is an active meditation on the earth as our original mother. It is generally done somewhat often in the beginning stages, and then less frequently as the training commences. Play with it, and see what it brings up for you.

After doing the previous exercise, imagine that with every breath you are drawing up from the earth a sense of strength and power... and every exhale sends down love and gratitude. Feel that your grounding cord is like an umbilical cord connecting you to the Mother in your deep core. With seven exhales, chant the following in a long, vibratory drone, becoming slower with every repetition:

*Hail Earth! Mother of all!*

## Opening the Way 3: The Holy Flame Exercise (Engaging the Star Goddess Candle)

Items needed:
A black Star Goddess candle
Matches

Now that we have established a simple inner practice, we can begin to bring ritual into the mix. Sit in front of your altar and perform the previous exercises. Once they are complete imagine that your whole body begins to vibrate and shine with a liquid, diamond light—the presence of your own divinity. Once you feel that you are brilliantly shining with this light, imagine sending a portion of it into the wick of the Star Goddess candle as you light it, your own divine presence merging with the candle flame, becoming one. Take a moment to contemplate how the flame that burns before you and the flame that burns within are one and the same... all flames are one flame. Then, open your arms before you with your palms facing upward and recite the traditional prayer:

*Holy Mother!*
*In you we live, move, and have our being.*
*From you all things emerge*
*And unto you all things return.*

On the last line cross your arms over your chest (left over right) and bow in reverence to the flame. This posture is reminiscent of the ancient Egyptian "death pose" and reflects the fact that all life returns to her. We are not bowing in the sense of subjugation, but out of respect and acknowledgment of the divine source, of which we all partake. Take some time (here in the beginning at least a few minutes, otherwise a few moments) to observe any sensations you may have.

Later, we will add here whatever more specific things we are working on, but for now, imagine calling back the power you sent into the candle flame, feeling it flow through your breath and into that space beneath your navel. Now, recite the Holy Mother prayer once more, and then snuff out the candle. Remain still and silent for the span of three breaths.

Once you have mastered the exercises (meaning, once you have memorized their forms and are able to regularly perform them satisfactorily from memory), then you may add the next technique to your spiritual toolbox.

---

## The Personal Temple

The personal temple is an astral construct that can be used in order to provide a deepened experience during trance. By utilizing personal symbols and visualizations, we can create a space in which our own power is more fully realized, and then use this as a starting point for whatever other trance workings we are wishing to engage in.

To begin this exercise, it is important to have a general idea as to what elements should be present in the temple. For example, will it be inside a building or outdoors? If outdoors, is it in a forest or on a beach? Will it be underground or in the heavens? You are only limited to the confines of your imagination and to what feels right to you. It's okay if it looks straight out of a fantasy novel or a science-fiction movie or even just a simple nature scene. The point is to imagine an environment in which you can see yourself performing great feats of magic. If you were the most powerful [Witch/Warlock/Wizard/fill-in-the-blank] in the world, where might you see yourself working your spells? What elements do you feel should be here for you? Certainly an altar … maybe a garden full of magical herbs? A bookshelf with an impressive collection of ancient tomes? Or consider that whatever you come up with now might change considerably in the course of your evolving practice. For now, just play with some different imagery and see how you feel in relation to it. The *feeling* is the most important factor here. When you are feeling powerful, then you are better able to become powerful. We will here use our imagination in order to train our energy body in the art of feeling, and thus becoming, as powerful as we can be.

I recommend performing the Summoning the Temple exercise several times while in the process of building one's personal temple. With each successive visit you will likely find that there are changes to the environment that may result in a better experience as time goes on. After you have done this several times, you may also wish to create a visual representation of your personal temple as a sort of meditative mandala.

### Summoning the Temple Exercise

Items needed:
Your black Star Goddess candle
Matches

Begin with the Four-Fold Breath and Grounding of Opening the Way. Imagine that you can feel the directions all around you—north, south, east, west, above, below—and, finally, feel yourself perfectly centered in between them all.

Breathe three deep breaths of power, and imagine that with every exhale you are breathing the power into the world around you, giving it form. Notice what form it takes. Look around you … to the north to the place of earth … to the east and the place of air … to the south and the place of fire … to the west and the place of water. Look above you and below into the places of aether. In the center of this place is an altar: *your* altar. Notice what objects or symbols are on it. What does it look like? How big or small is it? What is it made from? How do you feel about it? Take in every detail. This is your place to make magic! It can look like whatever you wish it to be.

In your mind's eye continue to look around, paying attention to all the details and using all of your senses to make the experience feel more real for you. Does this place have a scent? What can you hear? If there are walls, what color are they?

What does the wall texture feel like? Explore all of the objects in this place in a similar fashion until you are familiar with every little detail of this place.

Once you have done this, spend just a little more time paying attention to how *you* feel in this place. Are you calm? Energized? Anxious? Happy? Sad? Notice how the energy of this imagined place affects you. Spend a few moments contemplating this, and then perform the Holy Flame exercise as before, imagining that as you are lighting the candle in your physical working area that you are also lighting it in your personal temple. The two candles—and the two flames—are but one flame.

When you are able to call up this place in your mind and the details are vivid, then you know that it has begun to take on a life on the astral. Each visit will strengthen this place and make it more powerful for you. From now on, each time you light your Star Goddess candle you will simultaneously be lighting the candle in your personal temple. Eventually you won't need to go through every step to "make it more real" for yourself, as the repeated visits will have made this place strong for you. But for now take the time to really explore your temple and see how it might change over the weeks and months to come.

---

By becoming proficient with these exercises and techniques you will have begun the process of strengthening your energetic foundation, your container for magical energies. Once you feel comfortable with these, you may move on to the next section in which we will begin the process of invoking the Faery fire.

# CHAPTER 3
# SUMMONING THE FAERY FIRE

*We are the living links in a life force that moves and plays around and through us,*
*binding the deepest soils with the farthest stars.*
—ALAN CHADWICK

In the lore of the Faery Tradition, it is often taught that the basic component of magic is life force, the active principle that vivifies and animates every living thing. Drawing from the lore of many other cultures and traditions, we can begin to see a fuller picture of how this life force presents itself to us and how we might better be able to cultivate it, thus improving our lives and our magic. The Hawaiians call this force *mana*, and perhaps because of Victor's own past-life memories of being a kahuna, this concept, along with other bits of Hawaiian language and lore, became part of the foundation that he taught to his initiates.

This gives us an opportunity to confront an important issue, that of cultural appropriation. This is the (all too common) practice of taking something from another culture, adapting it to suit one's personal needs, and then presenting the practice or oneself as a legitimate representative of that culture without regard to the lives and heritage of those who are rightfully part of it. While we in the Faery Tradition adopt (and might even adapt) certain magical models and methodologies from various cultures into our own practices, the line drawn is that of representation and respect. Though I may use concepts from Huna, for example, to further illustrate my work in Faery, I most certainly do *not* represent myself as a kahuna, nor am I claiming to be teaching a form of Huna.

I know full well that there are some who would criticize this approach, saying that I—as a white man—have no right to call upon Polynesian gods, Middle Eastern angels, or African orishas. To this I respond that while I would never claim ownership or special knowledge of a culture that is not my own, in my personal practice I am committed to pursuing whatever spiritual techniques and relationships speak to my soul. The experiences that I have when using these practices, or communing with these beings, are my own, though I acknowledge that my experiences and relationships with them will likely be quite different than for those who originated from those cultures in question.

When practicing my Craft, I often draw inspiration from the practices of other cultures and will explore concepts from them in order to deepen my understanding of the human-divine connection. However, out of respect for those cultures I will not remove them wholesale from their context, for in doing so they not only lose their original meaning but also are in danger of being misrepresented, which in turn causes harm to their culture of origin.

For me, this becomes a very fine line that must be carefully walked. As a practitioner of Witchcraft, my drive is to learn as much magic as I can from whatever sources resonate with me. In those instances in which a practice, symbol, or deity speaks to me and demands my devotion, I make a commitment to honor the cultures from which they originated by pledging to study their histories, to listen to the voices of those who identify as part of those cultures, and, where possible, to support the living people who belong to that cultural group. In practical terms, this may mean speaking out against racism or discrimination, engaging in political actions, or even donating money to organizations designed to assist in the advancement of those people from whose cultural heritage I am benefitting. When teaching the Craft, I will give examples of what has worked for myself, but I encourage my students to do their homework and to follow the guidelines that I have set for myself in regards to whatever outside cultural practices may be calling to them personally.

Moving forward, we can look at those cultures that have for themselves defined the subtle powers and we may learn something from their approach, noticing where different traditions have arrived at similar conclusions as well as where they may differ completely. Each teaches us something more about the nature of reality and how we might continue to navigate the landscape of the numinous. We needn't imitate the practices of another in order to pursue a valid spiritual path. Instead we can allow these different methodologies to inspire our own unique approach as we tread our own route toward understanding and power.

Toward this understanding, we begin with a basic lesson on the nature of life force. Hawaiian *mana*, Chinese *qi*, Hindu *prana*, Grecian *pneuma*, even the Force of Star Wars fame all describe this type of vital energy that is unseen but that can be tapped into in various ways and directed toward increased health, vitality, and magical efficiency.

In some of the lore of what has been called Old Faery, this magical power was sometimes called wraith-force. This references its invisible and insubstantial nature, while acknowledging its close association to the human body. A wraith, to the folklore of ancient Scots, was a ghost or an apparition, but one that often appeared in the form of a living person, usually to act as a portent of their death.[13] It is the life force personified; its potency is evidenced by the mythological description of it surviving even death itself. It is the very stuff of life; the insubstantial, quintessential energetic blueprint for life before it actually becomes manifest. This is what nourishes and empowers us, not just in our magic, but in our mundane existence as well.

This life force is cultivated and gathered naturally by certain actions, such as eating, drinking, meditating, spending time out in nature or in sacred spaces, engaging in sex, and certain other types of creative, physical, mental, emotional, and/or social activities. The type or vibration of the force is different, depending on from where it is received. For example, the life force that I gather from eating a fresh carrot is quite different from that which I might get from eating, say, a piece of cake. And this is also altogether different than what I might take from spending time in the redwoods or by creating art or by making love. Each is different, and yet at their core they are also the same.

This force is the very same one that we, as practitioners of the Craft, will first utilize in order to work our magic, so we are well advised to become masters at its cultivation and direction. To do anything in this life requires energy, and magic is no different. This basic life force is consumed and then transformed according to the needs of our body, mind, and soul, and then it is directed where it is needed in order to complete the various tasks before us, conscious as well as not. Sometimes our goals require no more than what we may normally have at our disposal or are able to generate through our own means via practice and ritual. Other times, however, we may need to seek out additional sources of energy in order to make our magic manifest. This is where we usually find that working with a spirit, deity, demon, or ally will provide us with what we need to make it happen, as these sources are immeasurably more potent. And because of this greater potency,

---

13. OED Online, "wraith, n." Oxford University Press, accessed August 28, 2015. http://www.oed.com/view /Entry/230504.

they are also immeasurably more dangerous, in much the same way that working with a live current of electricity is dangerous; less so for one skilled in the art of electrical engineering, but dangerous nonetheless. The electrician respects electricity, and the Witch respects magic all the same.

It is through the development of an agile skill in working with one's personal power that we become capable of dealing with that of the transpersonal. Before we can effectively run a marathon we must first learn to breathe, to stretch, and to walk. Gathering personal power is part of the fundamental practice for the effective Witch, Faery, or otherwise. A great deal of what we do magically is for the express purpose of gathering power. "Raising energy" or "raising a cone of power" are Craft terms that refer to this process of gathering force with the purpose of directing it toward a magical goal. Often this force is raised from the participants themselves by dancing, singing, chanting, and performing ritual actions designed to trigger altered states of awareness that are more conducive to engaging and gathering this power. But no matter what methods are used to cultivate this force, it all begins with something as simple as the breath.

## The Breath Is Life

It is worth considering that the word *spirit* derives from the Latin *spiritus*, which means, "breath."[14] This is a theme that plays out in many other cultures and languages throughout the world. In Hawaiian, the word *ha* means both "breath" and "spirit," as does the Hebrew word *ruach* and the Greek word *pneuma*.[15] In Arabic the root of the words for both spirit and breath is *ruh*,[16] again pointing us in the direction of what the ancients held as common knowledge: that breath and spirit are one and the same.

The first and most fundamental way in which we gather life force is through breathing. As you have probably already learned with the Four-Fold Breath exercise, deep conscious breathing generates more power than our all too common habit of taking shallow and unconscious breaths. This is the first and foremost way that we can begin to cultivate greater amounts of personal power.

---

14. Dictionary.com, "spirit," Dictionary.com Unabridged, accessed August 26, 2015. http://dictionary
   .reference.com/browse/spirit.

15. Stanislav Grof, "The Healing Power of Breath," Omega Institute, 2013, accessed August 26, 2015.
   http://www.eomega.org/article/the-healing-power-of-breath.

16. Edward Clodd, "Theories of the Nature of Spirit," in *Animism, the Seed of Religion* (A. Constable &
   Company, Limited, 1905), 37.

In times of stress or prior to any spiritual or magical working you will wish to perform the Life Force Breathing exercise, or a similar exercise, as this will bring a sense of peace and calm as well as increase your personal power and mental focus.

At this point you should definitely be making sure that you are recording your experiences in your magical journal. The experiences you record now can positively affect your magical work later on, so it is definitely worth your while. Even the smallest detail that may seem insignificant now may prove to be invaluable later on.

### Life Force Breathing Exercise

Begin with the Four-Fold Breath. Now imagine that the area surrounding your physical body is filled with a luminous mist or fog. As you inhale, imagine that this fog is entering your nostrils and flowing into your lungs. With each exhale whisper the sound *Haaaa* until your lungs have been emptied of air while imagining that you are retaining the light. Your exhale should be slightly longer than your inhale. With each successive breath, this light slowly fills your lungs, chest, belly, etc., until your whole body is full and glowing.

### Directing Life Force Exercise

Begin with the Life Force Breathing exercise. When you are full and shining with this power, begin imagining that this inner light is coalescing into a small ball of light, about the size of a golf ball and roughly three-fingers width beneath your navel. As you continue to breathe, softly focus your awareness on this ball, imagining it pulsing in light and power with the rhythm of your breathing. When you feel that you have cultivated a sufficient charge, begin by imagining this ball as it slowly moves upward. With every slow, deep breath, this ball of life slowly rises up your central column and comes to rest in a space between your heart and throat. Again, see it pulse and shine with the rhythm of your breath. After a few breaths, the ball again slowly rises, now resting in the center of your head, where it again pulses with your breath.

After a few to several seconds of this, reverse the process so the ball slowly descends back to the chest and then finally beneath the navel once more. End by imagining that this light is being dispersed and absorbed throughout your body over the course of three breaths.

# Life Force and Food

We also gather life force from the food we eat. The less processed the food the more life force it is likely to contain. Fresh vegetables and fruits contain a higher quantity (and quality) of this force, while a pastry, for example, contains far less. Another thing to consider when eating is the environment in which the eating occurs. Meals should be happy, relaxing affairs. Good food and good company both positively affect the quality of the life force gathered. Stressful topics should be avoided while eating, as we will internalize the negative energy and it could cause us problems later on, such as increased anxiety or even disease.

Ritual observances for the eating of a meal are simple yet potent pieces of practice that offer us more than what we might first believe. When we have formed the habit of conscious engagement with the spirit of our food, then we will be in a better place to make food offerings to our spirits and allies that are more potent and thus readily accepted.

## *Attuning the Sacred Meal Exercise*

When about to eat a meal, we can use this simple technique to align our consciousness to the life force within it, thus increasing the amount and the quality of the force that we will receive. This also serves to prevent any other spirits from being able to potentially steal the energy before you have a chance to absorb it.

With the meal before you, place one or both hands palms down over it. Imagine that in the center of each of your palms is a star that radiates starlight down into the food. Simply allow your consciousness to focus on the food … imagine the vegetables as having grown in the earth … the bread as a growing grain, milled and worked and baked … the meat raised and sacrificed to feed another life. No matter what you eat, a life was sacrificed to feed your own. It's a simple fact of life. Life feeds death and death feeds life. Contemplate the life cycles of each of the foods you are about to eat and affirm to yourself that you will gather all of the life force that these foods offer. This can be a simple, silent observance, or you can create a ritual around it if desired.

## *Deepening the Sacred Meal Ritual*

Considering that we also gather force from ritual actions, combining the previous exercise with a simple ritual observance, such as the following, could positively affect your results.

Follow the Attuning the Sacred Meal exercise as given. With your hands over your meal, imagine the starlight is flowing deep into the very molecules and atoms that comprise the food you are about to eat. Imagine that you can see down into the empty space that exists between the molecules of the food ... and that in this empty space you can begin to perceive a faint light that seems to emanate from the dark emptiness itself. Continue to breathe, allowing this light to build into a brighter force. "See" this light filling the food until you imagine it pulsing with power. Say:

> *From fertile earth, this rising life,*
> *Into myself, I take this power.*

Eat the food with a genuine sense of reverence. With each bite contemplate the life force within it, experiencing it in the textures and flavors of the meal as you savor it fully. Imagine this force as a great light that then merges with your own inner light, nourishing and strengthening you.

As mentioned previously, the Hawaiian word for life force is *mana*. While this is often used as a generic term, there are other more specific forms of life force referenced in the Hawaiian language. Normal mana can be raised to another form, called *mana mana*. This refined form of mana is more mentally focused than the normal mana, which is more primal in nature.

In turn, another higher form of mana exists: *mana loa*. This is the "fire of the gods" or "star fire," as it is sometimes known in Faery.[17] It is a particularly powerful form of life force, one not commonly encountered in normal or mundane life. This power can harm as well as heal and is the divine power that is associated with magic, miracles, and deep enchantment. When we touch this power, we ignite into ecstasy. It opens us up to the voices of the spirits and the gods, and we can learn

---

17. T. Thorn Coyle, "South: Engaging the Flame," *Evolutionary Witchcraft* (New York: J.P. Tarcher/Penguin, 2004): 106–107.

much from this state. In it, we have access to an interconnected web of possibilities, threads of association and connection upon which the Witch may gently and skillfully tug in order to weave her will into the cosmic pattern. It is a wonderful state of being for short bursts of creative impulse and magical power, but it is unhealthy if maintained for too long and eventually collapses.

## The Blue Fire

In the Bloodrose line of the Faery Tradition, wraith-force (mana) is taught using a visualization device known as Blue Fire. This was reportedly introduced into Faery practice from that of pranic yoga, where it served as a means to be better aware of vital energy with the body and mind. Great care was taken to ensure that each student was visualizing the *correct* shade of blue—the electric blue of a gas flame—even going so far as to advise staring at such a physical flame beforehand so as to "seed" the visual memory. With each person trained in focusing on this particular frequency of thought, this would provide a methodology to psychically plug in to each other and to the group's *egregore* via shared praxis.

Like most things within our tradition, this simple act caused its share of controversy. Victor Anderson warned of the dangers of "playing" with Blue Fire:

> *Blue Fire occurs within magical ceremonies ... That happens, accept it. As long as the god self is controlling it, it is very beneficial. It contains so much of energy, so much of life, so much of power. But to just deliberately play with it and try to breathe it and say that it is the only thing that's important is like sticking your hands in radioactive material. The result is like taking LSD, you can start hallucinating, start feeling like you are so busy with the spiritual things that you can't think of the so-called mundane. If you go along like that, you can just go completely off your nut. That's exactly the price you pay for it. So don't misuse it. Blue fire is deadly dangerous, but it's also very beneficial, and very necessary in magic, but it has to be used properly.*[18]

His own experiments had led him to work with this flame not as simple wraith-force but as star fire. He also reportedly taught that it was "safe" to work with life force in "any of the colors of the rainbow."

---

18. Victor Anderson, "Speak of the Devil," *Witch Eye #3 (2002)*.

After years of working extensively with the Blue Fire, I have come to the understanding that this is *not* the same as simple life force. But neither will I assert that it is the same as star fire. Like the elusive realm of Faery itself, this flame is both and neither and also something in-between. It is primal and civilized and wild and calm. It illuminates the mind and excites the body. It is the fire of creation—the stuff of *life*. Make no mistake: it *is* dangerous. But only if it is not respected, much as with *any* fire.

My current thoughts are that the Blue Fire is an otherworldly vibration of wraith-force that is more aligned to magic. It is the hot alchemical fire that transmutes substances from one form to another. It is the ecstatic pulse of electric arousal we feel when we experience sexual attraction. It is a living consciousness as well as an inexhaustible source of creative energy. It is the "Faery fire." It is of the earth and the dead, but it is also of the stars…and the gods. It is of the body. But it is also of the mind and the spirit. It is the flame of the *will of the practitioner* and by extension *the will of the gods.* This is a major component of the Witch Power, awakened through initiation in numerous covens, lodges, and lineages and tracing back to our otherworldly spiritual ancestors. But before it can be fully (and more safely) awakened, it must first be engaged.

### The Blue Fire Breath Exercise

Begin with the Life Force Breathing exercise. When you are full of shining light, exhale and begin to empty yourself of it. Allow your exhales to be slightly longer than your inhales and allow yourself to become completely emptied. There is only dark emptiness within, and you float in the gentle darkness without.

Take a moment to bask in the peaceful darkness both within and around yourself. Now imagine that you can see into the energetic blueprint that forms the foundation of the matter that comprises your immediate environment—ground, floor, ceiling, furniture, trees, rocks—anything and everything around you. Imagine delving between their molecules, where you perceive the empty space that actually comprises most of the object itself. In this empty, dark space you begin to see a faint blue light emerge. With each breath build this light up into a steady glow. See it as the color of a gas flame, an electric blue, alive with vibrancy and life. Imagine it not simply as a light…but as a *flame.* A flame is *alive*…it pulses and dances…it is in motion…it is active.… Now imagine this flame filling the matter of the objects around you so that their entirety shines a brilliant electric blue. Imagine that this fire also fills the air around you … it is in all things … the hidden light within all matter … pulsing and alive.

Now, in the span of at least six breaths, imagine that you are breathing in the blue fire from the air and objects around you with each inhale. Like a luminous blue fog of flame, it enters your lungs, where it is subsequently spread out into your blood and into the rest of your body. Continue until you are full of this light and you feel yourself throbbing and thrumming with power. When you feel that you are at your limit, take one more breath of Blue Fire, and then on your exhale release this light back into the environment around you. With each subsequent exhale, release a little bit more as you relax and come back into a space of calm balance.

## Invoking the Blue Fire Ritual

Again, we add a ritual element in order to focus our power and precision. Perform the Blue Fire Breath, only now when delving into the empty space and perceiving the darkness there, call out to the spirit of the Blue Fire:

*Hidden light within the dark*
*Ignite in bluest flame!*
*And through my breath I take thee in*
*My will I now proclaim!*

Cultivate and gather the Blue Fire as before, taking note of any differences you may experience from the previous exercise. Release the flame as before, returning to a space of calm and full presence.

## Directing the Blue Fire Exercise

Perform this exercise while sitting down. Place your hands comfortably in your lap, palms facing each other and about 6 to 8 inches (15 to 20 cm) apart. Perform the Invoking the Blue Fire ritual. Once you are filled with this flame, over the span of at least six breaths imagine coalescing the flame into a single ball of blue fire within a space between your heart and throat. Breathing through this ball, imagine sending it over and into your left shoulder, moving down into your left hand. Imagine your hand being engulfed in a blue fire that empowers but does not burn or consume. Breathing deeply, imagine this flame leaping across from one palm and into the other as you breathe it into the palm of your right hand with your next inhale. Continue to breathe deeply as you bring this flame up your right arm, into your right shoulder, and back into your chest where it began. Continue this practice of moving the flame down your left arm and over to your right as you gain speed with every pass until the flame begins to whirl within you, spinning like a top, the ball of flame now resembling a ring of blue fire pulsing in a circle of your arms and chest.

When you feel that the fire is humming strongly within you, open your eyes to gaze at the space between your palms. Some people can see the blue fire jumping between their palms and fingers. Even if you do not physically see the blue fire, just notice how you feel it as it spins through your body with your breath.

After some time with this, begin to slow down the spinning of the flame and return it to a ball in your chest. Release the flame as in the previous exercises.

---

Having learned to invoke and cultivate the Blue Fire, now we will work to absorb greater and greater amounts of this power. By performing this or similar exercises on a regular basis, we will gradually increase our capacity for magical power, learning to control it as we go. Think of these exercises in the same way you would physical exercises at the gym: repetition builds results. There is no way to really skip ahead of these types of workings. Either you cultivate the necessary skill to work effective magic through experience and perseverance, or you don't. Either way your work shows for it.

### Absorbing the Flame Exercise

Perform the Invoking the Blue Fire rite. When you are full of the Blue Fire, take one more breath to "stretch" your capacity, feeling this stretch through the exhale. On the next inhale, imagine the flame within you being absorbed into the cells of your body … your molecules … your atoms … and the empty space in between them. Imagine that this empty space absorbs the Blue Fire like a sponge absorbs water.

---

The desired result of the previous exercises should be some variant of a space of energized calm. If you are feeling agitated, confused, dizzy, unfocused, or the like, you may wish to perform a Grounding exercise and potentially eat something healthy, especially protein. Another tool might be to use an exercise such as the following.

### *Skeletal Grounding Exercise*

This can be done whenever you are feeling amped up by the presence of magical energy but want to try and keep it for its benefits as opposed to sending it away into the earth, as many ritualists often advise. While this latter technique is fine and even useful at times, it should by no means be the default for how we are to treat altered states of energetic awareness.

Perform this exercise while standing. Using the techniques learned in the previous exercises, focus on the excess energy that is giving you the sense of agitation or distress that you are experiencing. Then use your breath to move it slowly through your body, gradually moving it into your skeleton, where the minerals in your bones will "ground" this energy deep in your stone nature and safely away from your animal nature (flesh/physical body).

When you feel that this energy has been fully absorbed move your arm out in front of you, make soft fists, and turn your wrists upward. Take a deep breath and pump your fists inward as you stomp down with one foot, imagining the energy in your skeleton locking into place. Take another breath and repeat the process, stomping with your other foot. On the third breath, repeat this process now slightly jumping in the air and stomping both feet down. Imagine this power stored within the minerals in your bones, like an intricate crystal that holds power and secrets. Take three more breaths and allow the power to disperse as you redirect your attention to other things.

### *Skeletal Grounding Ritual*

Perform the Skeletal Grounding exercise. When it comes time to absorb the power, assume the appropriate stance and say:

> *Shining, buzzing, blinding light,*
> *Into the darkness of the stones*
> *With three breaths I here absorb*
> *This flame into my very bones!*

You may wish to recite this incantation before each of the three times you will be performing the pumping gesture and stomping, or just the once before beginning these repetitions. End as before.

---

As we work with the practices of cultivating and gathering power, we begin to learn better ways to keep the power that we already have, as opposed to allowing it to leak away. We also learn to cleanse and refine our own power, lest we become wasteful and thus diminished in capacity. A basic tenant of Faery Tradition has always been that of good energy ecology: basic awareness of how much we are using, how much we are wasting, and where our various sources of power come from, as well as methods for reusing or recycling power that would otherwise be deemed negative and likely banished in some well-meaning but thoroughly depreciating ritual, completely ignorant of the real harm being caused. Exercises such as those dealt with here are one step toward cultivating that awareness for ourselves. This awareness is greatly expanded once we learn of the community that comprises the self and the various layers of the soul structure of the human being.

## CHAPTER 4
# THE PERSONAL TRINITY

*Many Gods have three faces, or aspects.*
*Feri Tradition reminds us that we, too, are a trinity.*
—T. THORN COYLE, *EVOLUTIONARY WITCHCRAFT*

Though small, the Faery Tradition has been strikingly influential to modern Neopagan Witchcraft. The core teachings of the Three Souls are like "faery seeds" scattered to the winds like dandelions and taking root in even the most Wiccan of places. Now, many Witchcraft traditions use some form of the Three Souls in their workings, but for the most part this is a relatively recent development.

A casual perusal of the books published up through the mid-1970s will confirm that no such concept was being taught in Witchcraft circles, at least not widely. It was certainly Starhawk's 1979 work *The Spiral Dance* that was responsible for introducing a wider Pagan audience to certain Faery concepts, tools, and lore—the Three Selves being perhaps chief among them. This concept of human/divine triplicity forms what could be called a cornerstone in the foundation of the spiritual and magical technology that is taught in the various lineages of the Old Faery Tradition.

This is a model of a tripartite cosmology, describing a divine as well as human triple nature. On the level of the human/personal, this triplicity manifests in the Three Souls, while on the divine/transpersonal this manifests as the Three Worlds much as described in Irish magical tradition.

While having its own philosophies and styles of practices for knowing and interacting with these souls, Faery Tradition teaches this basic concept by drawing from many different streams of cultural mythos. Several cultures, philosophies, and magical systems have long recognized the multiplicity of human beings' spiritual nature. Ancient Egyptians described multiple souls, each having their own unique position and role within the community of the self. Jewish kabbalists recognize four souls, one of them being the life force that feeds the remaining three. Practitioners of Huna work with three selves. Mongolian shamanism works with three souls. Even modern psychology identifies different layers to the psyche, such as the Freudian threefold model of ego, id, and super-ego. Each culture, system, and philosophy differs in its approach, yet they all hint at a deeper and singular truth: we are much more than what we think we are.

Many cultures likewise illustrate a concept of a divine trinity. To the Egyptians, who built the pyramids, a sacred triad was honored in the worship of Isis, Osiris, and Horus. Ancient Celts were very fond of the number three, recognizing three elements, the three realms of land, sea, and sky, and of numerous manifestations of a triple Goddess. Of particular interest to many Witches is the triadic figure given to us by the ancient Greeks in the form of Hecate, the threefold Titan goddess of Witchcraft and the crossroads.

Christianity also recognizes the sacred power of the number three with its concept of the Holy Trinity. Representing God in the triple forms of Father, Son, and Holy Spirit, this esoteric concept describes the dynamic relationship between three interrelated divine forces that have been recognized and variously named throughout history. Having characterized divinity as existing in triune aspects, is it then such a cogitative leap to perceive humans in the same way? If humanity is made in God's image, then why not?

The Irish folkloric "Three Cauldrons of Poesy," a poem attributed to the celebrated bard and hero Amergin, describes three metaphorical cauldrons as residing within the human body. Each exists to catch and hold the inspiration, power, and blessings that are bestowed by the gods.

The cauldrons are symbolic points within the human body that facilitate the accumulation and refining of various frequencies of life force. How these cauldrons are positioned within us determines the amount of poetic and spiritual power that we possess. Depending on the individual person they are often turned to different orientations: upright, on their side, or inverted. An upright cauldron is better suited to receive and contain the blessings of power we may receive. The work of the practitioner is then to cultivate experiences that will encourage these cauldrons to move into the upright position, where they can better receive life force, instead of spilling most of it away or rejecting it entirely. Traditionally, these experiences are said to be born of great joy or great sorrow, and they serve not only as energetic catalysts for inner change but also of poetic (divine) inspiration, which in Irish magical tradition equates to great power.

Faery Tradition describes the three selves or souls in a manner similar to that of Polynesian Huna. Each soul has its own drives, desires, quirks, personalities, as well as strengths and weaknesses. In the BlueRose line, these are usually referred to as the talker, the fetch, and the holy daemon. Even just within the Faery Tradition these souls are given various names, and divergent practices are encouraged for getting to better know and align them. What is constant is how each of them is described.

| Table of Three Souls | | | | |
|---|---|---|---|---|
| NAME | TYPE | SYMBOL | CAULDRON | AFFIRMATION |
| Talker | Mental | Golden Sun | Vocation | I Think |
| Fetch | Primal | Red Moon | Warming | I Feel |
| Holy Daemon | God Soul | Blue Star | Wisdom | I Am |

## Talker: The Mental Soul

We begin the journey into our tripartite nature with what feels closest to what we already know about ourselves. Known in Huna as *uhane*, the middle self, and to Kabbalists as *ruach*, what Faery calls the *talker* can be experienced through what we psychologically describe as the ego, or the personality. It is that part of ourselves that we recognize as our*selves* when we look in the mirror, when we hear ourselves speaking, and when we recognize our own handwriting … these are points of contemplation for getting to know your own talker.

Since the triple soul model can be seen as comprising multiple spiritual energy fields and not simply psychological designations for aspects of the psyche, we can proceed with the knowledge that we do so by way of association and metaphor, and not of direct equation. The talker is not the same as the ego. But in making the comparison we begin to understand something of talker's nature.

Talker is rightfully associated with communication and with language. Talker operates within the rules of logic and reason. It is our intelligence in the way that we normally understand that word. It is talker who is largely in control of our actions when we are calm and present-minded.

As a spiritual energy field, the talker is said to reside in the outer layers of the human aura, or "nimbus." In those who are highly evolved or otherwise particularly strong in the Power, this appears as a bright, luminous fog surrounding the individual.

Talker's function is to cultivate awareness through perception. Talker gathers information—in the form of various types of energy through the senses: light through vision, vibration through hearing, sensation through touch, etc. Talker takes this sensory input and assembles this chaotic cacophony of light and sound into a discernible perception from which to base an observation. Talker is constantly taking in these energies from the immediate environment and then making judgment calls based on logic, but also through the memories and relationships of the fetch, another soul in our trinity.

The term *talker* reveals something of this soul's nature, and also of its inherent challenge. A large part of our work is to learn how to *silence* our talker. This is not because of some innate flaw or moral judgment, but instead because when talker is silenced its power becomes much more focused. When talker is silent, it becomes the *listener*. Only when we have listened to all possibilities can we make an informed decision.

Talker is often described as residing (i.e., being physically anchored) somewhere in the head, or alternatively between the heart and the throat. According to the doctrines of Chinese medicine, this last area is one of particular power in the body, a *dantian* or "elixir field" in which the energetic meridians of the human body interact. Much like the Hindu chakras (of which talker can be related to the third, fourth, and fifth) this point of power can be engaged spiritually and magically in order to bring about various effects such as, in the case of talker, increased concentration, focus, and mental acuity. Placing talker near the heart also helps to associate it with the Cauldron of Vocation, the essence of the poet's "vision" where they receive their inspiration and skill.

Most of us are born with this cauldron tipped on its side, so that only a small portion of power is retained. Those who possess no artistic vision or poetic nature are born with it inverted. Talker, like the Cauldron of Vocation, must be trained in order for it to be strong and as powerful as possible. My own experience in working with and teaching this material for nearly twenty years is that talker is most often firmly anchored in the head *and must be consciously moved* into the heart. This moves our consciousness from a space of ego into a space of centered openness. This allows for talker to become the listener and be better able to communicate with the other souls in our structure.

### Knowing Talker Exercise

Items needed:
Your black Star Goddess candle
Matches

This set of exercises should take roughly three weeks to complete. Each of these three exercises should be performed at least four times in a one-week period before moving on to the next step. Begin each by first performing the three parts of the Opening the Way exercise. When you are finished with the specific working you may end your rites by taking back your power from the candle flame, as in the Holy Flame exercise.

1. Spend five minutes sitting in meditative space, simply paying close attention to your immediate environment. Notice the sounds of the space you are in … the temperature … the state of light or darkness. Pay attention to all of your senses and try to really listen to what they are telling you. Especially if you are already familiar with your environment, then you may be tempted to give less than your full attention. *Don't skip over this.* Expand your awareness beyond your immediate environment and see what you can learn about the surrounding areas. Write down your observations in your journal.

2. Twice a day choose an object to visualize for two to eventually five minutes at a time. It should be something relatively simple, like an apple, a spoon, or a candle. Experience as many details as you can about the object, and engage all your senses (touch, smell, taste, etc.).

3. Recalling the familiar sense of talker and all it represents to you, imagine that you can focus this sensation in the center of your brain. Just imagine that this area is shining with a warm, white-golden light and that this light fills your entire body, shining outward into your nimbus. Maintain this sensation and awareness for at least the span of seven breaths, and eventually work up to maintaining it for several minutes, paying attention to this sensation while simultaneously being aware of your environment.

## Fetch: The Primal Soul

The second part of our soul structure is called variously the wraith or *fetch*. This is the *unihipili*, or lower self. It will become familiar if we approach it as the Freudian id or subconscious, as long as we remember that these terms refer to aspects of the psyche and not to spiritual presences of which the psyche is but a part.

Fetch is preverbal, communicating not in words and sentences, but in gut reactions, symbols, and dreams. It is our animal and sexual nature … as well as our innocent child nature. It is primal and uncivilized. It is fetch that desires something even though we may know it is not good for us. It is that part of us that experiences delight and joy, and, according to Cora Anderson, is the first part of our soul that falls in love.[19]

To fetch there is no reasoning, just desire. Fetch has needs, and it communicates those needs to us primarily through the physical body. We crave foods, people, drugs, and other experiences that make fetch feel secure and more powerful, while we instinctively avoid certain things and situations that would make fetch lose that power. This makes getting to know your body essential in learning to effectively communicate with fetch.

According to tradition, fetch is the part of our soul structure that stores our memory. Within fetch is what modern psychology has termed "the shadow"—the Jungian idea of an unconscious aspect of the personality that is disassociated from the ego and effectively hides away our least desirable traits. Many things lurk in the shadow, such as buried memories of things we've done or were done to us, secret longings, secret fears, grief, guilt, or shame. All of our secrets lurk within the shadow, just out of sight. Waiting patiently and never quite forgotten. Fetch has a long memory.

Faery Tradition recognizes this part of the soul as the first layer of subtle energy in the human aura that is closely connected to the physical body. This layer is said to permeate the physical body and extend outward roughly one to one and a half inches (2.5 to 4 cm). While this layer can change its form for the skilled or naturally gifted practitioner, it most often mimics the form of the physical body and can appear to others in this form without regard to the body's location. This is most evident in cases of astral projection. The phenomenon of seeing an apparition of a living person most probably became associated with their impending death because the wraith body is said to be more likely to dissociate from the physical body near death. In many of these cases it is possible that the person's wraith body was already in the process of preparing for physical death, causing the apparitions in question.

---

19. Anderson, *Fifty Years in the Feri Tradition*, 16.

*Fetch* is the "soul of the body." Its primary concern is the gathering of life force to fuel and feed the physical body and then to distribute anything left over to various other tasks and causes. Fetch already knows how to do this; it is a basic, natural function of fetch, much as your heart's natural function is to pump blood. No one needs to explain to the heart how to do this; it simply does, thus enabling your life to happen, beat by beat by life-giving beat. Fetch works in much the same way. However, using exercises such as those given in the previous chapter will teach fetch how to work under the conscious direction of talker. This will allow us to better harness the power fetch gathers, to collect *extra* power than what we might normally gather, and then to direct that power where *we* decide, and not only where fetch's impulses might otherwise determine.

Fetch's first and foremost job is to keep the physical body alive—to make sure the heart is beating and the lungs are breathing and our other internal organs are functioning properly. Fetch directs life force to those organs, synapses, and nerve endings that are responsible for making this happen. Generally, fetch gathers what it needs to from the environment, but has little else remaining for whatever spiritual or magical tasks we may wish to engage.

The *dantian* associated with fetch is a spot usually described as being "three-fingers width" beneath the navel. This corresponds with the folkloric lower Cauldron of Warming, which is upright in all people at their birth and is associated with raw life force and vitality. Fetch can be related to the first two and even the third of the Hindu chakras, this last being shared with talker.

### Knowing Fetch Exercise

This set of exercises should take roughly three weeks to complete. Each of these three exercises should be performed before moving on to the next step. Begin with the Opening the Way exercise.

1. Each day this week, for five to ten minutes, re-create the sensual awareness from various memories. (Example: If you have ever been on a roller coaster, you might recall the sensation you experienced as you slowly approached the top, and then began the inevitable descent … see how well you can "feel" the experience now. Sensually recall other experiences, both pleasant and unpleasant.) Record your observations in your journal.

2. For the second week: Get a small portion of a food that you are particularly fond of. This should be something special, something that is a type of treat. Spend five

to ten minutes enjoying this food while you do nothing else: no talking to others, no listening to music or TV, no texting on your phone, no checking the dreaded Book of Faces. Just be *present* with the flavors and the textures of the food you are enjoying. Feel the food in your mouth as it moves over your taste buds. Feel it moving down your throat as you swallow. Let every bite, every chew, every flavor, and every texture be a type of devotion to the present moment that only exists *right now.* Try a similar approach this week with music, with art, with dance, with sex... This is fetch, not a sterile, mental idea, but the actual living, breathing, dancing, sweating, and sexual soul of our wild, divine physical bodies.

3. Using what you have learned about fetch over the past two weeks, recall its presence and imagine this sensation as being anchored in a space about three-fingers width beneath your navel. Feel a red warmth building in this area. Your primal blood pumps in your gut. Allow this presence to open up and deepen within you. Explore your deep feelings. Pay attention to what fetch wants... what *you* want... on a deep gut level. Are you uncomfortable? Relaxed? Angry? Bored? Hungry? Sexually excited? Pay attention to what your body is telling you, as this is the first way that fetch has to communicate with us. This isn't about acting on those impulses (sometimes our fetch wants things that are dangerous, inappropriate, or even violent). This is about observing and giving fetch a clearer space in which to communicate its own needs and desires. When fetch feels *heard,* then our inner workings will go much more smoothly. Allow yourself at least a few minutes to fully be aware of fetch.

End by placing your hands on your lower belly as you think of something happy. Close your eyes and really picture it... feel the emotions of happiness and then physically smile wide. Allow your heart to open and see this opening facilitating the light of talker to shine down from your head as a white-gold light. Allow this light to shine down into fetch as a type of self-blessing. Send this smile and this happiness to fetch.

---

Besides a deeper understanding of our own primal nature and the complexes it contains, we must also learn how to communicate effectively with fetch because it is only this part of our soul structure that is able to directly communicate with the third, and highest, of our three souls: the *holy daemon.*

# Holy Daemon: The "God" Soul

This part of our soul structure has been described by the myths of numerous cultures and has appeared in countless works of art that span the globe. The halo of Christian and Eastern art is an artistic attempt to capture the essence of the in-dwelling divinity that is present in all humanity, but it is most often seen in those who are spiritually enlightened. Usually appearing around or above the head (though sometimes around the whole body) the halo was the representation of the divine light, associated with Christ, Buddha, and numerous other divine figures throughout history.

Sometimes called the "Deep Self," this is the part of ourselves that flows back into the fullest presence of the Star God/dess, God Herself. In BlueRose we use the phrase *holy daemon* to describe this soul, in reference to the ancient Greek *daimone*, which referred to a type of tutelary spirit or one's personal genius. This was seen as a type of intermediary presence, between one's human nature and that of the gods. In Faery, this is seen as our own "higher" or "deeper" nature, our very own piece of God/dess through which we may more safely commune with spirits and intelligences from other planes of existence.

From the perspective of talker, the daemon is something akin to a parent, in that it is a more highly evolved form of consciousness, has a more far-reaching perspective than talker, and is a guiding and protecting influence. The daemon, it is said, loves the talker (and fetch) with "the same love that a perfect parent has for a perfect child, raised to the power of divinity."[20]

According to Irish magical tradition, the Cauldron of Wisdom is located in the head and is for most people turned upside down at birth. Only those who have undergone the true initiation are able to turn it upright, and be fully open to the wisdom of the God Soul.

In Faery Tradition, this soul is said to symbolically reside just over the head of the physical body. In this it is our own transcendent nature, our higher self as described in the New Thought movement, or the Holy Guardian Angel of Ceremonial Magick fame. It is part of our work in Faery to draw it down into our body where it can become embodied. Once this embodiment of the daemon becomes habitual, we are better able to be in control of our magic, and are able to touch sources of power that would otherwise elude us.

It is through the daemon and the spirit contacts made through the daemon that the deep magic of our Craft occurs. It is only through the conscious embodiment of our own divine nature that we are more safely able to traverse the worlds and engage with their inhabitants *as equals*, a foundational approach for the practitioner of Faery Witchcraft.

---

20. Faery oral tradition.

Consider this poetic piece of Faery teaching offered by the late Grandmaster Victor Anderson: "*God is self and self is God and God is a person like myself.*" Underneath its almost silly singsong composition lies a hidden piece of contemplative wisdom.

"God is self and self is God…" begins the teaching. I interpret this to mean that God and self are two sides of the same divine quality, that being *consciousness*. It is consciousness itself that is the divine spark that exists with us. This is what makes gods (and ourselves) holy. We may be small, but we must recognize this inherent holiness, our own authority as caretakers of the divine spark of life that we each contain within ourselves. We are all God Herself made manifest, the Luciferian in-dwelling divinity, the spirit-within-matter, the stars within the earth. "I am a cell in the body of the Goddess. And I demand my rights!"[21] We approach even the gods, as we would other people, neither higher nor lower than ourselves, as equals. "God is a person like myself." We recognize the divinity within all things. Through this recognition we make connections. And it is through these connections that we make magic.

One of the (many) traditional images associated with the holy daemon, one that is particularly pleasing is that of an unfolding flower, ever in perpetual bloom, as if to express its innate quality of openness and pure beaming radiance. It is this imagery that Victor drew from when he taught what can be thought of as a core prayer of the Old Faery Tradition:

### The Flower Prayer

*Who is this Flower above me?*
*And what is the work of this God?*
*I would know myself in all my parts!*

This prayer is often taught to students of our path as a means to poetically engage the daemon and be open to our calling, that spiritual message or drive toward which our personal daemon is here to guide us in this life. While the flower is not specified in the prayer, we might be forgiven if we were to draw a page from the ancient Hindu who often used the symbol of the lotus flower and its multitude of petals to symbolize the ever-unfolding mystery that is spirit. The lotus also symbolizes a dual nature, as it grows in the dirty muck and then blooms in the clean, sunlit air above the mud, thus representing the evolution of pure spiritual enlightenment born out of the grossest of forms.

---

21. Oral tradition attributed to Victor Anderson.

While the lotus is the archetypal spiritual flower of the East, its Western counterpart is definitely the rose. An even casual perusal of the literature associated with Western Magical Tradition will yield many results of the rose being held as a symbol of the unfolding mystery of magic and spirit. It also represents a dual nature, what with its delicate and fragrant blooms, and its sharp and foreboding thorns. It is a flower of spirit, love, power, and mystery…and the dangers that accompany them.

The name of my lineage of Faery Tradition, *BlueRose*, stems, in part, from a visionary experience with my holy daemon. In this vision, I saw my own daemon as a rose of cobalt blue flame, in perpetual, unfolding bloom over my head. From its center emerged the Dian y Glas, the youthful Blue God of love, sensuality, and deep spirituality, who is equated in our tradition with one's personal God Soul, or daemon.

Think of your daemon as your own personal pipeline to the gods. It is through this deeper and higher nature that we are able to connect with forces outside of ourselves; powerful spiritual forces that might otherwise cause us harm are made less dangerous through the embodiment of our own daemon.

In the Faery Tradition we are taught never to allow anyone or anything to come between ourselves and our own daemon. In the Old Craft we do not "bow down" to anyone or anything, and that includes the gods and spirits with whom we work and offer our devotion. In fact, the honoring of our own daemon is *required* before praying to any other deities or spirits. When we draw down our daemon into our bodies and into alignment with our other souls, we step into a focused magical space from which we can walk between the worlds in shamanic fashion, and better direct the powers we seek to summon.

The daemon is always at the ready to answer our prayers. This is the first god to whom we pray, before all others. But often our prayers are muddied and our intentions are not made clear. All too often both fetch and talker will disagree about how to go about certain things and so will "fight" in their own way. Talker may wish to proceed, but fetch will drag its feet. All the while, daemon hovers above us patiently waiting until the "kids" stop squabbling. This makes getting to know each part of our soul structure and clearing away any complexes that may be present essential to working effective magic in our tradition.

In the lore of the Old Faery Tradition, this soul is often referred to as the Bird Spirit, referencing the symbolism of the bird as being of heavenly environs. This bird shows up in various forms in Faery lore: a falcon, a peacock, and a dove, to name a few, each linking this soul to a major deity revered in Faery Tradition, Dian y Glas.[22] In fact, *Dian y Glas* is said to be the Faery name for the God Soul, as well as being the name of a deity. This paradox is not uncommon in our tradition, which we might be reminded draws its name from the beings and workings of the liminal otherworld. We will delve more deeply into the nature of the Blue God (as well as other deities) in the chapters to come, but for now suffice it to say that the Faery concept of the daemon is that it is one and the same as the Blue God and yet is also our own personal God Soul.

The Hawaiian name for this soul, *aumakua*, gives us a hint into its evolutionary nature. In Hawaiian mythology, the aumakua is an ancestor spirit who has risen to a deified state. In this we are exposed to the idea of the aumakua as an evolutionary process, rather than a static state of being. Old Faery Tradition teaches that the three souls continue to live and grow after physical death. The souls are known to sometimes split apart after the death of the body, and each may go on to follow their own paths. According to oral tradition, a fetch can evolve over lifetimes and become a talker, while a talker can eventually evolve into a daemon. With this in mind, the idea of one's daemon also being a type of ancestor might take the form of a soul living several lives, gaining experiences, and evolving over time. This evolution is following family lines in some cases, while in others manifesting perhaps in an unseen lineage, one that is mapped not in bloodlines but in spiritual connections. The holy daemon is the center of our shamanic web, by which we find connection with every other spirit, being, planet, star, and particle in the universe. The holy daemon is our personal *mystery*. It is that part of us that is still out of reach … a dream not yet fulfilled, a potential yet to be realized.

## *Knowing Daemon Exercise*

This set of exercises should take roughly three weeks to complete. Each of these three exercises should be performed before moving on to the next step.

---

22. This has usually been taught in Faery circles to be Welsh for "God of the Blue," which is demonstratively incorrect. While it *may* have been an attempt by an English-speaking person who was learning the Welsh language, it is also likely (based on Victor Anderson's penchant for gaining knowledge from spirits on the astral as well as relying on his knowledge of past lives) that this phrase is an "intuitive reconstruction" of the (long lost) language of the ancient Picts, an early major spiritual influence on our tradition.

Items needed:
 Your black Star Goddess candle
 Offering candles
 Matches

1. Open the Way. Imagine a brilliant blue light shining in a space roughly 10 to 12 inches (25 to 30 cm) above your head. This light takes the form of a many-petaled flower—a lotus, a rose, a cornflower, etc.—made of blue fire. Know that this is your highest and deepest self and that it loves you unconditionally. Recite the Flower Prayer. Imagine that the light of the sun or stars in the heavens above shine down upon and through the petals of your flower, shining down into your crown and slowly filling your body as you breathe twelve breaths of power. With each exhale, chant "*Iao!*" in a long, drawn-out drone, feeling the light of the daemon shining within and around you, surrounding you in a bubble of love and protection. Stay in this state for at least several moments and pay attention to how you feel and whatever messages you may receive. Journal your experiences before ending the session.

2. After one week of the above, prepare an altar to your daemon. Include objects and art that feel in resonance with your higher self. Each day light a candle in its name and speak aloud an invocation to your own daemon, detailing its beauty, power, and other precious qualities. Burn incense as an offering and meditate on your daemon for several minutes while you gaze at the candle. Imagine a shower of stars falling down around and through your head; allow yourself to truly listen to what messages you may receive.

3. After one week of performing the first two steps, add the following: Choose a spirit or deity that you wish to work with or one with whom you already have an active relationship. While in the receptive listening state of communion with daemon, reach out with your awareness through your daemon and out into the universe and seek audience with this being. Imagine your daemon shining brightly above your head and illuminating the outer darkness. Be aware of any spirits or beings that you may sense. If you feel a connection to your chosen deity or spirit, then project an aura of respect and power to them through your daemon. Communicate with them and see where it leads you.

---

While each of the souls have traditional anchors in the physical body that correspond roughly with the Irish Cauldrons, the *dantians* of Chinese medicine, and certain of the Hindu chakras, they are not identical. Victor Anderson reportedly taught that it was possible to open up energy centers at any location within the body, and not just those used in various systems. With this in mind, various lines of our tradition each may differ in their placement of these anchors. This also further validates different approaches, which may place these souls in different physical locations.

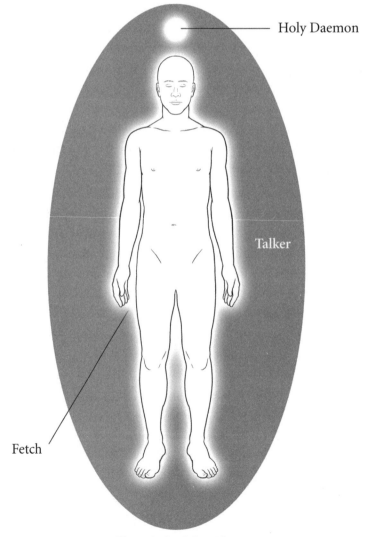

*Figure 2: Auric Locations*

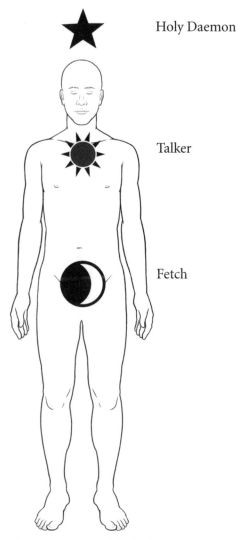

Holy Daemon

Talker

Fetch

*Figure 3: Stations of the Body*

## The "Ha" Prayer Exercise

In the form given here it is a prayer to align our Three Souls. This it does by its very nature, but later—once proficiency is gained through its repeated engagement—we can work it toward a more specific goal.

This exercise is actually a spell. In fact, it is sort of *the* spell in Faery Tradition, in the sense that it forms the basis for all energetic transactions in our practical philosophy.

As with most of the exercises within our tradition (even the core exercises) there are different approaches, which come to us from the Hawaiian stream of cultural mythos. This is a version that is used in the BlueRose lineage.

As mentioned previously, *ha* means "breath" and "spirit" in Hawaiian. It is also the sound that is made when making an audible exhale, a key component of this rite.

Begin by breathing the Blue Fire. With every breath, pay attention to how you feel this charge is building up. The result should feel like an almost electric tingling, and it may manifest especially in the genitals, stomach, and fingertips.

Mentally (talker) ask fetch to gather and store this wraith-force. It can be a simple thought, or you may wish to speak a more formal declaration, such as:

*I now gather wraith-force to align my Three Souls.*

Take four deep breaths—inhaling for the count of four and exhaling for the count of eight—in through the nose and out through the mouth, imagining that fetch is gathering wraith-force. Just before the fourth exhalation, cock your head backward and imagine sending the power from fetch up to your daemon as you exhale the sound *HA!*

For some, when performing this exercise, this exhalation will be short and forceful, a sudden *HA!* For others this will be gentler, perhaps the soft exhalation of a lover's sigh, a breathy *haaaaaaa…* Experiment with both and remember to record your observations in your journal.

## The Rite of the Bird Spirit

This is a slight reworking of a traditional Old Faery rite to align the souls and manifest one's desires. It can be seen as a ritual extension of the Ha Prayer. The overall approach is nearly identical to the traditional form, but the form and poetry given here are my own and preserves the symbolism of the original. (This can be altered to better suit your needs.)

Items needed:
Your black Star Goddess candle
Matches
A light blue candle
Some copal incense
A short length of red cord
Two medium-sized stones

Begin by Opening the Way. Light the blue candle and the incense. Pass the red cord through the smoke of the incense, and then tie it into a loose slipknot. Place it gently aside.

Take four deep breaths of power. Pause for a moment, and then imagine what it is that you wish to manifest. Take four more deep breaths, and then knock the two stones together nine times, in three groups of three. (This is taught as a method for getting the attention of your fetch.)

Be aware of your daemon above you in the form of a bird made of blue fire.[23] Take hold of the (knotted) cord, holding it loosely in your hands.

Take four deep breaths, contemplating how you are gathering life force into your fetch as you do. Pause for a moment and then chant the following in a single, low, vibrant tone:

> *The spirit hovers over me*
> *The bird now spreads its wings*
> *I draw the waters into me*
> *And the power that it brings*
> *Store, O fetch, these waters now*
> *As four times I will breathe*
> *And when I pull the red cord tight*
> *The blue falcon is released.*
> *As arrow fleeing from the bow*
> *As semen from the phallus flows,*
> *I breathe again, I speak the word*
> *And give the water to the bird.*

---

23. The original called for the visual of a silvery-blue sphere.

Take four breaths while again contemplating the gathering of life force, and then recite the chant again. Do this again for a third time.

Once you have completed the three recitations, take an additional deep breath of power while focusing on your daemon. Exhale forcibly and quickly while you exclaim the sound *HA!* and project a sense of power from your fetch to your daemon as you also quickly and tightly pull the cord from each end, pulling loose the knot and holding the cord taught. Pay attention to your experience of alignment for at least a few moments, while you hold the cord in front of you.

### Opening the Way 4: The Inner Constellation Exercise

This exercise will become a staple of your Faery practice and should be considered to now be part of your Opening the Way exercises. As you become more proficient with it, you may take less time to perform it. Initiates with years of experiences are trained to be able to align their souls with a single breath. But we would be foolhardy to think that this would be all that we will ever need to do to align ourselves. Though I often align with a single breath (and I do so multiple times each day) I still practice the formal forms in order to keep myself skilled. Otherwise it is far too easy to become lazy and inaccurate with our work.

In a relaxed state, focus your awareness softly in your head … in your talker. Become aware of your thoughts as they arise … just notice them without judgment. Continue to breathe, slowly and deeply in a rhythm.

As you breathe, begin to notice the spaces of stillness and silence that exist at the ends of your breath. Allow them to wash over you with every pass as they grow larger … each breath bringing them closer together toward the center of your breath where they meet and merge into one eternal moment of stillness and silence. Feel the presence of the Void as you breathe slow and deep. Allow your mind to clear. … Do not force your thoughts away; just notice them as they gently float away from you like leaves on the wind on your exhale … free of distraction, allow your talker to become cleansed and charged as you breathe.

Now, imagine a brilliant golden yellow light begin to form in your head. As you breathe, it becomes the sun in miniature, shining brilliantly and radiating out into your outer aura … the auric realm of the talker. In your mind … in your talker … form the intent to align your Three Souls. Feel this intention shining in the heart of the sun within you and allow it to become stronger and clearer with every breath.

Breathing deep, allow your awareness and your intent to slowly sink down inside your body … deep down into your belly … into your guts … into your sex … into your fetch. Imagine that your intent has now become a symbol of your Three Souls aligned, and notice how you feel about that symbol.

As you breathe allow yourself to feel the presence of your fetch … your emotions, your desires, your drives … and your power. Imagine a primal red light begin to form in your lower belly, becoming a blood-red full moon in miniature. As you focus on this image and sensation, notice how your fetch feels … notice what it wants. It will speak to you in emotions, impulses, or in symbols. Take your time with this.

Now begin to breathe the Blue Fire. Allow this power to flow into your fetch where it is stored. Feel your fetch alive with the conscious energy of the Blue Fire, first in your belly and genitals, but then all around you in that first layer of your aura, your etheric body … the auric realm of the fetch. Focus on your symbol of intent and feel how it is being charged with life force with every breath.

When you are feeling charged and powerful, open up your awareness to your holy daemon above you. See it as a brilliant star made of Blue Fire surrounded by all the stars and galaxies in the cosmos. Imagine this central blue star as containing the collective light and brightness of all the stars in the heavens concentrated into a single point.

Take four deep breaths of power, your inhale focusing and concentrating the life-force in your belly, and then send that power up—along with your symbol—to your daemon as you exhale the syllable "*HA.*" Feel a charge of energy rush out of you, through your breath, and into your daemon above you. As your symbol flows into the daemon, feel that your prayer for alignment has been made and imagine that your symbol begins to radiate outward, morphing into a pearlescent glowing light. Feel this pearlescent light as a liquid energy that begins to flow down from the daemon over and through you until it begins to gently fill your fetch. Breathe this power deep into your fetch. Feel how it is being healed and charged with divine presence and guidance; fetch guided by daemon.

Now breathe this power up into your talker. Allow your consciousness to absorb this power. Notice that the power flows out into your outer aura. Allow the light of talker to slowly move from your head into your heart, leaving room for the daemon to descend. Feel the power move freely between the Three Souls, bringing them into alignment as each of them moves into your heart center, so that the moon eclipses the sun that is surrounded by celestial brilliance. See them come sharply into focus. See the resulting eclipse and feel how it is your own Black Heart of Innocence[24] shining bright—your own divinity aligned within you. Hear their particular energies like individual sustained resonant notes and listen to them sing now in perfect harmony. Recite the following incantation, feeling strongly that each of your Three Souls are speaking it in their own language:

*Shining star and moon and sun*
*Aligned within this vessel of the earth*
*Together now the Three made One*
*Our single voice in union given birth.*

Take a deep breath and feel the unity and strength of your Three Souls. After a moment say, *"We are the Three who speak as One!"* Feel strong and centered. It is done.

---

24. The Black Heart of Innocence is a unique Faery Tradition symbol for the natural sexual state of the soul and will be discussed further in chapter 12. Many thanks to Faery priestess Morpheus Ravenna for the suggestion to include a reference to the Black Heart in this exercise.

# CHAPTER 5

# PURIFICATION WORK

*Whatever purifies you is the right path.*
—RUMI

The more we work with the primal soul of fetch, the more we begin to realize just how much of that soul remains unseen. Like an iceberg, fetch only reveals the tiniest part of its mammoth self to the conscious eye. The vast majority of it lies beneath the surface. Fetch is definitely a "behind the scenes" sort of soul. All day long, while we are busy with other (talker-ish) tasks, fetch is busy as well, gathering life force from our environment. And herein lies the problem.

While it is indeed the mark of a good fetch that it gathers and stores this life force, it becomes slightly more problematic when we begin to see exactly what else is being gathered up. As mentioned previously, mana comes in many forms. There are messages in that mana that we receive from others around us in the form of attitudes and emotions ... these are "frequencies" of life force that we pick up all the time.

Anyone who has ever walked into a room of people and immediately felt a sense of tension can attest to this. This tense energy is still a form of life force ... its just life force that is at a frequency that we experience as tension. Life force is not always as benign as many would like to think. It can be just as destructive as any other force. Whether it comes in the form of traumatic events, bad news, disease, malicious gossip, or just bad vibes, not all of the life force that we accumulate is good for us. And yet we are taking it in all the same.

Think of this extra bad mana as the psychic pollutants that are just part of the environment. If we live or work in environments in which there is a lot of negative energy (abuse in the home, alcoholism, drug addiction, anger issues, hostile work environment, etc.), we are constantly taking that type of vibration inside of ourselves, and this could mean that we are being "psychically poisoned" little by little.

Even just living a somewhat normal, happy, middle-of-the-road existence doesn't mean that we have avoided our share of the poison brew. Besides the unavoidable occasional hard times that we each may experience during life, the messages that we constantly get from our culture through the Internet, TV, magazines, etc., are all telling us what we are supposed to look like, how we are supposed to act, and just how we are inevitably falling short. The corporate, ad-driven economy requires us to feel inferior so that we will turn to whatever wrinkle cream or boner pill we think will fix our (largely manufactured) problem. And once we feel we do have a problem, it will fester in the shadow of fetch, waiting for the right moment to come out and make us feel inferior, confused, or weak just when we need our strength the most.

A Witch cannot afford to be burdened with complexes and demons and fears. When we travel the astral worlds we need to be free and precise in our concentration. If we are harboring fears and complexes, they could arise in the middle of a trance and ruin our work. This can mean the difference of a successful spell or a bout of anxiety, depression, or worse. No matter who or what we are, there is negative life force that we come into contact with every day. And knowing this, we need to learn how to make ourselves free of it.

As alarming as this may sound, it is nothing new. Spiritual and religious traditions have long held the concept of spiritual contamination. This is the idea that certain objects, foods, activities, animals, areas of land, buildings, people, or states of being are disharmonious and can cause our souls to become ill or even injured if we engage or come into contact with them. This is where one might find observances and superstitions, such as those regarding touching the dead or entering a graveyard. To avoid the negative spiritual outcomes predicted in such a system, many traditions require sometimes elaborate cleansing rituals to be observed after coming into physical contact with a dead body, after having sexual relations, after spending time in a graveyard, or after eating certain foods, etc.

Spend any time with a group of Faery practitioners and you will soon realize that many of us are quite serious about the art of spiritual and magical purification. We are often performing cleansing rites, and it can seem, at times, as if we are in a never-ending cycle of the stuff.

This can be disconcerting for the new student, however, as the concept of purity has been co-opted by the church of the false god to mean a state of sexual ignorance, leading us to a plethora of societal ills that stem from the shame of our own bodies and a fear of our own sexuality. When we hear the word *purity* we might be forgiven if we think of purity rings, abstinence-only programs, and the other nonsense that the religious right in the United States had pedaled to the masses. But true purity is not a moral judgment. It is a clear and scientific fact.

Consider that a bar of pure gold is just that: pure. Meaning, it has nothing in it that is not gold, no "impurities." Should we analyze the bar of gold and determine that it is actually 2 percent brass, this says nothing of the gold's morality. The 2 percent of impurities in this scenario would need to be filtered out in order for the gold to retain its "pure" status.

When I am feeling that I am in a state of purity, this is when I feel that I have no obstacles, no blocks, nothing weighing me down. I am simply able to be myself, to allow my own natural life force to flow unencumbered. This is true purity. No adherence to some misguided political ideal—just being 100 percent who I really am.

I once had a student who refused to do the cleansing work that I assigned. They had performed the exercise once and then declared themselves "clean" and went on further to say that they felt that stressing the importance of such repeated cleansings was giving their fetch the negative message that it was *unclean*, and therefore they decided not to do any more of the cleansings. They were not dealing with any particular trauma or stress in life and so they thought it was better to just leave well enough alone.

I explained to them that—like bathing—one couldn't simply do it once and then expect that they were now "cleansed for life." Just like we pick up dirt and oils on our skin throughout the day, so too do we pick up psychic and spiritual contaminants that should be cleaned away regularly so that we don't become weighted down by them. It's up to us to take matters into our own hands and transform the situation we are handed into the one that we want. Leaving well enough alone has never made a good motto for Witches.

Part of our working in an energetic ecology is that we strive to not waste any life force, if possible. With this in mind, it should come as no surprise that instead of banishing negative energy, it is the main approach of Faery Witchcraft to make the attempt to transmute said negative energy into a form that is more useful. Toward this end we may use the following rites, the first being an exercise in the alchemically transformative powers of fire.

## The Fires of Purity

In the times of historic plagues, fire was often employed for its purification properties. As a means to combat disease, clothing, bodies, and even structures were burned in an effort to stop the spread of infection.

At some point in our lives we have all likely heard the phrase "purification by fire." This usually refers to a difficult or a painful period that ends in a successful outcome or some type of personal development or epiphany. Fire can burn, and it is precisely because of this fact that it is utilized in the purification ceremonies of both Witches and Pagans alike.

In our tradition, we can call upon the cleansing powers of fire in the form of a simple exercise that can be used by anyone in order to help transform whatever obstacles or noncongruent energies may be at play. We identify fire with life force and also with the spark of divinity. When we inwardly nurture that spark into a flame we are better able to stay free of the negative and even corrupting forces with which we come into contact every day.

### *The Fires of Purity Exercise*

This exercise can be used at any time you wish to help transform negative or stressful energy into a neutral form. It can be used daily, or even multiple times a day, if needed. Or you can use it when you are dealing with a particular situation that is stressful, such as paying bills or engaging in a difficult phone conversation. Once you have mastered the energetic techniques, you can augment the form to better suit you and your particular situation.

Items needed:
Your black Star Goddess candle
Matches
A white candle

Begin by Opening the Way, including the fourth step that was added in chapter 4. Recall something in your life that you feel to be negative. It can be a bad habit, a trait, a feeling … it can be large or small. As you continue to breathe slowly and deeply in a rhythm, allow yourself to truly feel the fullness of this negativity. If you have an emotional reaction to it, allow yourself to feel that emotion. If it is a memory, allow yourself to become totally immersed in it. Take some time with this. When you can feel it to its fullest extent allow yourself to maintain the sensation for the span of *at least* three breaths.

Cup your hands in front of you at heart level and take three deep breaths of power ... with every inhale allow this feeling to coalesce, becoming concentrated in your chest. Feel how this negativity becomes charged with your inhale, how it becomes magnetized and flows together from all the places in your body and aura and moves into your heart center. With each exhale, breathe this negativity into your empty hands, and imagine that it becomes a dark ball of negative energy, heavy and black. It becomes stronger with each breath, becoming like a dark star whose gravity draws out from you all that is negative, unhealthy, or impure. Feel it crackle and vibrate with darkness.

Now, take one more breath and send this dark power into the light of the Star Goddess candle with your exhale and a wave of your hands. Imagine the dark power as it collides with the candle flame and notice what you might feel as it does.

While concentrating on the light of the Star Goddess, begin to slowly chant *"aum"* as you light the white candle from the flame of your Star Goddess candle. Imagine that this sound is transforming the negative energy and that whenever you take a breath, you are breathing in this power, now transformed into a brilliant white holy fire. Continue to chant for as long as you feel it is appropriate. Then say:

> *By the light of the stars I am pure.*
> *By the flame of my own being I am whole again.*
> *By the holy fire I am charged and strengthened.*
> *And by my will, so must it be!*

Now, in silence, breathe in this fire, allowing it to completely fill your body until you are absolutely shining with it. When you feel you are ready, allow the holy fire to flow into your fetch, where it will be stored. If you feel that you are holding too much power, you may allow some to be sent to your daemon, or even be grounded into the planet. Extinguish the white candle. Breathe in silence for three breaths. It is done. End as normal.

Eventually this exercise should be performed (perhaps in an abbreviated form) each time you light the Star Goddess candle to begin Opening the Way, but practice with it as given here consistently (at least four times per week) for at least a month before making that change.

---

## The Waters of Purity (The Kala Rite)

The Waters of Purity is a stylistic adaptation of a core spirito-magical purification practice taught in our tradition. Known most often in Faery by its Hawaiian name, *Kala*, this word means "to loosen, untie, free, release, remove, unburden, or absolve."[25] It is arguably one of the most important pieces of Faery Tradition praxis.

This simple ritual provides us with a means of mental, emotional, and spiritual absolution to free up entanglements of our own life force. These entanglements are most often created by something like an injury, trauma, or otherwise intense or long-term feelings of guilt, shame, anger, etc. We take on destructive messages from the world around us that do nothing to serve our highest good and everything to tear us down and make us feel small and disconnected from the divine. Often we are our own worst enemies in this regard, unable to really let go of the past so that we can move into a space of true healing. This is the true meaning of *forgiveness*, another meaning attributed to Kala. Forgiving is not the same as forgetting nor is it condoning bad behavior. It is simply valuing oneself enough to no longer accept the negative conditions of being attached to a particular person, issue, or complex and finally cutting the cord that would bind us to whatever dark fate accompanies them.

Even if we are not ready to forgive the acts of another, something else to consider is that most often the person who really needs to be forgiven is *ourselves*. The Waters of Purity becomes a ritual in which we can forgive ourselves in a way that includes our daemon. In essence, it is a spell for spiritual absolution.

Besides those born of our own complexes, we also can experience these blocks or negative energies at the hands of another. But lest we feel we need to immediately turn to more drastic measures, be aware that Kala is effective in dealing with all types of negative energies, external as well as internal. A hint of this is revealed when delving a little deeper into the word *Kala* itself, for it also means a "prayer to free one from any evil influence"

---

25. Ulukau, the Hawaiian Electronic Library, accessed July 15, 2015. http://goo.gl/6X2uTB.

as well as "to practice counter-sorcery."[26] Whether through mundane actions such as aggressive or inappropriate behavior, or less often through magical actions such as a manipulative spell or a curse, the Kala rite deals with these blocks all the same. In those instances when "bigger guns" are called for, the performing of the Kala rite becomes a highly recommended first step.

The practice of personal cleansing is not only for when we feel we have a specific problem. It is an integral part of the regular practice for the Faery practitioner, as it provides us with a means toward a type of "spiritual hygiene." At times we may think we are immune to the poison the world constantly tries to feed us. We may decide that through sheer will alone we will avoid the pitfalls that accompany the onslaught of negative energies that we experience on any given day. But our mental self is only one aspect of our whole being. Our fetch gathers up energies from the world without judgment and often takes on these negative messages, storing them away where they fester in our shadow, unseen and sometimes unknown.

As a regular practice, the Waters of Purity gives us an opportunity to transform negative energies and blockages within ourselves, as well as to reclaim the power that these blocks have tied up within our energy bodies. This process of taking back our (now transformed) power is an essential point of distinction when comparing cleansing practices of most other spiritual traditions. We are not banishing the negativity, we are literally *transforming* it into a form that is more useful and healthy. This is a healing rite above all else.

In its simplest form, the Kala rite is the simple act of charging a bowl or glass of water with life force while saying a simple prayer for one's own purification. Once the water has been charged, it is then drunk in order to physically imbibe the blessings invoked upon it. This physical act of drinking the charged water acts as a visceral symbol to the fetch that we are changing our being. We are literally taking this intention into our physical bodies. It becomes the Witches' potion, brewed in the cauldron of the Goddess.

Some have asked if other liquids may be used in lieu of water. While much of my own practice with Faery Witchcraft has led me to explore the edges of practices and what constitutes "tradition," to this I must answer with a firm "no." While one may wish to perform a similar rite using another beverage, the rite of Kala is traditionally done with pure water and nothing else. One reason for this customary insistence is that this is a traditional rite and if we were to change this core element then it would cease to be

---

26. Ibid.

Kala (or the Waters of Purity) and become something else. But there are other reasons more substantive to our query. Consider that each of us is comprised mostly of water. It is a basic element and is associated with cleansing, both physical as well as spiritual. We bathe in water. We are baptized in water. We drink water to help cleanse and flush our internal systems. It is a basic need for life to exist. It is simple. It is the water we need to live. Nothing more. Nothing less.

One last note about the process of Kala that comes from the lore of the Old Faery Tradition: it is said that the Kala rite is only "finished" upon the first urination performed after the rite itself. My interpretation of this traditional lore is that this is the instance in which we are releasing what does not belong to us. Having transformed our own complexes and impurities, those negative energies thrust upon us by others are likewise transformed during the rite and then released back into the cycle of water, where this transformation may continue to take place, sending ripples of healing out and into the world.

## The Waters of Purity Exercise

*Simple Version*
Items needed:
Your black Star Goddess candle
Matches
A glass of pure, fresh water

Begin by Opening the Way. Charge yourself up with the Blue Fire. When you feel that you have a sufficient charge built up (you may begin to feel a slight tingling sensation and/or become sexually aroused) place both hands palms downward over the surface of the water and *will* some of this charge into it with your exhales. See the water shining with a crystalline luminescence, humming and singing with sheer and pure power. Take your time with this and encourage your imagination to use all of your senses to make this experience seem more "real."

When you feel that the transformation is complete (or as complete as it can be for this session) drink the entire glass of water, imagining how this light is now merging with your body's fluids and spreading out to every part of you. Feel how this power—your power, now transformed and purified—is breaking down all blocks within you … spiritual, emotional, physical, and mental … and is making you strong, whole, and healthy. Take a moment to bask in this inner light.

*Complex Version*

This version takes the previous simple version and introduces the concept of calling forth one's negative energies or blocks. It also expresses the rite through a more formalized ritual to focus and increase its effectiveness. Once you have performed the above several times, try this version at least four times, taking notes on how you feel they differ.

Items needed:
Your black Star Goddess candle
Matches
A glass of pure, fresh water
Some sea salt

Begin by Opening the Way. Hold the glass of water in front of your lower belly, which is the anchor point for the fetch, our primal soul. Recall something that you wish to be free of … a bad habit, a negative trait, a fear, a bad relationship, etc. Allow yourself to really feel the presence of this thing, along with any emotions that may be attached to it. As you continue your meditative breathing, allow these sensations to build within you.

When you feel that these feelings are at their peak, breathe three deep breaths of power, and will this negative energy out of your energy body and into the glass of water, which now appears to your mind's eye as thick, black, heavy, and toxic. You may wish to make a sound of release on your exhale, perhaps visualizing the negativity as a black smoke or some other symbol that feels appropriate. If you still feel that there is more negativity within yourself take three more breaths and repeat the process until you feel it is time to move on.

Now, raise the glass up to heart level so that you can see the light of the Star Goddess candle reflected through it. While opening up to your own daemon, call out to the Star Goddess to come and assist your transformation:

> *I invoke the Mother of the Stars*
> *Who was and is and ever shall be*
> *Androgynous source of all creation*

*All seeing. All knowing. All pervading. All powerful.*
*Shine in me your holy flame!*

See her emerge from everywhere, and then step behind you to place her arms around you ... her hands now resting upon your own. Feel her presence move through your daemon and into every part of you. Say:

*Mother ... yours is the cup of the wine of life;*
*the cauldron of transformation and rebirth.*

Now hear her say back to you:

*Behold! I am the Mother of all living. And my love is poured upon the earth.*

Now, sprinkle a small pinch of sea salt into the water with the knowledge that it will now assist in transforming the negative energies. As you breathe silently intone the phrase *Holy Fire* on your inhale. On your exhale blow out upon the surface of the water, feeling the Goddess's presence moving in the form of a white star fire though your souls, through your own breath, and into the water. Imagine how the energy of the water is now being transformed ... what was toxic and dark is now beneficial and light. Allow the star fire to explode within the water, imagining it flaring up with each exhalation until you perceive it as a constant, steady, and brilliant glow. See the water shining with a crystalline luminescence, humming and singing with sheer and pure power.

When you feel that the transformation is complete, drink the entire glass of water, feeling how the light is now merging with your body's fluids and spreading out to every part of you. Feel how this power—your power now transformed and purified—is breaking down all blocks within you ... spiritual, emotional, physical, and mental ... and is making you strong, whole, and healthy.

Place your hands over your lower belly and send your fetch love and support. Physically smile and allow the associated feelings to arise. Say three nice things about yourself and send the feelings of these things down into your fetch, along with the energy of your smile. Give thanks to the Goddess for assisting you. Extinguish the candle and breathe in silence for the span of three breaths. It is done.

———————————

Observances like the Waters of Purity are important in our tradition because of the deep introspective work that is done in the training process. The path of Faery is a dangerous one, populated with our own demons and fears. As we continue to open our awareness and make spirit contacts, we will rely more and more on our ability to surrender the ego and more fully engage these beings in the trance worlds. In these states, our skills of alignment and concentration are essential to being able to maintain the integrity of our spirit connections and thus our magical work. In these states we are also more vulnerable, making the ability to transform negative or disharmonious energies into a more useful form, vital for keeping ourselves safe and balanced.

## The Holy Bath Ritual

This is a reworking of a traditional Faery rite. This simple observance can be a powerful one in times of need, so don't discount the importance of bathing magic. We will discuss other types of magical baths in chapter 9, but for now familiarize yourself with this basic approach. Try it at least once or twice this next week and journal your experiences.

Items needed:
A bathtub (a shower and a small basin for water will also work)
Your black Star Goddess candle
Matches
A white candle
Some incense
Salt or soil
An essential oil blend of your choosing

Go to your tub and draw a bath. (Alternatively, if you are using a shower, you may use a small basin of water to perform the ritual and then pour its contents over your head at the end.) When it is ready, light the Star Goddess candle and Open the Way.

Feel your own divinity aligned within you. Say the following while performing the stated ritual actions for each line of text:

*We are the Three Who Speak as One!*
*Water, by my life force I join you*
*With earth* (sprinkle some of the salt or soil into the water),
*With air* (blow one long breath through the incense smoke over the water's surface),
*With fire* (light white candle from Star Goddess then plunge flame into the water),
*And with aether* (pour some of the oil into the water).

Open yourself to the Star Goddess. Say:

*Water, be purified in the Name of the Mother of the Stars*
*Who was and is and ever shall be*
*Androgynous source of all creation*
*All seeing. All knowing. All pervading. All powerful.*
*Shine in me your holy flame!*

Imagine and feel her within you. Place your hands just over the water so that your palms are facing down. Take three deep breaths of Blue Fire and feel it, along with the presence of the Goddess within you, flowing from your hands and into the water below. See it glowing and becoming vibrant. Say:

*Mother of all the worlds,*
*Make holy these waters*
*That I may be purified.*

Draw a pentacle over the water with your fingers. See it flow into the water, charging and binding it to the purpose of what you have intended. Bathe in silence by the candlelight. When you are done give thanks to the Goddess.

------

Becoming proficient with various purification techniques will be essential to keeping balanced as we encounter the inhabitants of our shadow. The Waters of Purity should be done at a minimum of four times per week, and ideally every day. The other rites given in this chapter may be used as needed.

# CHAPTER 6
# THE WITCHES' FORGE:
## THE WARRIOR'S WILL AND THE IRON PENTACLE

*Anything worthwhile is dangerous.*
—VICTOR ANDERSON

Toward the realization of our own godhood the Faery practitioner cultivates an internal code of ethics that forms what is sometimes called "the Warrior's Will."[27] This is our true will, honed and sharpened razor-fine, forged in the hot flames of conflict and transformation, shaped by our strength, practice, and skill, and finally tempered by the cool waters of compassion and love. We hone our magical skills through our regular practice, and with months and years of diligence we are rewarded with a greater capacity for power as well as the proficiency necessary to wield that power effectively and responsibly.

Where the untrained individual would most often mindlessly react to certain situations, the Warrior is trained to mindfully respond. "Right action" is the key concept here, in that the Warrior (or the Witch) must do what is effective, not necessarily what might feel good in the moment. Only children (and some would argue, bloggers) can get away with throwing tantrums, and even then they are often punished. Functional adults need to be able to be effective at dealing with problems. And this means knowing our strengths

---

27. There are Faery initiates who do not like the term "Warrior" applied to our tradition. To this I must point out that Victor Anderson himself referred to Faery as a "Warrior's Tradition" on occasion and even likened Faery to a martial art. This does nothing to assert, however, that we should be forced to adopt the Warrior terminology if we do not wish to. I will remind the reader that our tradition is quite diverse, and very few formal rites or philosophies are shared by all lines. If the term bothers you, ask yourself *why* but then find a term that better represents this concept.

and weaknesses. "We do not coddle weakness," a popular saying in our tradition begins. So we search for our own weaknesses and then we strive to transform them.

It is vital that we become strong in the Power if we are to be successful Witches. Many of us have been practicing the Craft for several years, but may have plateaued in much the same way that one might with a physical exercise regime. After some time of doing certain practices, we can get to a place where we seem to not be able to progress any further, and we might start to imagine that we have come as far as we can go. This can be discouraging, to say the least, and is one of the main reasons that some might leave a formal practice of the Craft, feeling that perhaps, and with respect to Gertrude Stein, "there is no there there." This would be, in my opinion, an unfortunate mistake.

While the Craft is certainly not for everyone, there are many who would benefit from a deep magical practice to assist in honing their natural skills. Many of us are drawn to the Craft because of some inborn ability or spiritual quirk—something that makes us different from others around us, some quality that marks us as Witches. True Witchcraft is more than just the practice of it. It is the result of the practice. The Witch herself is the embodiment of the Craft—a living, breathing affirmation of it. A regular practice enables us to move slowly and steadily into that space of embodiment, that we may progress further upon our chosen path and have the strength and skill necessary to do so more safely.

The Faery Tradition teaches that the body of the Witch is a vessel for the Power. Our job then becomes one of shaping that vessel and making it a sound one so that it is able to effectively hold that Power. If our vessel is misshapen, then that Power could spill away or worse, such as cause damage to the vessel, which in this context could mean physical discomfort or pain, or even emotional trauma, and in extreme cases, even a psychotic break. Here, then, is the hidden danger of the Old Craft truly revealed: Through our engagement of the Witches' Fire we run the very real risk of burning ourselves.

If the notion that the Craft is dangerous gives you pause, it should. Our practice is literally one of harnessing primordial powers and inviting possession by spirits to assist in our magical work, and these powers and beings can easily wound or even kill if they are not approached with the razor-fine edge of balance and discernment that is the War- rior's Will. Our job as practitioners of the Witchcraft is to venture beyond the firelight of normal human perception and into the Outer Darkness of the unknown. While a few may legitimately make such a venture, even fewer will return unscathed.

The old lore tells us that when encountering Faery we are changed forever, and there are only three possible outcomes. If our constitutions are weak, we could be killed by the encounter, and folklore provides many examples of mysterious deaths supposedly occurring at the hands of the Fae. The power being too great for the body to contain, the death could come in many forms: a heart attack, an aneurism, or interestingly even a freak accident, suggesting that there might be an element of choice involved on the side of the Fae, and that our own strength alone might not be enough to withstand them should they move against us.

If we are not killed by our encounter with Faery, then folklore tells us we might simply be driven to madness. On this the old stories have no doubt: Faeries will drive you *crazy*. The expanded consciousness that is telepathically contacted during the Fae encounter is too great for the average, untrained human mind, and so the mind cracks. Many tales speak of those who "were never the same" after their encounter with the Fae. If our vessel is not a sound one—if we are not grounded in the physical world—then, when encountering the numinous, we could be easily tipped over the edge of our own sanity. It might be instant or it might take time, but once the sleeper in the shadow awakens it will rise and, like the devil, take its due.

Should we survive with our sanity intact we are given the Faery prize: the gift of poetry. We have previously seen that in Irish magical tradition *poetry* is a term synonymous with spiritual and magical power, and indeed the folkloric traditions speak of the poet also as being a prophet. In the ballad of Thomas the Rhymer, our hero Thomas, a folk minstrel, is taken by the Queen of the Faeries to her realm where he is in service to her for seven years under very specific instructions on how to conduct himself while there. Upon completion of this service, he is granted "the tongue that cannot lie," a poetic gift of prophecy. Thus Thomas becomes Thomas the Rhymer (a poet), his other traditional title being "True Thomas," a reference to his role as speaker of the truth, for whatever he predicted would come to pass. This was not only a gift of poetry or even prophecy but also that of manifestation: of spell craft and of magic. Whatever he *spoke, came to pass.* He had been initiated into the magic of Faery, and had been forever changed by the encounter.

As an initiate of Faery Witchcraft Tradition, I too have been changed by my encounter with the Faery Power. My experience is that this particular Power is one intimately connected to creativity in all forms, which is why our tradition has such a high number of artists and bards. Those who naturally have the Fae gift are drawn to our path like a moth to flame. We are inflamed by the passion of Faery and know that our souls sing with their eternal song. And so we follow that siren's song, wherever it takes us. And sometimes that path may lead us to dangerous places, and it might be safer if we had an experienced guide along the way. The training that has been developed in the various lines of the tradition has sought to make the journey into Faery safer for the experiencer, but by no means has it made the journey safe. In much the same way that there is only saf*er* sex, there is only saf*er* Faery, and the risks that we take are real and ultimately our own.

Not even amongst initiates is everyone equally capable of harnessing the powers that we seek to control. Many of our own have not come back from in between the worlds intact. Ours is a path of deep shamanistic power in which we travel to other worlds and engage the beings there. Sometimes those dealings are simple and easy. Other times they are arduous and can leave us feeling broken and wounded. Such is the life of the Witch. There is always a price to pay. But this work will strengthen us. If we are diligent in our workings we will gather that strength little by little, and we will grow in our endurance and skill, becoming experienced, confident, and strong in our magic. This is when we become a competent Witch. Not at our initiation (which is truly just the beginning of our journey, as the word suggests) but after living the life of the Witch, after having worked with the tools and the magic, and having experienced the highs and the lows that a life in Witchcraft has to offer.

Much attention is given in the Craft for traditional roles, such as midwife or healer. While these are both important and noble roles and professions, there is another role within Traditional Witchcraft that often gets overlooked. And it is precisely this role that we need to—at least symbolically—take on for ourselves if we are to gain strength and power.

To those who depended on them, the blacksmith was a magician. Literally. Who else could take the very bones of the earth and—through fire, water, strength, and skill—shape them into the needs of society? To ancient peoples the blacksmith was an integral figure, providing much needed tools for farming, building, and everyday simple living. Every buckle, every sword, every plowshare, every horseshoe, and each and every nail had to be worked by a skilled smith to provide the basic necessities of life.

The Greek god of blacksmiths and fire, Hephaestus, was depicted as being crippled, as were some other early forge gods. This is perhaps due to the harsh chemicals used by the blacksmiths of antiquity, which we now know could cause crippling damage to those who worked with them over long periods unprotected. Drawing from this lamed smith god folkloric imagery, some forms of Traditional Witchcraft enact a sort of dance representing the Witch blacksmith god Tubal Cain as being crippled, dragging one foot behind as he circumambulates the "compass round."[28] This could also be representative of a gruesome alleged folk practice: the blacksmith, being so necessary to the survival of a village, would be literally hobbled to prevent him from being able to leave.[29]

As a master alchemist, the blacksmith was able to cause solid objects to bend to his will, a sorcerous act to be certain, though the magic didn't necessarily stop there. Enchantments were often woven into the objects being shaped upon the forge—a sword empowered by a god of war or skill, a shield ensorcelled for protection, a cooking pot blessed in the name of a bountiful goddess.

The Faery Tradition is both old and new. As inheritors of the Old Craft, we take very seriously the responsibility of preserving the myths, art, spells, and lore that have been handed down to us, while at the same time acknowledging that this traditional lore forms the beginning of our magical understanding, and not its end. We take these stories and teachings of old and strive to find new meaning in them. With this in mind, perhaps what we need is to become the blacksmiths of our own lives. Enter, the Iron Pentacle.

## The Iron Pentacle

One of the most recognizable tools of the Faery Tradition is also one of the most misunderstood. While some still insist that its origins are in the Harpy Coven of which Victor was a member in his teen years, there has never been any evidence of this, and according to those closest to Victor he never made the claim himself.[30] The Iron Pentacle is a means to help address some of the concepts that caused psychic wounds that the over-culture has inflicted upon us all. These five concepts in particular being especially problematic or "hot" areas in our psyche that need be refined and tempered were the ones that Victor felt were hurdles to living in the Black Heart of Innocence, a major goal for the Faery practitioner.

---

28. Laurelei, "The Lame Step," American Folkloric Witchcraft, accessed September 14, 2015. http://afwcraft .blogspot.com/2011/06/lame-step.html.

29. Glaux, "Tubal Cain: an Introduction," American Folkloric Witchcraft, accessed September 14, 2015. http://afwcraft.blogspot.com/2012/04/tubal-cain-introduction.html.

30. From a private conversation with an initiate of Victor and Cora Anderson, who was also a member of their final coven.

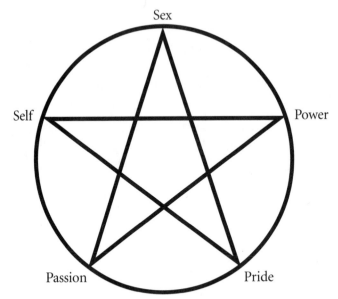

*Figure 4: Iron Pentacle*

At first glance, the Iron Pentacle may seem like a simple mnemonic device to assist the student in remembering certain concepts integral to the tradition. While it certainly possesses this benefit (and this alone has the potential to help us cultivate and maintain the Warrior's Will, if we are diligent in its contemplation), the Iron Pentacle is so much more. The Iron Pentacle is the soul-forge of the Faery practitioner. With it we expertly craft ourselves into finely honed tools of the Craft.

It is a pentacle both because it is the largest symbol of the Craft (with its interlocking points that represent the five elements of life) but also because the pentacle represents the human body.

The pentacle is iron because this element is essential to virtually all life on this planet. It is a "star metal" in that it was created in the stellar forge that is the heart of a star. When that star died in an unimaginably powerful explosion, that iron was spread out across the universe and eventually formed into the cores of planets, including our own Earth. Iron is a metal related astrologically to the planet Mars and represents the male principle of divine creation, inseminating the female principle who is the earth mother. It is a magnetic metal and played a major role in early magic and the development of science. It became associated with power and healing.

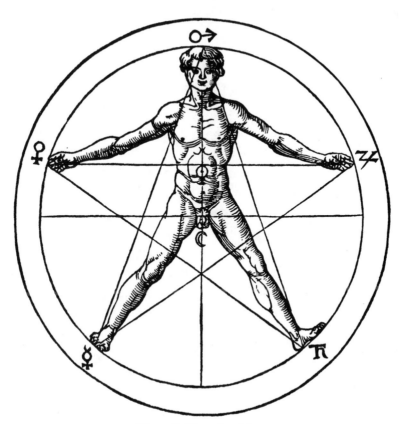

*Figure 5: Vitruvian Man*

Around 1050 BCE the Chinese created the first magnetic compasses using lodestones, magnetically charged pieces of iron ore. While they were used primarily for divination, it was much later, in the fourteenth century, that the magnetic compass became essential to the sea-faring peoples of the Mediterranean, who could now use this tool to help chart their course when they could no longer see the stars due to bad weather, thus opening up a new world of travel and trade.

Its symbol on the periodic table is Fe (from the Latin *ferrum*). This last detail forms one half of a "poetic etymology" invented by Victor to give symbolic authority to his preferred spelling for our tradition, "Feri" (the other half being *ferus* the Latin origin for the word "feral"). In doing so, the importance of both iron and primal wildness to our particular branch of the Craft is poetically suggested. Like the planet, iron is at the core of our tradition.

Iron is also a major component of our own blood, and it is essential to the transfer of oxygen from our lungs to the tissues of the body and helping to remove waste on a cellular level. For us iron is blood; it is breath; it is purification; it is *life*.

Iron is also, the blacksmith knows, quite a soft metal. But it can be hardened, strengthened by the process of tempering—which is heating and pounding and shaping and cooling and starting the process over again and again.

Iron also, interestingly enough, plays an important part in Faery folklore where it is said to dispel or counteract Faery magic. This would at first seem contradictory; why employ the symbolic use of a metal that would avert the very magic we are trying to embody? The answer is that Faery Tradition is first and foremost about *human* magic. We have a relationship with the Fae realms, but we do not physically reside there.

Iron is a grounding metal; our lore speaks of its uses for anchoring someone in the physical realm during astral travel work. Victor recommended keeping a piece of iron on one's altar for just this purpose. Using the Iron Pentacle, we spiritually activate the iron in our own blood in order to excite our own life force but also to maintain our sense of physical reality, which will keep us safer as we traverse the other realms and deal with the denizens there.

The pentacle as a whole is a map to how we are engaging life force—namely, where in our lives we might be cultivating it effectively, as well as where we might be leaking it away. It is a psychic diagnostic tool, and one that can be quite effective if we allow ourselves to commit to a regular practice with it. Even if taken as a meditative mandala, the Iron Pentacle is more than just a mental tool. It is an energetic practice designed to refine our consciousness.

As we explore the points of the pentacle, we will be given an opportunity to discover where our own internal energies might be blocked or where our vessel might not be strong enough to contain the powers we seek to invoke. Through the lens of the Iron Pentacle we can more easily be made aware of our own complexes and weaknesses, and then through using the Iron Pentacle as an energetic and magical tool we can work to remove those blocks and refine the impurities we find within.

Each of the points of the Iron Pentacle has its own unique qualities and practices associated with it. To this growing body of traditional material BlueRose offers its own contribution: meditative "emblems," or visual symbols that act as keys when engaged in trance.

# Sex

## *Emblem: A Spiral Galaxy*

It has often been said that everything in Faery begins and ends with sex. In fact, Faery Tradition is most definitely a "sex cult,"[31] but only in the strictest sense of the term. While some might be disappointed to learn that this does not necessarily translate into wanton orgies, the true meaning of this is demonstrated in our creation myth. The universe's creation was a sexual act. The point of Sex on the Iron Pentacle represents that creative power and reveals itself in both the differentiating polarity and ultimate resonance of divine energy. It can be found in that moment of our own orgasm in which we shed the restraints of the ego-mind and open to the universal dance, participating in its creation and destruction with every flash of pleasure. The big bang was the universal orgasm. And creation has been unfolding ever since.

We recognize the act of sex going on all around us. Not just in the literal birds and the bees, but in the *experience of being moved* by a wondrous sight or event such as a stunning sunset or a work of art, the flavor of a fabulous meal, or the sense of rapture that may come from listening to an opera or other moving piece of music. This is a profound opening up of the soul and senses, an exhalation of the physical that both embodies and transcends. It is simply a state of ecstasy.

The eager student of the Craft should take note, as this is an important aspect of our Craft that goes back to the ages. Sex is beautiful. Sex is holy. Sex is *powerful*. There is a reason that it is often through sexual intercourse that many of the older traditions pass initiation from teacher to student. Sex allows us to achieve an ecstatic state, a state of power in which we can communicate in a deeper way than mere words. It lies outside of the logical. It is sensual. It is intimate. It is energetic. It is *mysterious*.

On a deeper level, the presence of Sex as seen through the lens of our pentacle goes even further. Even now, gentle reader, as your eyes glance over the page or the screen, and you glide your gaze over the letters I have chosen to use to communicate these ideas to you, be aware that my message, my words, my *will* have, in some sense, entered into you. Going further, we know scientifically that we are always exchanging molecules with other bodies of matter. To a Faery Witch this too is a sexual act. Sex is a sharing of energies, a blending. And sex embraces all of the senses, as all are equal pathways through which we can receive power.

---

31. I use this term deliberately, as this was the term that Cora Anderson herself used during a private conversation with me at her home circa 2004.

Its placement at the top of our pentacle reminds us first and foremost that we are sexual beings, and that any attempt to escape this basic fact flies in the face of reality. If we map the pentacle to the human body, the point of Sex occupies the head. This is a reminder of the old saying that the biggest sex organ in the body is the brain. In the act of sex, we merge physically with another, but this is just one layer of the sexual experience. We become energetically *permeable* and thus able to open to outside energies and influences. In the ecstatic state, that heightened sexual consciousness opens and we are able to touch powers greater than just ourselves. In Sex we open up to life force. In ecstasy we surrender the ego and are fully in the present moment and yet transported. We are between the worlds, and this is where the magic really happens.

## Journaling

Contemplate the following and then write in your journal for ten minutes.

*What does sex mean to you? How are your sexual relationships? If you are not partnered, self-sex is a valid way to run sexual energy. What does your sex life consist of? Are you satisfied? Do you feel connected or disconnected before, during, and after sex? What nonphysical sexual acts have you engaged in recently? If none, what can you make happen this next week?*

---

# Pride

*Emblem: A flower blooming in the sun*

Once we have opened to the life force in the point of Sex, we allow that life force to move through us, unimpeded. This truly is Pride, which is our own deep nature, allowed to shine forth unrestrained. The Abrahamic religions have often demonized pride by conflating it with arrogance, but true pride is not arrogant; it is noncomparative. It is simply the natural unfolding of who we are, laid bare unashamed. To be proud is to be free of the chains of sin and shame that have shackled humans for thousands of years.

To stand in our pride is to deny the hold that the false god has upon us. It is, quite simply, the claiming of our own divinity. The flower doesn't worry if it is as pretty or smells as sweet as the others in the field. It simply unfurls its petals and proudly displays its stamen, for all to see in a literally shameless sexual display. It is in the point of Pride that we begin to see the Black Heart of Innocence come into view. It is the state of being *before* being self-aware. It isn't "I am," it is simply "am."

## *Journaling*

Contemplate the following and then write in your journal for ten minutes.

*In which of your own qualities do you take pride? What activities do you particularly enjoy? What about those activities brings you happiness? Where do you feel shame? What part of you has been made to feel small? How do you think you would be if you allowed yourself to be big?*

---

# Self

*Emblem: An open eye*

Now the "I" comes into play. As life force moves from Pride and up into Self it blooms into our consciousness and we become self-aware. It is at this level that we become conscious, the divine fire of the gods made manifest in the form of our own sentience. Self is the full and true knowledge of our own limits and potentials as well as exploring the edges of who we are in relation to others.

We often think of self as a singular monolith, as if we are unchangeable as we move through our lives and interact with others. But a closer look reveals just how changeable we really are. We are not what we *do*. We are not our jobs, our religions, or our sexual identities. We are not defined by our relationships, though they can give us special access into deepening our understanding of Self. We may only show it in little ways: how our tone and demeanor softens when a certain person enters the room; how we adopt a particular mode of behavior when we go to work, as opposed to when we are with family or at a movie theatre or at a nighttime bonfire ritual on the beach. Depending on the situation and the other people involved we adapt; we change. The Open Eye of Self asks that we look closely and examine where these adaptations occur so as to better know where our triggers and complexes may be.

## *Journaling*

Contemplate the following and then write in your journal for ten minutes.

*Ask yourself, Who am I? When you release your job, your relationships, your likes, your dislikes, etc., what is left? Also, consider yourself in different social situations in which you have noticed that you behave differently. What triggers or prompts those changes? Do they serve you effectively?*

---

# Power

*Emblem: A tree, a lightning bolt, or a lightning-struck tree*

Like all of the points on the Iron Pentacle, the point of Power is problematic. Most often we have a culturally enforced negative view of power. "Power corrupts," we are told. But what we are often *not* told is that this is only one type of power. This type of corruptive power is often called "power-over." This type of power is coercive and often allowed to flourish in hierarchies where the few have authority over the many. The type of power that we are engaging through the Iron Pentacle is that of "power from within." This is the *true* power. It is simply "the ability to do something," and with this as our focus we begin to see just exactly where we are already directing the power in our own lives. With this awareness we might be able to discern how to revise where we are directing it, so as to better accomplish what we wish to do. "Power management" might be a focus on this point.

Power is changeable. What is powerful in one situation might not be effective in another. This is why the emblem is changeable as well. Sometimes we need the slow, steady growth of the oak tree, slowly forming rings and reaching its branches to the sky, unfurling each green leaf. Sometimes we need the lightning bolt to strike and destroy all we have built so that we may start anew. And sometimes, in those special times, we need the magic of the lightning-struck oak, a particular symbol of power for Druids, who carried pieces of this magically charged wood for the purposes of protection.

## Journaling

Contemplate the following and then write in your journal for ten minutes.

*Where in your life do you feel powerful? Where do you feel powerless? What things—great or small—have you been able to accomplish on your own? Even if just looking at small accomplishments allow yourself to contemplate a sense of power that comes from seeing your actions through and causing some form of change, big or small.*

---

# Passion

*Emblem: An ocean wave*

Passion, it is taught, is the gateway to ecstasy, a recurrently sought-out state in Faery Tradition praxis. Passion is our ability to *feel things deeply*. It is through engaging our emotions head-on instead of stifling them to be better palatable by society that we are able to truly step outside of ourselves as in the Greek meaning for the word *ékstasis*. On the road to ecstasy, Passion is a signpost pointing the way.

Passion only requires that we feel, it doesn't require *what* we feel, as all emotional states are equally viable portals into the ecstatic state. Consider "the passion of lovers" and the likely pleasurable feelings that phrase might evoke. Next, "she has a passion for teaching." Now consider "a crime of passion," a stark example of how emotions can—under the right circumstances—take complete control of our lives. Passion can be born out of joy and euphoria just as easily as out of grief, rage, seething hatred, or soul-wrenching despair. While my own personal preference is to induce states that are pleasurable for this work, it is equally valid to induce those that are born of discomfort. But either way, passion is like that ocean wave; if we are prepared to face it, we can get up on our surfboards and—through balance and skill—ride the wave to new vistas. Or the wave can crash over us, maybe even causing us to drown.

## Journaling

Contemplate the following and then write in your journal for ten minutes.

*Where is your passion? What excites you? What gets you out of bed in the morning? What do you fear? What makes you angry? What makes you sad? What is the root of your apathy? Explore your emotions as you ask yourself what in particular has the power to be "louder" than the others, and which ones remain quiet or even silent.*

---

## Running the Iron Pentacle Exercise

Once we have contemplated each of the points with our journals, it is time to engage more than just talker. While Victor taught his students the pentacle, he didn't offer a step-by-step method of energetically engaging and moving energy between the points. Here then is arguably one of the best innovations that the Bloodrose coven had to offer: through their creative process they created just such a method, and it is this technique from which BlueRose draws its initial steps in working with this traditional tool.

The process itself is a simple one. In the aligned state, we focus on the iron in our bodies, forming an energetic presence that we then use to draw the pentacle upon our physical form, tracing the points together as we draw the star within ourselves. We then invoke the presence of each point of the Iron Pentacle into a point on the star and then move energy by force of will between each point, continually drawing the star as it grows with intensity and speed with every repetition. We make whatever observations we can, and then we slow it down, and finally reabsorb the energies raised.

As this is one of the foundational practices of the Faery Tradition, you will want to make sure that you are giving it enough attention to really make it work. Doing it once or twice and then deciding that it's not useful really only demonstrates an inability to commit to a discipline. One Faery teacher that I know requires all new students to perform a similar exercise every day for thirty days with the additional requirement that they journal their experiences each day. If they miss a day then the thirty-day period starts over and they continue until the assignment is complete. This serves to both ensure that the student was really working with the pentacle in a meaningful way and to "weed out" those who were not cut out for such a rigorous practice. If Witchcraft is not for everyone then Faery might be even doubly so. A teacher (or this book) can only lead you so far. Ultimately, whether you are just a reader, or a long-distance or in-person student of an initiate, you will only get out of the practice what you are prepared to put in.

### Simple Version

Items needed:

Your black Star Goddess candle

Matches

Open the Way. Feel how with every breath, oxygen is activating iron in your blood. Feel the iron within you surge and swell with every breath. Feel how it takes life force from the air around you to feed your souls. Notice how it takes impurities from your body, and how it helps to break down the blockages within you. Every breath makes currents of power within your body pulse and throb and glow with a deep humming energy. Molten iron fire rushes through your veins.

Focus this iron energy into a pinpoint of red fire shining in the center of your forehead. With every breath this light gets stronger ... brighter ... hotter. Feel its intensity, focused like a laser. As you breathe into this light it begins to travel downward toward your right foot, leaving a trail of red fire where it rests for at least one breath. It continues onward and upward to the left, reaching your left hand. Breathing deep, it moves over toward your right hand. Feel the lines of energy as they vibrate and hum. Moving with your breath, the trail travels downward to the left, reaching your left foot. And then finally it returns to the center of your forehead. A five-pointed star of red iron fire is now shining over (or directly in front of) your body. Feel it throb and thrum with power. Feel its heat ... like molten stone. Sense its vibration ... notice how it is pulsing, like a slow, steady heartbeat.

Starting with the uppermost point, and moving in the order in which they were drawn, contemplate and invoke the presence of each point by chanting:

*In the name of [Sex, Pride, Self, Power, or Passion]!*

Hear each name ring like a great bell whose deep and clear resonance charges and purifies the point so that you may then breathe it in transformed. See the point glow brighter for a moment. Absorb this light and the resonant sound with your breath and feel it spread throughout your entire body and into your aura. Breathe this power back into the point on the pentacle. Contemplate the qualities of each point as you complete the other four. Repeat the entire pentacle at least seven times.

Now, still breathing slowly and deeply in a rhythm, silently run the energy between the points while increasing speed. Do this until the points are glowing steady and begin to merge until the entire pentacle is glowing with power. Feel the Iron Pentacle shine and vibrate before you! Notice how its light shines deep within you, bringing you into resonance with its aligned and powerful presence. Maintain this sensation for at least the span of seven breaths.

With three slow deep breaths, allow the Iron Pentacle to melt down within you, and on your fourth breath absorb the pentacle into your heart, beneath your navel, and in the center of your brain. On the fifth breath it moves out to flow into your whole body. On the sixth breath it flows into each of your Three Souls and your aura. On your seventh breath you have completely absorbed and embodied the pentacle. It is done.

### Complex Version
Items needed:
Your black Star Goddess candle
Matches
Five red candles

Place the candles on the ground around you to mark each of the points on the pentacle. You may wish to perform this exercise lying down with your body aligned to the position of the candles, or you may wish to sit in the center of them facing the top point.

Open the Way. Begin to breathe power into the iron in your body. See it shine and glow within you. Invoke the Iron Pentacle into your body … feel it shine with power. While focusing on the point of Sex, *will* this point to stretch and flow into the corresponding candle on the floor. *See* it shine with an inner luminescence. Say:

*By the fire of my will I invoke Sex!*

Light the candle and feel how its flame is really the physical manifestation of the light of Sex. Breathe your power into it, and then breathe it back. Feel the point of Sex as being stronger than before. When you are ready, feel the power move from your Sex point to your Pride point. Imagine a connecting line of energy traveling from one candle to the next. Focus on Pride and see its candle now glowing with an inner light. Continue this entire process for the remaining three points until all the candles are lit.

Now, sitting (or lying down) between these lit candles run the points of the Iron Pentacle. If you are lying down, then feel how the candles are making the pentacle stretch just beyond your physical body. If you are sitting, then be aware of the pentacle as the power moves between the points around you, parallel to the floor. Imagine that the candles are magnifying the energy, keeping each point in perfect balance. Breathe in the light from the candles, and see it fill your body and move freely between your Three Souls. Imagine there are rays of red light streaming from each of the five candles and converging in your center. Invoke the Star Goddess in the center by saying:

*I invoke the Mother of the Stars*
*Who was and is and ever shall be*
*The androgynous source of all creation.*
*All seeing. All knowing. All pervading. All powerful.*
*Shine in me your holy flame!*

Feel her presence emerge from all around you. Feel her light shining from deep inside you and allow it to build within you with your breath. As you maintain her presence within you, ask her to teach you more about the Iron Pentacle and how to embody it in your life. Be prepared to make her an offering or to sacrifice something in order to learn more. Continue to run the points of the pentacle, feeling the power increase with each pass. See the pentacle glow and vibrate! Maintain this for several minutes.

With three slow, deep breaths, allow the Iron Pentacle to melt down within you, and on your fourth breath absorb the pentacle into your heart, beneath your navel, and in the center of your brain. On the fifth breath it moves out to flow into your whole body. On the sixth breath it flows into each of your Three Souls and your aura. On your seventh breath you have completely absorbed and embodied the pentacle. It is done.

As we continue to work with the Iron Pentacle, we will have opportunities to focus on each of the points in relation to other elements and practices. But for now, simply engage the Iron Pentacle using the exercise version for at least a month at four times per week, remembering to journal your experiences. The ritual version should be done twice in the month.

---

After you have completed the ritual, begin engaging the pentacle in different ways: Victor taught his students a different method, contemplating the points not in the "star" but around the circle. Beginning with Power, one is to contemplate each point in the following order as the circle is mentally drawn: Sex, Self, Passion, Pride, and Power. This method has the added benefits of "sealing" the energy inside the body in a way that the star method does not. Also, this method allows us to end on the point of Power, which is a means to specifically conjure the presence of that point. This way we are moving through a progression of energies that culminate in the affirmation of our own Power. This is also one method I have seen for raising energy for spell work: to end on Power and then perform some specific spell can further intensify the working. This is true of the other points as well. Try invoking them in a different order, ending on the one that most aligns to you particular goal. Experiment!

You may find that certain emotional triggers may be heightened in the period in which you are engaging this work. This type of introspective magic will reach deep into our psyches and dredge up those things that had previously been buried away. Remember your purification work and make sure you are engaging a regular practice of it. When specific things arise you will want to make sure that you are addressing those issues with the Waters of Purity. Remember to take back your (transformed) power from the situation. This is the constant work of the magical practitioner. We must forge ourselves into the perfect instrument for the deeper powers or else they will break us. Slow and steady goes the work. Slow and steady we build our foundation.

### *Prayers of Iron*

Sex:

*Primal throb! Unfolding flower!*
*Spirit of radiance rejoice!*
*Embrace your writhing spiral lover*
*Our souls made one in wraith-born tryst.*

Pride:

*Flower open to the sunlight*
*With delight and upraised stem you shine*
*Grant your simple wisdom gleaming*
*That I be the flower in my heart.*

Self:

*Open eye, reveal thy truth*
*And cast thy gaze within the dark*
*To conjure forth the light of knowing*
*That I may see beyond the veil.*

Power:

*Vital sap that slowly rises,*
*Forming circles one by one*
*Lightning striking down from heaven*
*To me your strength and skill bestow.*

Passion:

*Heart that's open fierce and wide*
*That knows what few else ever will*
*Through me let your river flow*
*And guide me to a distant shore.*

All:

*Iron Star within my body*
*Iron Star within my blood*
*Life force rise and flow unhindered*
*Shine like fire, strong and sure.*

# PART TWO:
# THE HIDDEN POWERS

The work of Witchcraft is not just a mental exercise. If our intention going in is that it is just a mental talker game, then that is most likely all we will get out of the experience. But if we approach this work as if it is *real*—as if the beings and what they do to us in the trance worlds are not "just our imaginations" but actual occurrences taking place on what might be described as "another plane of existence"—then we will be able to get the most out of what it has to offer. (And honestly, if you do not want to get the *most* out of the Craft, then you probably shouldn't be here anyway.)

At this point, I feel compelled to insert into this narrative a personal story from my own training in Faery Witchcraft and one that I often cite in my own classes. I call it "My Most Humiliating Moment." After having spent nearly four years of weekly sessions in arduous Craft training, and having been formally dedicated to the Faery Tradition, my teacher revealed to me to a particular inner temple—a temple-space on the astral planes in which I was introduced to certain beings and symbolic presences. After we returned from our trance, I was then instructed to revisit this temple and those beings on my own and report back my observances the following week. When I next engaged my personal altar, I re-created the symbolic keys necessary to engage this particular temple and to petition the guardian spirits that stood vigilant at its gate. But they did not move. Again, I engaged the keys, thinking that I had somehow made an error, that my concentration was not sufficient, or that somehow I was not worthy. Still they did not move. Frustrated, I told myself that it was my own mind that was tripping me up, that whatever impediments I was now facing were of my own mental construction, and so—in order to move beyond obstacles of my own making—I decided to force my way in.

I had no reason to believe that this would cause any issue, but my immediate experience of the temple was off; my perception was that I was slowly swimming through the space as if through some unseen, thick fluid the consistency of molasses. My feet never touched the floor, and it was an effort in concentration to manipulate myself across the room and to engage the particular objects and symbols that were part of that week's homework. I eventually did so successfully, and I made my way out of the temple and closed my rites. I was pleased that I was able to move beyond what obviously had been a mental block.

The next week I went to class and sat with my teacher and proudly gave the account of my week in my regular check-in. I will never forget what he said to me.

"I cannot believe you were so disrespectful."

I was stunned. I had gone from feeling so powerful to feeling so power*less*, the rapid extreme of emotional sensation was too much for me to bear and so the shock prevailed. It was if I had been smiling and happy and then suddenly slapped across the face. And it *stung*.

"You are treating your trances as if they aren't *real*, as if they are simply a mental construct. If you continue in this way then this is just for entertainment, and then you will never go any further than that."

Mortification erupted over my face in hot flashes. I had been so sure, so *proud*. How could I have been so blind? I was embarrassed because I knew it was true. I had been treating the work of the Craft as if it was a mental toy, a thing to idly pass the time, as entertainment. I hadn't really committed to its Mysteries. Even having been dedicated to the priesthood, I still was only taking it so far, but not quite far enough to believe it was *real*.

I can distinctly remember that as my teacher continued to calmly explain his observations of my behavior, I mentally resolved to never come back to class. Even having spent *years* coming to class, doing trances, projects, assignments, rituals, participating in community rituals and events, I was prepared to throw it all away because I was embarrassed.

Fortunately for me, my training had not been done in vain. After a few breaths, I remembered that training, and so I decided to "breathe through" the immediate feelings of shame and embarrassment to see what lay on the other side. And when I did, I realized that it was my ego that was bruised, and that *of course* it would want me to stop coming to class and stop doing this work, as this is the *very work* that would allow me to be free of the ego's death grip on my consciousness and keep me from being the most powerful Faery Warlock I could possibly be. With this realization, I decided that I *would* continue my studies and, not only that, I would now make certain that I treated the trances as being *real*.

Toward that end, I resolved to make amends to the temple that, in my arrogance and ignorance, I had inadvertently desecrated. I visited and petitioned the guardians there. I made offerings there and offered real-world actions to back it up. After some time the damage was healed, and I walked away from the experience a bit wiser than I had been before. What happened in the trance *was* real; it was just a "different kind of real" than what is *physically* true. I had gained an awareness of the *poetic* and with new eyes was able to see the truth that up until that point had eluded me.

Having now resolved to approach the Craft and its Mysteries as *poetic truths,* we may step more assuredly upon the path as it begins to deepen in strength and power. Only when we release the arrogance of the ego and surrender to the possibility of magic are we able to finally find it, hidden in plain sight—where it has always been.

# CHAPTER 7
# THE HIDDEN TEMPLE OF AIR

*If you surrendered to the air, you could ride it.*
—TONI MORRISON

Though Faery is its own unique strain of Witchcraft, thoroughly independent of British Wicca in terms of lineaged connection to the old Witch Power, it is an open, syncretic system and as such it adopts models and tools of power wherever it finds them. The model of the five elements of Western Magickal Tradition is one of those tools, and while some of the associations will be familiar to students of the occult, there are others that are not necessarily in the "norm" as the model is expressed through Faery Tradition.

The model of the five elements is that of a wheel, our sacred circle that takes us through the cycles of the seasons. We travel along that circle to describe the process of thought as it moves into manifestation.

It all begins with a thought. Whatever projects or activities we wish to engage in, we must think it first to make it happen. So we begin our journey into the elements with the processes of the mind, which poetically places us in the realm of air, which is traditionally placed in the east,[32] where the sun rises and where the day begins.

---

32. A note on directional associations: Faery Tradition was born in the Northern Hemisphere, and specifically the West Coast of the United States, which has influenced how the elements are directionally arranged. Practitioners in other locations may wish to make adjustments for where they feel the power better wishes to be aligned directionally. Ultimately any element can be any direction. The directional model is just a convenient means to allow us to physically engage our environment and our place within it, as well as make poetic connections to further engage the consciousness of the elemental presence. Those associations given in this book are traditional to Faery.

We engage the elements in a multilayered fashion. By taking the seasonal wheel of the year and dividing it up into four sections we are able to assign each of the four physical elements, which lets us engage them physically while also giving us an opportunity to align ourselves with the seasonal rhythms of the land on which we live. In the case of air, we associate it with spring, with sunrise, and the color golden yellow.

Air moves, lifts, clears, and brightens. Poetic air teaches us discernment. It is the most talker of the elements, being associated with communication and language, as well as logic and reason. Its tool is the wand, which immediately is at variance with what most people are familiar with. In the popular model, the tool of air is the sword, as evidenced in most symbolism in tarot. In Faery, the wand is air because it retains the spirit of the wooden branch it came from, which once stretched out toward the sky in adoration and felt the wind and breeze. It is also because a wand denotes skill; it is a precision instrument for friendly invocations and the precise direction of attention and power.

In the physical body, we say that air rules the respiratory system, reminding us that we are in a constant relationship with an invisible and nearly omnipresent force without which we would literally cease to be. With every breath, air cleanses us, removing impurities from our blood and vitalizing our bodies. We take a breath in … we let a breath out. We are all a part of the cycle of air, one breath at a time.

As we are moving now into areas that are not universally shared by all lines of the tradition, I must make a brief note on what I call the Bloodrosian Recension. This is a term I coined that seeks to make plain the very many (and valuable) innovations that Bloodrose coven and linage has offered the overall Faery Tradition while also understanding that to some who are outside of this line and its influence those innovations are considered to be "outside" the Faery Tradition altogether. Faery is not a singular body of material, but a way of life. As such it is likely to look very different for each of us. I offer this explanation here to stress that it is ALL Faery, as the tradition continues to grow and evolve.

In addition to the more common associations of communication and the like, there are key concepts that are meditated upon for the purpose of deepening our relationship with the elemental powers. For air these are Resonance and Clarity.

The state of resonance is when two or more objects are vibrating at the same frequency. When a tuning fork is struck over a piano, the piano wire that corresponds in musical note to the tuning fork will vibrate, as it is in a state of resonance. This concept can be applied to people, emotions, ideas, relationships, etc. We have all experienced at least a glimpse of this sensation during our lives. That person with whom you just clicked or that poem or story that really spoke to you are examples of you feeling this type of resonance.

Clarity is the poetic key toward coherence, a state of understanding. We experience this when we are focused and able to really listen, as well as speak effectively when necessary. We have all had those moments of clarity in which attitudes or behaviors were suddenly revealed to us in a new light. We could see clearly where once we had not been able and perhaps didn't even realize our limitations.

## Journaling

Open the Way and then ask yourself how you feel when you hear the word *resonance.*

*Write down anything that comes to you, anything at all. It doesn't have to make sense. Spend at least five minutes writing about resonance. Then, do the same for the word* clarity.

## Air Incense Recipe

For many of these exercises, you will be asked to burn air incense. You are welcome to use whatever you'd like or you can use this recipe.[33]

1 part eucalyptus
2 parts lavender
1 part mugwort

Combine together and store in an airtight container. This blend can then be burned on a lit charcoal to fumigate the area for your workings. This will shift the energetic vibration of the atmosphere and will allow for a deeper connection to the powers we are invoking.

---

# Magical Singing

The spellwork of air leads us into the realm of the voice. As air is communication, we use our voice to embody this elemental principle in our magical work. Singing and chanting allows us to use this element to move us into a place of ecstatic openness.

---

33. Devin Hunter, "Elemental Incense Recipes" in *Modern Witch Magazine Volume One* (Living Temple Media: Walnut Creek, California).

You don't have to be a great singer to utilize the power of magical song and chant in your work. Even just singing in the shower can be beneficial. When I am using magical song in my own work, I will often start humming and then singing, articulating the various qualities of the thing that I wish to invoke and putting it to song. You can easily use the tunes of songs that you already know and love and simply replace the words with whatever ones describe what you are trying to manifest.

Alternatively, you can write out chants, perhaps using the names of spirits or deities that you work with. When put to song, these words take on a new life of their own. Give yourself the space to experiment with song.

Begin by just chanting *aum* in a long, slow, drawn-out note. Feel the vibration in your throat and notice where else you feel it. When you are familiar with this, experiment with using different tunes … and perhaps allow the tunes to become free-form, just feel the energy of the vibrations moving though you. Be aware that these vibrations are currents of energy that you are putting out into the world, causing ripples in the aethers. Evolve into singing songs that really emotionally move you, and allowing yourself to really feel those currents moving through your body as you sing.

## The Magic of Scent

When dealing with the air element we must also pay attention to the power of scent. Scented oils and incense have been used for centuries in religious and magical rites. We use scent in our rites because we wish to engage the sensual. Faery is a very sensual tradition, and we use sensation in order to gather life force in many forms.

Every scent chosen for a ritual is a message to our fetch. We choose a scent that puts us in a particular mood. Notice how you feel when you smell the scent of roses. Now how do you feel about lavender? About lemon? How about sandalwood or tea tree? Each of these have very distinct scents and are associated with various magical and healing properties. But how they smell *to you*? It is your fetch that will ultimately determine if you can work with a particular scent or not. If you really hate the smell of rue, for example, then chances are rue is not your plant ally. Sometimes a person just "doesn't smell right," which means their pheromones are communicating to our fetch something about that person. Pay attention to what fetch has to tell you about scent. Go with our gut.

Try making a conscious effort to bring more scent into your magical work. Especially for those who might find the smoke of incense to be irritating, I suggest working with essential oils in a diffuser, as this method is smokeless and clean and will not aggravate the lungs. Also the essential oil is the highest vibration of the spiritual essence of the plant to be found in its physicality. By working with the oil, you are working directly with the plant spirit.

Oils are used as a physical catalyst between our own energy bodies and the object or person we are anointing. Our magical intentions and prayers align with the plant spirits within the oil, and by the magical law of contagion the oil transfers this intention to the person or object in the act of anointing or dressing.

Experiment with using oils in your work. Try wearing certain scents when you perform your Faery exercises and see if you notice any difference. Remember to record your results in your journal.

### Opening the Golden Road Exercise

This exercise will train your fetch to begin the journey into the hidden temple. Work with it at least a few times as given before proceeding to the next exercise.

Items needed:
Your black Star Goddess candle
Matches
A yellow candle, placed in the east
Air incense

Open the Way. Turn to face the east. From the flame of the Star Goddess candle in the center, light the yellow candle in the east. Feel how the light of this candle calls the elemental realm of air closer to you. From this candle light the incense. Close your eyes and imagine a door appearing in the east that has the alchemical symbol for air etched upon it: a golden yellow upward-pointing triangle with a horizontal line dividing its middle. Take a moment as you charge yourself up by breathing the Blue Fire. When you feel you have a sufficient charge, say:

> *I summon forth the eastern door:*
> *Open now, reveal the road of air:*
> *Golden yellow, sunlight's glow,*
> *Bring thy knowledge, bring thy notion!*

With your exhale send the Blue Fire out and into the symbol on the door, which you imagine shining bright in response. Imagine that this door opens wide before you, and you can now see a golden yellow road that stretches off into the infinite east. As you continue to breathe, this road also stretches toward you, through the door, right to where you sit or stand in the center. Imagine yourself standing on this road and feel yourself in relation to the east. Look through the open doorway to gaze down the length of this golden road. You can see the rising sun at the very end of this road before you. Take some time—perhaps only a few breaths to a few minutes—and then give a silent prayer of thanks, imagining the road receding back though the door, which then closes and is gone. End your session as you would normally.

---

## The Guardian Beast of Air: Eagle

This work will introduce you to one of the many guardians of the Faery Tradition, specifically the first of the guardian beasts. These totemic beings are part of the Faery Tradition by way of the Vanthe line, a noble lineage founded by the late Alison Harlow, and can also be found in the book *Mastering Witchcraft* by Paul Huson. They are different (yet resonant) beings than what most of the rest of the Faery Tradition works with as guardians (and what BlueRose calls "the Watchers") and best serve, in my opinion, as introductions to both spirit work and the hidden temples. The guardian beasts are emissaries of the elemental realms, which act as spirit guides, assisting us in traveling to the many, many places in and beyond the hidden temples that we will be visiting as part of our work.

The eagle is the spirit guide of the east, the Faery emissary to the realm of air. It is the herald of the dawn who will protect and guide us on our journey into the hidden temple. As a totem, the eagle brings us clear sight and the ability to rise above a situation in order to gain a better vantage point, a perspective that is far-reaching and better informed. Eagle brings the power *to Know*, the first of the four foundational points of the Witches' Pyramid.

### Invoking the Eagle Exercise

Items needed:

Your black Star Goddess candle

Matches

A yellow candle, placed in the east

Air incense

Begin by Opening the Way. Perform Opening the Golden Road.

Continue to look through the open door, allowing your gaze to flow along the golden road and out into the east. Imagine that you are opening up through your holy daemon and that you can reach out through your daemon and into the east … into the vastness of the rising sun. Say:

> *Golden eagle of the east!*
> *Bringer of the cleansing winds*
> *And the breath of life,*
> *Emissary of the powers of air!*
> *Come to me, and bring your knowledge!*

Breathing deep, you see a golden eagle flying in the distant sky before you. It flies before the rising sun, proclaiming the majesty that is the new day. It circles in the sky several times before swooping down toward you, flying through the door and then circling directly above. Watch it as it flies in circles overhead … feel how as you are following its motions with your sight you are falling deeper into a trance … you are getting lighter … floating … and you feel yourself gliding in the sky on feathered wings … in the body of an eagle you fly and soar! Look with your eagle eyes to the ground below. Look with your keen sight! What do you see? Feel the wind flowing over your feathers as you dart amongst the clouds. Take your time with this.

After a while, when you feel it is time to come back, allow yourself to descend slowly and back into your own human body as you touch ground. The golden eagle circles overhead, watching and guiding you. Give it thanks and notice if it flies away. Allow the golden road to recede back through the door, which fades away. End your session as you would normally.

## Entering the Hidden Temple of Air Ritual

This rite should ideally be performed at dawn or in the morning hours. Build an altar in the east. It should be draped with an altar cloth and adorned with your symbols that represent the air element, as well as the yellow candle and the incense.

Items needed:
Your black Star Goddess candle
Matches
A yellow candle, placed in the east
Air incense
A golden yellow (or other appropriate color) altar cloth
Air symbols (feathers, flowers, etc.)
A wand

Open the Way. Perform the Golden Road exercise followed by the invocation of golden eagle. Take some time to commune with eagle before moving on.

At some point, the eagle will guide you through the door of the hidden temple of air … the doorway is filled with brilliant silver and golden light. It is bright, reminiscent of bright sunlight reflecting on rippling water … take another deep breath, and step through into this light.

The light opens up all around you and you now see a great meadow before you. The scent of wildflowers is on the air and the cool spring breeze caresses your skin. There is dew on the grass and everything feels fresh and pure. The sun is rising just over the horizon before you, its golden yellow light filling the air with luminescence.

With your wand, trace a half-circle with an upward curve in the space before you—like a glyph of a rising sun—made of golden yellow fire. Say, *"By my mind, I invoke air!"*

Imagine the rising sun expanding to fill the sky, becoming a huge golden half-sphere of luminescent energy that is so huge that even the enormous curvature before you is actually only its very tip rising above the horizon.

Take three deep breaths and feel your body become empty and hollow.

Take seven deep breaths and feel your body filling with the elemental powers of air in the form of a golden yellow light, which embodies the qualities of Resonance and Clarity.

Take seven deep breaths and imagine the golden yellow half-sphere projecting into your throat, where it becomes a golden half-circle. Feel the freshness of air moving within and through you.

Take seven deep breaths and imagine that your respiratory system, lungs, tongue, throat, and skin become filled with shining golden light. Take some time (at least a few breaths) to fully absorb the powers of elemental air into your physical and energy bodies. Say, *"I am air"* seven times as a long, drawn-out vibratory note, becoming slower and longer with each repetition.

Continuing to breathe deeply, focus your attention on that golden half-circle within your throat. Notice how it shines brightly throughout your physical body, and how it spills out into your aura. Maintain this presence for the span of at least several minutes.

For the span of three breaths become aware of the meadow and your working area existing simultaneously. With three more breaths allow the meadow to fade. Extinguish the yellow candle. End as normal.

---

# Sylphs

Sylphs are the nature spirits of the air element. As with all of this type of nature spirit they exist in the etheric region that we often refer to as the realm of Faery.[34] They are the animating force that infuses life force into the air that we breathe and that keeps the processes of the planet alive and functioning. These are the spirits that most children think of as "fairies." Swiftly moving and often appearing as winged, they flit about making love with each other, thus vitalizing the air. They can also sometimes appear as little silver spirals.

Without their involvement, the air we breathe wouldn't give us life force and we would soon wither away. Their presence cleanses and nourishes us with every breath and we can learn much from studying them and building personal relationships.

## The Breath of the Sylphs Exercise

Items needed:
Your black Star Goddess candle
Matches
A yellow candle, placed in the east
Air incense

---

34. Anderson, *Fifty Years in the Feri Tradition*, 56.

Open the Way. Invoke the golden road and the eagle. Move into the hidden temple and engage the elemental power and the glyph.

Remember your soul alignment and reach out through your daemon and into the molecules of the air around you. Imagine that you can see little motes of light sparking and fling about … here and there … little silver lights … or they may appear winged, or like spirals. Notice how they come to you. Notice how they collide with each other and how when this happens little flashes of light occur. This is them having sex and creating vitality. Take a deep breath and breathe them into your lungs … they vitalize your breath … giving you life … now breathe them out again, and they return … spiraling into the atmosphere.

Maintain this practice for at least several breaths and then ask them, "How can I connect with you more deeply?" Pay attention to any feelings or thoughts you may have in response to this question. Whether or not you feel that this answer is coming from yourself, or not, just observe what arises. You can judge its worthiness later. For now, just pay attention to whatever comes up. End as you would normally. Record your experiences in your journal.

---

## The Wand

In the Faery Tradition, the tool of air is the wand, contrary to what is found in most permutations of Western Magical Tradition and modern Craft, which, like the symbolism found in the tarot, uses the blade as the elemental tool. The wand can be seen as a manifestation of one's intellect, reaching like the branches of a tree into the higher realms illuminated by the solar light of consciousness. In practical terms, it is used to direct energy and to invoke friendly spirits, acting as an extension of one's consciousness in the realm of one's ritual space.

There's something so delightful to fetch about holding a wand. From childhood we are raised with images of Witches and Wizards using magic wands to cast their spells (*Expelliarmus!*) and so it feels natural for fetch to use one in a magical setting.

### Enchanting the Wand Exercises

For each of the following exercises you will need the following items:
Your black Star Goddess candle
Matches

A yellow candle, placed in the east
Air incense
Your wand

Begin each exercise by performing the following:

Open the Way. Light the incense. Focus your attention on the golden road of the east and light the yellow candle. Connect with the eagle and journey through the door into the hidden temple of air. Spend some time breathing in the presence of the element, filling yourself with the golden light. Allow the half-circle in your throat to shine brightly.

### Awakening the Wand

Holding the wand so that the bottom is positioned at your throat and the tip is pointed out away from you, begin to breathe the golden light from the half-circle in your throat and out through the wand and into the east, imagining this energy flowing out to greet the rising sun. Allow the wand to become the embodiment of Resonance and Clarity. Do this for twelve breaths and then on the next twelve, breathe the golden light back from the sun, through the wand, and into the half-circle in your throat. Now, reduce this pattern to six breaths. Now three. End with several instances of doing this with a single breath, exhaling the power into the sun through the wand, and inhaling it back the same way. After you have done this for several minutes call the power back into you to integrate it, extinguish the candle, and return to normal consciousness.

### Drawing the Pentacle

As when awakening the wand, breathe through the wand to charge it with the elemental power. Now, holding the wand in your projective hand draw a pentacle in the air before you, imagining it shining with golden yellow light. Exhale the power though it: one breath per line of the pentacle. After the pentacle is complete, draw the power back to you by retracing the pentacle in reverse, breathing back this power on each inhale. End as normal.

### Triangle and Wand Purification [35]

While in the hidden temple, remind yourself of the physical space in which you are working. Open your eyes and maintain the energetic presence of the temple, you "walk between the worlds." Physically cast a simple circle around yourself by pointing your wand to the ground and turning clockwise, imagining your holy fire streaming through your body, through the wand to form a circle on the ground around you. Feel the moment this circle is completed and feel how it is a perfect shape and that within it you are perfectly protected and your power is focused. Affirm to yourself that this circle will remain in effect on the astral for the duration of your session here.

Identify a particular negative feeling that you have about yourself. It can be anything, big or small. Allow it to coalesce into a symbol or an image. Notice how you feel about it.

With the wand, draw a triangle of blue fire on the floor outside of the circle so that it points toward you. See it shine and pulse with power.

With seven breaths imagine placing the symbol or image into the triangle.

Draw a golden yellow pentacle in the air with the wand. When it is complete, stab the wand though the center of it and hold it in place for the span of three breaths. Imagine a beam of energy pouring forth from the wand and into the image. When it reaches the image, see and feel that it becomes a whirlwind, destroying the image and transforming the energy that it represents into a purified form. See it shine and glow. Take some time to really feel this power.

With seven slow breaths call this now transformed power from the point of the triangle into your circle so that it permeates the very air of your ritual space. See and feel it swirl around you, noticing how it feels on your skin, but also the emotional sense that it brings. With nine more breaths breathe it in, seeing yourself shine with this power. Take some time to feel this power within you, radiating out from you in all directions. Feel how you are now free of whatever block or negative energy you transformed. When you feel you are done close your circle as normal.

---

35. Based on a traditional exercise from Coven Korythalia, 1984.

# The Watcher of Air: Star Finder

The Watchers are the spiritual ancestors of the initiates of our tradition. It is from them that the Witch Power—and the Faery Power—originates. They are ancient beyond reason. At the birth of the universe they were born first, moving out from the womb of the Star Goddess in all directions and forming what we understand as three-dimensional space and time.

The Watchers, in one sense, are stars. They are the four royal stars of antiquity, the guardians of heaven. Our lore states that "we do not know if the names we have for them are their own, or to those beings that they themselves hold allegiance."[36] This often forgotten piece of lore underscores the fact that—even to the initiates—these beings are *mysteries*. Their names aren't even names at all, they are job descriptions. The Star Finder, if you could tell by the title, has associations of mapping the stars and traveling between the worlds.

They are ancient, primal beings. And they seem to want to help us evolve into our own godhood. When we work with the Watchers, we are allowing them to make subtle changes to our energy bodies. Often we experience symbolic representations of this while in trance: imagery of being taken apart and put back together again … having strange objects removed from our bodies and replaced with crystals, stones, jewels, or other power objects. I once had a student who experienced a Watcher pulling out a junk drawer from their midsection, organizing it, and replacing it. The realm of the symbolic is not always as cryptic as it is sometimes made out to be.

Even if we do not consciously perceive an energy exchange taking place, the effects are happening on the level of the fetch. Continuing to meet with the Watchers is key to allowing them to build and deepen an energetic relationship. There will be no substitute for actually doing the work and forming the bond. Once formed, the Watchers will guide and protect you. They are the familiar spirits of the Faery Tradition, here to guide and teach the next generation that we may do better than our forebears. And so on. And so on.

In the Bloodrosian lore, it is said Star Finder may appear in vaguely humanoid shape, his body a transparent golden yellow, the color of bright morning sunlight. His[37] eyes

---

36. Oral tradition.

37. According to Faery oral tradition, the Watchers may appear in both male and female forms. While Victor spoke of them primarily as masculine presences, in the Bloodrosian Recension, air and fire are represented as male while water and earth are represented as female.

are bright and tinged with blue, reminiscent of stars, and as if to underscore his angelic origins, he has enormous wings, often described as being lavender in color. He stands or flies before the light of the sunrise, which is seen shining brilliantly through him. In his right hand he is often depicted holding a sapphire-blue wand or staff, capped at the top with gold, and at the bottom with silver, which are obvious solar and lunar references. He may also appear as a slash of soft sunlight, carrying a gentle wind, or simply as a golden star shining in the east.

The Star Finder wields the power of Knowledge. We call upon him to act as an intermediary and teacher, guiding us when dealing with the deeper mysteries of air, but also of the realms of knowledge and the mind.

*Figure 6: Star Finder Sigil*

## *Invoking Star Finder Exercise*

Items needed:

Your black Star Goddess candle

Matches

A yellow candle, placed in the east

Air incense

Your wand

Open the Way. Invoke the golden road and the eagle. Step upon the road and move through the door and into the hidden temple of air where you connect with the elemental powers and activate the glyph in your throat.

Place your palms together at heart level in front of you, fingers pointing up. With a deep inhale, breathe in the power of the spring meadow and the rising sun. With each breath allow that power to fill you and become concentrated in the glyph of the golden half-circle in your throat. This should span at least three breaths.

With your next exhale, allow a thread of energy to flow forth from the glyph in your throat as you extend your hands outward into the east, fingers pointing outward. Imagine the energy thread as flowing outward into the realm of air in the east and rising up above eye level and reaching an infinite point. This may take a few breaths to achieve.

Imagine that this thread is connecting you to the elemental realm of air. Open your hands so that they are cupped in front of you and gesture as if you are gathering this elemental energy. With your next inhale, bring your hands back so that you now cross them over your chest, left over right. While this is happening you are pulling the elemental energy into the glyph via the energy thread. Bow in reverence to the direction.

With your wand (or even simply your fingers) trace a five-pointed star of golden yellow fire in the space before you. Repeat the invocation:

> *Star Finder, Star Finder, Star Finder!*
> *In darkness deep between the stars,*
> *You glide and soar on wings of light*
> *Watcher of the rising sun,*
> *We call your knowledge and your sight!*

Imagine the Watcher emerging from the yellow pentacle. Take several deep breaths, feeling the presence of the Watcher before you. Take three deep breaths and feel your body become empty and hollow.

With six breaths, imagine the Watcher projecting into the half-circle on a beam of golden yellow light. Breathe in the presence of the Watcher along with the power of Knowledge, and imagine an image of the Watcher in miniature forming within the glyph in your throat. Know that the Watcher within you and the Watcher before you are one and the same, two sides of the same coin.

Maintain this presence for at least the span of six breaths.

You may spend as much time as you like working with Star Finder, allowing him to guide you. Or move on to the next step.

Take a deep breath of power, and imagine taking a step closer to the Watcher before you. As you do, the Star Finder within expands in size and power.

Ask him, "Who am I?"

By asking this question we form an energetic space into which the presence of the Watcher may flow. Simply pay attention to whatever may arise or transpire during this time, whether it makes logical sense to you or not.

Repeat this process, stepping closer and closer, while the Watcher within expands to eventually fill your whole body. When you next take a step you then merge with the Watcher before you. Now all three of you have merged into one shining being. Maintain this awareness for several breaths, and then imagine stepping out of the immediate presence of Star Finder so that he is before you once more. Allow him to guide you. You may sit in silence or he may speak or show things to you. Allow him to guide you as he will.

After you have spent several minutes in communion in this manner, end by giving thanks to the Watcher for his assistance. Say:

> *Star Finder,*
> *Watcher of the rising sun,*
> *I thank you for your power and your presence.*
> *Stay if you will, go if you must,*
> *But ere you depart I bid you:*
> *Hail and farewell!*

Pay attention to whether or not you feel if he stays or goes. Either way, release your connection to him as if letting go of a thread or a tether. Imagine the pentacle dissolving and scattering like smoke on the wind. For the span of three breaths feel the meadow and your working area existing simultaneously. With three more breaths allow the meadow to fade. Extinguish the yellow candle with a silent prayer.

---

## The Flower Maiden

Nimüe, sometimes called the Flower Maiden or the Corn Maiden,[38] is the most common name given in Faery for this strange and interesting goddess. She is the essence of new life: the birth and growth of plants and animals, as well as the embodiment of the Holy Grail of Faery praxis, the Black Heart of Innocence.

In the traditional lore, it is said that she may appear as a young girl anywhere between six and twelve years of age, naked or dressed in white or pink, occasionally with green snakes that writhe in her radiant red hair. Despite her soft appearance, she can be one of the most dangerous of the gods. Her emblem is a six-day-old crescent moon, which she wears upon her brow. She is the great arouser, and she represents the innocence of sexual being. It is her holy lust that arouses the powers of nature to arise out of the depths of winter. She is associated with both caves and wells, obvious symbols of the sacred yoni. She is the fierce protectress of the innocent, especially that of children.

Nimüe is sometimes said to be the reflection that the Star Goddess sees when she gazes into the curved mirror of black space as described in many permutations of the Faery creation myth. In this we are made aware that Nimüe is the same being as the Star Goddess, just seen from a different perspective, one of the many paradoxes at the center of Faery Tradition.

That Nimüe is a goddess seen in the aspect of a child can be disturbing to some when one considers the sexual nature of the myth; the Star Goddess is said to make love to her reflection, which is the poetic retelling of the big bang. Certainly a human relationship of this nature would be abhorrent, but the gods are not role models, they are energetic currents that are the conscious powers of the natural world. When we fully understand that Nimüe is the same person as the Star Goddess then we begin to understand that what the myth is relaying is actually an act of self love; the Star Goddess is using sexual energy as a means for self-integration and exploration, and the result is the birth of new consciousness.

---

38. *Corn* is a traditional word for an area's staple grain. So in the British Isles, this grain would most likely have been wheat.

### *Invoking Nimüe Exercise*

Items needed:
Your black Star Goddess candle
Matches
Flowers
Silver chalice filled with water

Create an altar to her with flowers (especially pink and white roses) and images of the beauty of nature. It is said that a traditional offering to her consisted of nine pigs (four white, four red, and one black). Place a silver chalice in the center filled with water.

Open the Way. Anoint yourself with a floral scent and connect to her through your fetch. Sing to her. Dance her into manifestation. You may wish to use the following invocation (or better yet, make up your own):

*Nimüe, Laughing One, dancing naked in the sun!*

You might see her dancing and rejoicing in a field of flowers, chasing butterflies. Notice how she feels to you, and notice your own deep heart. What passions stir within you? Without judgment, what do you wish you could be doing right now? Ask her to help you get in touch with those parts of you that have been denied ... shamed ... beaten down. Feel her presence and channel it into the water, drinking it down as a cleansing and a blessing. After you are finished, eat something sweet, offering half to her.

---

## The Blue God

The Blue God is known by many names: the Peacock Lord, Dian y Glas, Melek Ta'us, Lemba, Eros, the Christos, and Lucifer, to name but a few. He is one of our central gods, but in some myths he is an angel, while in others his origins as a djinn or faery are subtly revealed. He is a shape-shifter, a trickster, and a great teacher. He is paradox: the highest spirit but also the most primal and low. He is sexual as well as spiritual and is the embodiment of both beauty and darkness.

The Blue God is that spark of divinity that resides within us all, the hidden spirit within matter. According to lore attributed to Victor, the Blue God sometimes appears as a winged serpent underneath the left hand of the Goddess. Here, it is said, he is the most beautiful and beneficial of all spirits. But outside of her influence he becomes the most terrible and wrathful. To me this represents the divine masculine balanced by the divine feminine, and the terrible price that is paid when the god force is no longer balanced by the Goddess.

One distinguishing characteristic that sets this deity apart from the others in our tradition is that the Blue God is not simply an individual, but a type of collective, what can be called a Divinity Complex. Under this umbrella, we find many different yet resonate divine personalities, which are often addressed together simply as the Blue God. Though these beings are different and separate, they also are not; while one cannot be substituted for another, they can all be approached through any of the other forms, as each of them are reflected in all of them.

Because of this inherent diversity within the core of this spiritual being, the Blue God is—in my opinion—the most quintessentially Faery deity in our tradition. He is the color that runs outside the lines, the blurred edges, the dreamtime. Like the entrances to the Faery realm as described in traditional folklore, he exists in a state of liminality, that of being between the worlds. Where an entrance to the realm of the Fae might have been said to be found on a beach or the edge of a forest (the meeting points of land and sea, and of civilization and wilderness, respectively), our liminal god holds a space in-between masculine and feminine and as such is often depicted as a male with female attributes. He also holds that space between earthly and heavenly energies, most notably demonstrated by the dual symbolism of serpent and bird, symbols often associated in our tradition with the Divine Twins—the two bright spirits that were perfected into God within the womb of the Star Goddess, a direct reference to the Divine Twins being aspects of the Blue God.

As Dian y Glas, he appears to us as a beautifully alluring blue-skinned youth. Traditional lore depicts him with an erect phallus, the soft breasts of a young girl, a serpent around his neck, and peacock feathers in his hair. He is sometimes shown playing a silver flute. He is the initiating principle of life force, and the spiritual nature of love, beauty, and sexual passion.

He is associated with springtime as well as with the nourishing waters of rains and of springs. He is the starry-eyed wonder of the world, how a child sees the beauty of the world through eyes that have not been corrupted.

The name *Dian y Glas* is also said to be a name for our individual God Soul, the holy daemon. In this we find a paradox, in that we understand him as a deity in his own right but also as a part of our own individual soul structure. Recognizing our own divinity by identifying ourselves with the God, we find our spirituality to be one that is both embodied and transcendent, simultaneously.

When he comes to us as Melek Ta'us, our attention is drawn to the Middle East, most specifically to those people of Kurdish descent in the general area of northern Iraq known as the Yazidi. To them, Melek Ta'us, known as the Peacock Angel, is the first emanation of the light of God whose special color is blue: blue being considered the most powerful color and the origin for all the others, as all light comes from the sky. Beyond this "signature" color, he is said to embody all the colors of the rainbow, which is his special symbol. He is the first (and ruler) of the seven archangels, containing the other six within himself (just as white light contains all the colors of the spectrum). To the Yazidi he is the Soul of the World, the collective divine presence of humanity. They also believe that he belongs to the whole world, and not just to the Yazidi themselves.

In this form, the Blue God comes to us with the imagery that we are familiar with—peacock feathers, blue skin, serpents, etc.—but we see some differences, as well. Melek Ta'us tends to appear as somewhat older than the Dian y Glas: darker, with a sharper edge. While Dian y Glas is often associated with youth and with springtime, Melek Ta'us is sometimes seen as existing outside of the Wheel of Time altogether—a guardian of the crossroads, a psychopomp who, like the classical Hermes, is associated with magic and with snakes.

One of the most important themes represented by the Peacock Lord is that of free will. In some versions of his myth, the beloved first angel is charged by God to "never bow to anyone but God," a command the Peacock Lord takes so seriously that he later refuses to bow to Adam, even when God orders all the angels to do so. While some see this myth as evidence of his willful disobedience and transformation into the Iblis or "Satan," to the Yazidi and those others who worship Melek Ta'us, he is the embodiment of free will. Only humans and djinn—a type of mystical being that is often described in terms which are strikingly similar to the Celtic Fae—were given free will by God; angels are extensions of God's will and so have none of their own, making Melek Ta'us unique among angels to say the least.

According to Islamic myth, the Iblis was created by God out of smokeless fire, a detail that would suggest that his origin is actually as a djinn, as he is quite clearly described as having been created from this particular substance. Angels, by contrast, are depicted as being created from light, while mankind from earth, dust, or clay. This detail is seemingly contradictory since Melek Ta'us is quite clearly referred to as an angel in the traditional myths. While on the surface it would appear that two separate beings with strikingly similar histories are being described, each by a different culture in opposition to each other, the Faery Tradition recognizes them as being two sides of the same coin. Our Blue God is not always what he seems. Just as we have seen how he exists in a space of liminality in terms of the male/female and terrestrial/celestial discussed previously, he also would appear to occupy a space between that of faery (or djinn), angel, and god.

After he refuses to bow before Adam, it is said that he was cast out of heaven for his pride. This is a story that most of us are familiar with in its Christian form as "the fall from grace," which gives us the concept of the fallen angels. After the fall, he was said to repent for his sins, weeping for more than seven thousand years and filling seven jars with his tears which he then used to extinguish the fires of hell, thus establishing him as a savior figure not unlike the Christ.

Another way to look at this myth is to see the fall not as a fall from grace, but as a necessary descent, a Promethean display of spirit manifesting down the scales of density and into matter. In my understanding, the fallen angels have fallen *in love* with humanity, working with us to help us realize our own divine potential.

In my own trance experiences with Melek Ta'us, I have felt that he contains both good and evil, beauty and darkness, which only serves to further qualify him for his position as "lord of the world" (i.e., the collective daemon of humanity). He contains all human potential, as opposed to some popular savior deities who exist only in a half-formed state of supposed perfection, setting the bar impossibly high and then harshly judging those who cannot attain the same state of mindless, saccharine stagnation.

Whether he comes as the youthful Dian y Glas or as the virile Melek Ta'us, his avian and serpentine iconography represents a union of complementary forces that individually we can understand as the Divine Twins, the "two bright spirits" that the Goddess took into her womb and perfected into God.

### *Invoking the Blue God Exercise*

Items needed:

Your black Star Goddess candle

Matches

Flowers

Peacock feathers

Build an altar to him, adorned with flowers, peacock feathers, and symbols that represent your highest soul. Open the Way. Feel your daemon shining overhead and how you are aligned with it. Call to him:

> *Dian y Glas, with eyes of wonder,*
> *Fill the heavens with light and thunder.*

Imagine his presence shining within your own daemon, and feel his light shining down around and through your body. Ask him to guide you … to reveal your passions and your talents for expressing them.

## The Breath of Life Exercise

This simple exercise can be used to help align magical items—such as herbs, oils, incense, stones, bones, candles, and curio—and prepare them for use in magical work. Since this is an exercise and not a ritual, you need not use your altar tools and Star Goddess candle unless you feel it is appropriate. Often our magic needs to be done "out in the world" in settings in which it would be impractical or imprudent to perform overt ritual actions. We must become proficient in doing this work *internally* as a means to keep the power flowing but also not fall into the limitations of requiring special tools or environs.

Begin by choosing an object that you wish to empower. It can be anything you wish. Have it nearby.

Open the Way. Recall your connection to the hidden temple of air and imagine the glyph in your throat shining golden yellow. Take several breaths and imagine that with each you are filing yourself up with the golden light from this glyph, until you are shining and bright. Now, focus on whatever prayer or intention you wish to impart on the object. Allow yourself to really *see* and *feel* it as being a reality. Take at least three breaths while you maintain this sensation.

Now, take another deep breath and with an open exhale, softly breathe out upon the object, imagining it becoming infused with your prayer or intention. Imagine that the spirit within the object is waking up to your intentions. You may perceive a soft glow form within the object. Speak aloud some affirmation aligned with your chosen purpose. It is done.

### The Story of Melek Ta'us

*Born of beauty and of pride*
*Melek Ta'us, the Peacock Angel*
*Gleaming jewel amongst the stars*
*Created from the smokeless fire.*
*Chieftain of the angels seven*
*By God so ordered not to bow*
*Before another, before another*
*Adam's birth disturbs this now.*

*As other angels turn and bow,*
*The Peacock turns to face the sun*
*Righteous pride prevents his bowing*
*And so free will has now begun.*

*Confusion in the ranks of heaven,*
*Conflict born from unity,*
*A fall from grace, to fall in love*
*With precious jeweled humanity.*

*The world knows not his sacrifice*
*And condemns his act of will as evil,*
*And though he strives to save our souls*
*Still is he cast as the devil.*

*Even though they know him not,*
*The Peacock Lord maintains his place*
*The King of Earth, a light from Heaven,*
*The guiding star of the human race.*

*Seven jars have been thus been filled*
*With his tears to save the world,*
*To quench the fires of hell and loathing*
*To douse the flames; to wash them clean.*

*Melek Ta'us, the Peacock Angel*
*Spread your painted fan and make*
*The seven heavens with thunder tremble*
*And help us rise, so to awake.*

### Invocation of the Blue God

*From the womb of Mother Night,*
*The first star born to bring forth light*
*Falls to earth on angel's wings,*
*Watching, waiting, laughing, singing,*
*Strutting in His peacock dance,*
*Calling down the wild-eyed trance,*
*Shaking heaven, tearing hell,*
*The serpent rises from the well.*

### I Am (the Peacock Lord)

*I am ... the first-born of Her light*
*Who ushers ... forth the day from night*
*Bear witness to my starry might*
*And join my grand seduction!*
*Now hearken you unto my song*
*Of life within destruction ...*

*I am ... the serpent in the well*
*Who rises ... up to conquer hell*
*Calling heaven down upon the earth*
*And as the stars do fall ...*
*My precious jewels reside in thee*
*Rise and hear my call!*

*I am ...*

*Mine is ... the path of sacred love*
*The serpent ... twining with the dove*
*And as below so is above*
*All life in your reflection!*
*For each of you I'm in your heart*
*Your beauty-flawed perfection!*

*I am ... the lust that rises high*
*Into the heavens beyond the sky,*
*Who dares to stand proud without shame*
*And as the sun does rise ...*
*A new day dawns in paradise*
*And met with joyous cry ...*

*I am ...*

*I am beauty, I am pride!*
*I am the light that never hides!*
*I am the power without shame!*
*Holy power, yours to claim!*

*As we sing the universe*
*In concert with us now affirms*
*This sacred light within our hearts*
*Never dies, never departs*

*So we sing together now*
*To call that love and power down*
*Within our blood, within our bones*
*The song that's calling us … home …*


*I am …*

## The Points of Flame: Self Exercise

This is an adaptation of an old Bloodrose exercise, which focuses on specific points of the Iron Pentacle in order to cleanse our blocks and impurities that we may have in relation to them. While Victor did not teach specific elemental associations for the points of the Iron Pentacle, the Bloodrosian Recension explored this and came up with a useful system that we use in BlueRose to help keep us moving forward with the Iron Pentacle while we are in the midst of working through the elemental cycle.

Since we are working through the element of air, for this exercise you will focus specifically on the point of Self.

Items needed:
Your black Star Goddess candle
Matches
A yellow candle

Open the Way. Invoke the Iron Pentacle in the air before you. See it shine and feel it vibrate. Feel how the energy moves between the points in a current of energy. Notice what it feels like.

After a few minutes of this, focus on the selected point of the pentacle. Say:

*In the name of iron, I summon forth Self!*

Feel your consciousness projecting into the point and feel how it projects into you as well. Relax, and allow yourself to become empty and hollow with every breath as you contemplate the energy of the point of Self. Notice your thoughts and feelings in relation to it.

Allow the light of the point to shine through you, exposing any imbalances or blocks that may be present in relation to this point. Take some time to examine this in every detail.

Hold the candle in both hands and call up images and feelings of negativity associated with this point. Allow yourself to really feel them … memories … negative thoughts … dreams … sensations … allow them all to build in power with every breath. If you feel like screaming or crying or humming or moving, allow yourself the space to do just that. When you feel that the sensations and images are as strong as they are likely to get, take a deep breath of power, your inhale condensing these feelings and images into a single force, as your exhale moves them all at once into the candle, where you feel them merge and take hold. Know that this candle is now the very heart of that which is negative about your relationship to the particular point of the Iron Pentacle.

Become aware of your own daemon: your higher self. Opened to its presence, you make a prayer to God Herself to charge you with the power to transform your own negativity. Feel her descend within you through your own daemon. Feel charged with her power and her strength. Know that it is really your power. See it emanating from within you to illuminate the room. You are a shining being!

When you feel the height of this power, light the candle with the incantation:

> *As this candle brightly burns*
> *And shines into the Outer Dark,*
> *Blocks to* [NAME OF POINT] *now shift and turn.*
> *Purified, I claim thy spark!*

Feel the negative energy in the candle being transformed into light, and heat … into raw power. Reach out with your energy body to feel how it crackles and hums with electric energy. See the luminosity from within the candle and breathe it in, knowing that the energy is changed. What was heavy and dark is now light. What once held you back now assists you. Allow this power to feed you, to nourish your own spark of divinity, which slowly grows into a bright and shining flame. Bask in this power for a while as you continue to breathe it through you in a slow, deep rhythm.

When you are ready, take three deeps breaths of power and allow the energy of the selected point to flow into the next, and the next, and the next as the pentacle balances itself and you experience the power moving quickly between each point once more. Feel how this movement creates a type of rhythm that increases with speed as you continue your slow, deep breath. As it gets faster, allow the points to blur together as the rhythm becomes a drone. Again, bask in this for a while and notice how you feel.

When you are ready, imagine the Iron Pentacle melting into you, resonating with the iron in your blood and bones. As you continue to breathe, allow its power to spread out through you, but especially into your fetch, which stores its power and makes you stronger. You may either extinguish the candle with a silent prayer, or you may allow it to continue burning, knowing that as the candle burns your impurities of that pentacle point are being broken down and transformed.

## Air Art Project

Since Faery is a religion that draws heavily from art and poetry, only those who are prepared to engage the artist's muse can truly walk our path. Toward this end, construct an art project that expresses your personal experience with the air element. It should include (nonverbal) references to both your strengths and your weaknesses uncovered during this time. While you may include elements that draw from universal symbolism (such as including images of the glyph, Star Finder, the rising sun, etc.) this must not be a project of "generic" air, but of personal air.

Pay attention to what colors you choose and why. It's okay if the answer is "because fetch likes it." Just be aware that this is the reason. Once this is complete, write out a short essay describing this art piece as if describing it to a dear friend who had no idea what it was or the symbolism involved. Make sure to explain why certain symbols were chosen, why certain mediums were used, etc. This essay is the talker component of the fetch project, marrying them both together through the medium of your choosing. Only once you have completed this should you move on to the next chapter of work.

# CHAPTER 8

# THE HIDDEN TEMPLE OF FIRE

*Fire is to represent truth because it destroys all sophistry and lies [...]*
—LEONARDO DA VINCI

Ever since early humans first made their illuminating discovery, fire has played a central role in the spiritual, religious, magical, and mundane practices of mankind, regardless of culture. To these ancient humans, fire literally meant the difference between life and death, for the individual as well as for the tribe.

As we move clockwise along the edge of the circle from air in the east we move into the south with fire. Here our ideas become focused and charged with motion and energy. Here we begin to see how our thoughts become *will*. It is here that our magic begins to gain momentum. Fire transforms, excites, arouses, illuminates, and empowers.

In the physical body, we say that fire rules the digestive system. This is our own engine that transforms our food into energy, into life force. In Faery, we associate this process primarily with the belly and especially the area beneath the navel, that area of primal power that we have associated with the fetch. In the mind, fire represents our own survival instinct, further drawing associations with fetch.

The meditative concepts for this element are: Strength and Active Potency. Strength is a concept that most likely all of us can understand, though it can mean many different things to different people. It might appear as our own perseverance in the face of difficulty. Or it might be our capacity to direct our life force, our ability to endure and succeed. On one level it is a passive quality, a resource that we tap, when needed.

Active Potency is the complement to this power. These are two sides of the same coin, for strength is meaningless if it is not *effective*, bringing the necessity of potency into the picture. But not just potency, *active* potency. It is not just passive potential; it is directed, responsive, and alive.

## Journaling

As with the previous element, Open the Way and then ask yourself how you feel when you hear the word *strength*.

*Spend at least five minutes writing about strength. Again, it doesn't have to make sense. Then, do the same for active potency.*

## Fire Incense Recipe[39]

1 part tobacco
1 part cinnamon
1 part clove
1 part vanilla bean

Combine together and store in an airtight container. This blend can then be burned on a lit charcoal to fumigate the area for your workings.

---

## Candle Magic

The job of a Faery doctor is to do magical work on the behalf of others, and one of the easiest methods is the art of burning candles. Witches of all stripes should already be familiar with the basis of dressing, empowering, and setting a candle for magical work, but if not then you should definitely educate yourself on the subject. Too many Witches are forgetting about the basic *craft* of our Craft. But it is more than just memorizing candle colors and the proper directions to apply oils. It is about entering into the space of *enchantment*, the magical realm of the poetic in which we conjure forth our primal force and our deepest power. We call the trance upon ourselves; we conjure our Witch power. When we are in this state, our actions become a language of becoming, our rituals are symbolic enactments designed to engage fetch and enlist the aid of daemon.

When using candles for spellwork, it is customary to dress them with herbal oils to help align them to our desired goals. The reasons for this are multifaceted. The oils them-selves lend influence by way of their spirit, the in-dwelling consciousness of their par-

---

39. Devin Hunter, "Elemental Incense Recipes," *Modern Witch Magazine Volume One.*

ticular herbal makeup. Faery recognizes that *everything* is alive. All matter is comprised of energy. And all energy has consciousness. When we are casting a spell, the herbs and the bones and the curio that we might use are more than just symbolic containers for our own energy. We interact with them as *living beings*. We recognize the consciousness in them. In the plants, in the oils, in the candles, in the stones … our job as Witches and Warlocks is to communicate with that consciousness and enlist its aid in the work we intend to do. There are probably a million ways to do this, or more. This is but one of them.

### A Faery Way of Empowering a Candle Exercise

Items needed:

A taper candle

Some oil, aligned to your magical goal

A toothpick or other sharp object for carving into wax

Decide the purpose for which your candle will be lit and then choose one of an appropriate color. Take a deep breath and be aware of your triple souls. With another breath begin to bring them into alignment. Take as much time as you need to feel the effectiveness of the alignment. (Initiates and others who have practiced regularly for years learn to align in a single breath, when needed, but we maintain that ability with a continued, formal practice.)

One you have aligned, imagine you are standing in the spotlight that is your holy daemon. This light is exceptionally brilliant and you imagine it shining through you with an almost overwhelming force. Allow this light to fill you with a sense of confidence. (Even if this confidence is nothing more than make-believe on your part, allow yourself to feel this sensation … go ahead and "pretend.") Taking hold of the candle in both hands, and focusing *through* the lens that is this feeling, allow yourself to focus *on* your magical intention or prayer. If you are doing a spell for healing, then feel confidant as you pronounce the illness healed. If you are looking for money, then feel secure that it is manifesting. If trying to remove someone from a situation, then feel as if you have the authority to tell them where to go and what to do. Imagine that this light and this confidence are shining through you and into the candle.

With the toothpick begin to carve symbols, names, or words on the candle that represent your magical goal, all the while feeling this light shining through you and into the wax. While you are working, you may wish to softly chant something repetitive that reflects the nature of your working, some options may be:

*Her leg is healed. The bones are strong.*
*From far and wide, the money comes.*
*He turns away. He walks away. He moves away.*

Continue to chant as you work, allowing your focus and the power to build. Now take hold of the oil and imagine it also filled with this light that is coursing through you. This light is not *empowering* the oil; it is *communicating* with it. Our fetch is nonverbally communicating with the plant and herbal spirits when we focus our energy and chant and pray.

At some point, I often feel as if a soft light gently appears within the oil, and then I know that it is ready for magical work. Now apply some of the oil to the candle using whatever method you wish (generally from tip to base or toward yourself for spells of increase, or base to tip for spells of decrease), still chanting softly and allowing the power and feeling of confidence to flow.

Once this is done I often will trace a symbol over the candle with my fingers, as a sign to my fetch that this working is sealed. You will likely find your own method of knowing as you develop a hands-on practice. When lighting the candle, I will speak aloud some affirmation about it, such as in the case of a spell to remove obstacles and bring guidance I might say something like,

*I light this candle in the name of [----].*
*What blocks her path now falls away.*
*Her eyes are open; she sees the light.*

Herbs can be added to the oiled candle, if desired, to give added potency.

This observance can easily be modified to accommodate for a seven-day glass-encased devotional candle. Instead of a toothpick, you will use a permanent marker to draw your symbols or names. Use an instrument, such as a screwdriver or sharp dowel, to drill a few holes in the top of the wax as a place for the oils to go. Don't use too much oil, however, as you can drown the wick, thus putting more magical obstacles in your path. In my view, whatever happens to the candle (even if completely mundane in origin!) becomes part of the spell. So if the annoying neighbors' kid comes over and knocks your candle over causing it to go out, I would interpret that as outside influences causing problems and potentially disrupting your work. As with all magic, however, your mileage may vary.

## Movement and Dance

Another magical modality that we associate with fire is that of movement and dance. As with singing, dancing is a common practice in Faery circles. One reason for this is that these practices are fun! Our circles are like parties to which we invite our gods and ancestors. They are celebrations! They can certainly be serious, but they should never be *boring*. Even if a ritual is scripted (and most Faery rituals tend to lean toward the *un*scripted, at least the main event) then it is read with life force and passion! Likewise when we dance and move while enchanted we allow that enchantment to build in strength.

Folklore often speaks of the Faeries dancing in circles. Elf circles or fairy rings are names given to their circular dance, but also to a natural phenomenon that was associated with said dance, a naturally occurring circle of mushrooms. It is said that one should never step inside a fairy ring lest they be swept away by the Faeries into their realm, never to be seen again! Practitioners of the Craft, however, know that we must do all we can to form lasting bonds with the inhabitants of the otherworlds, and so we may seek these places out in order to dance with them, aligning their energies with our own.

Motion and dance are often used as a means to deepen the trance experience. One Old Craft technique, called seething,[40] uses quick, controlled movements and the rhythmic tensing and releasing of muscles in the body in order to facilitate a shift in consciousness. Related to the Norse tradition of *Seiðr,* a type of sorcerous practice that is often used for oracular purposes, seething is a way to raise power and enter into a deeper trance at will.

One simple way to do this is to stand perfectly straight and then begin to slowly tense and then release your lower leg muscles in a rhythm. Allow this rhythm to slowly flow up your body until you are tensing and releasing muscles in your legs, arms, belly, neck, and jaw. Begin to quicken your pace, tensing some muscles and releasing others faster and faster as your breathing speed also increases. Allow this to become almost chaotic, until

---

40. American Folkloric Witchcraft, "Seething." Accessed Sept. 21, 2015. http://afwcraft.blogspot .com/2013/03/seething.html.

you are literally shaking and trembling. To an outside observer it would appear almost as if you are having a seizure.

While seething, focus your attention on a magical goal as the power in your body is increased. You should feel the power being raised. When you feel it is reaching its peak, release all of your muscles at once and allow the power to be sent on its way. Some prefer to literally collapse to the ground at this point, or perhaps make a sweeping outward gesture with their arms and hands as if to send this energy off toward its goal.

Another, more historically accurate form of this practice would be a type of spinning dance. Using this method, one might obtain a staff or a pole, such as a broom or a stang, and then "ride" it in a wide circle, focusing their awareness on the central point of the circle. Alternatively, one might rotate around a central pole in order to keep this central focus while engaging in a circular motion. After some time revolving in this manner one will find themselves slipping into a trance.

Even simple dancing can provide us a means to enter more deeply into trance. Notice how movement and dance can immediately change your mood. If you are depressed or angry, sometimes engaging in dance can be just what you need in order to channel your energies in a positive direction. When working in the element of fire, try engaging in some dance as a type of personal devotion. And, just like the saying goes, dance like no one is watching.

### Opening the Ruby Road Exercise

This exercise will train your fetch to begin the journey into the hidden temple. Work with it at least a few times as given before proceeding to the next exercise.

Items needed:
Your black Star Goddess Candle
Matches
A red candle, placed in the south (or in the north, if you are in the Southern Hemisphere. Make the appropriate adjustments to the text based on your location.)
Fire incense

Open the Way. Turn to face the south. From the flame of the Star Goddess candle in the center, light the red candle in the south. Feel how the light of this candle calls the elemental realm of fire closer to you. From this candle light the incense.

Close your eyes and imagine a door appearing in the south that has the alchemical symbol for fire etched upon it: a red upward-pointing triangle. Take a moment as you charge yourself up by breathing the Blue Fire. When you feel you have a sufficient charge, say:

> *I summon forth the southern door.*
> *Open now, reveal the road of fire:*
> *Red as ruby, scarlet flame*
> *Bring thy action! Bring thy truth!*

With your exhale, send the Blue Fire out and into the symbol on the door, which you imagine shining bright in response. Imagine that this door opens wide before you, and you can now see a ruby red road that stretches off into the infinite south. As you continue to breathe, this road also stretches *toward* you, through the door, right to where you sit or stand in the center. Imagine yourself standing on this road and feel yourself in relation to the south. Look through the open doorway to gaze down the length of this ruby road. You can see the noonday sun at the very end of this road before you. Take some time—perhaps only a few breaths to a few minutes—and then give a silent prayer of thanks, imagining the road receding back through the door, which then closes and is gone. End your session as normal.

---

## The Guardian Beast of Fire: Lion

The lion is the spirit guide of the south and the Faery emissary to the realm of fire. It is associated with the zenith of the sun at midday and represents the peak of active power. Lion can help us to find our strength and our sense of pride. Lion brings the power to Will. Lion brings the power *to Will*, the second of the four foundational points of the Witches' Pyramid.

### *Invoking the Lion Exercise*

Items needed:
Your black Star Goddess candle
Matches
A red candle, placed in the south
Fire incense

Begin, as always, by Opening the Way. Perform the Ruby Road exercise.

Continue to look through the open door, allowing your gaze to flow along the ruby road and out into the south. Imagine that you are "opening up" *through* your holy daemon and that you can reach out through your daemon and into the south … into the blazing heat of the noonday sun. Say:

> *Red lion of the south!*
> *Bringer of the potent flames*
> *And the quickened blood,*
> *Emissary of the powers of Fire!*
> *Come to me, and bring your will!*

Breathing deep, you see a red lion sunning itself in the distance ahead of you. It stretches and stands directly underneath the noonday summer sun, proclaiming the majesty that is the height of the day. It begins to move toward you and then stops a few yards from your position. In your aligned space, open up through your daemon to connect with the lion, looking deep into its eyes. You begin to move into a deeper trance as you gaze deeply. Imagine now that you are on all fours, your feet transformed into paws as you stretch your muscular lion body and let out a great roar! Feel the strength of your muscles. Feel the power in your voice! Imagine leaping forward and running in your new lion body, feeling the musculature of your new body as you gain speeds you had never imagined. Feel the active power in your new form, the inner fire that blazes within.

After awhile, when you feel it is time to come back, allow yourself to slow down and return to your own human body as you find yourself back where you started. The red lion stretches on the road ahead of you. Give it thanks and notice if it moves away. Allow the ruby road to recede back through the door, which fades away. End as you would normally.

### Entering the Hidden Temple of Fire Ritual

This rite should ideally be performed at noon, in the afternoon, or the hottest daylight hours. Build an altar in the south. It should be draped with an altar cloth and adorned with symbols that represent the fire element, as well as the red candle.

Items needed:

Your black Star Goddess candle

Matches

Red or orange (or other appropriate color) altar cloth

A red candle, placed in the south

Fire incense

Fire symbols (obsidian, lava rock, pictures of a volcano or desert, etc.)

A knife or blade

Open the Way. Perform the Ruby Road exercise followed by the Invocation of the Lion. Take some time to commune with lion before moving on.

At some point, the lion will guide you through the door of the hidden temple of fire … The doorway is filled with brilliant crimson and golden light. It is bright, like dazzling sunlight reflecting on rippling water … Take another deep breath, and step through into this light.

The light opens up all around you and you now see a great desert before you. The air is dry and hot. The sand is hot beneath your feet. Small fires dot the landscape for as far as you can see. The noonday summer sun is blazing in the sky above you, its brilliance a powerful thing to behold.

With your blade, trace an upward pointing triangle in the space before you, like a glyph of an active flame, made of ruby red fire. Say, *"By my will, I invoke fire!"*

Imagine the blazing sun morphing into a huge ruby-red pyramid of light that fills the sky before you.

Take three deep breaths and feel your body become empty and hollow. Take seven deep breaths and feel your body filling with the elemental powers of fire in the form of a ruby red light, which embodies the qualities of Strength and Active Potency.

Take seven deep breaths and imagine the ruby red pyramid projecting into your belly beneath your navel, where it transforms into a ruby upward-pointing triangle. Feel the explosive power of fire moving within and through you, and yet easily contained within this triangle. This glyph serves to focus this fire, making it more potent.

With seven deep breaths imagine that your mouth, stomach, intestines, and esophagus becomes filled with luminous ruby red light. Feel how your body's energy is a type of fire. Take some time to fully absorb the powers of elemental fire into your physical and energy bodies. Say *"I am fire"* seven times as a long, drawn-out vibratory note, becoming slower and longer with each repetition.

Continue to breathe deeply and focus your attention on the triangle within your belly. Feel how it shines throughout your body, and how it shines out into your aura or nimbus. Maintain this presence for the span of at least several minutes.

For the span of three breaths become aware of the desert and your working area existing simultaneously. With three more breaths allow the desert to fade. Extinguish the red candle. End as normal.

---

# Salamanders

Salamanders are the nature spirits of fire. They don't just live in the fire, they are the fire itself, which is a type of consciousness.[41] They are the living consciousness of the plasmic state of matter. Salamanders are often said to look much like their physical world namesakes, only more reptilian than amphibian in appearance. They seem, to one with the Sight, as if they are small lizards within the flames, or even as tall, robed giants, when in the presence of larger fires. They can also appear as small blue orbs of light.

Not as much is known about the Salamanders as the other elemental spirits. Their explosive and trickster nature makes it difficult to study them safely for too long. They are responsible for every fire in the universe, from the tiniest match strike, to a bonfire, to a forest fire, to the nuclear heart of a star. It is their presence that causes fire to transform, purify, and to give life. When we light a candle or tend a flame, we are making a personal devotion to these spirits and so we should remember to pay attention to their presence, and we will learn much from them.

### The Heat of the Salamanders Exercise

Items needed:
Your black Star Goddess candle
Matches

---

41. Anderson, *Fifty Years in the Feri Tradition,* 60.

A red candle, placed in the south
Fire incense
A simple candle

Open the Way. Invoke the ruby road and the lion. Move into the hidden temple and engage the elemental power and the glyph.

Remember your soul alignment. Reach out *through* your daemon and into the wick of the unlit candle as you take a deep breath and light it. Pay attention to the flame as you softly gaze at it … delving into it. Feel the explosive power even within this tiny flame. Notice how it shines and radiates, and know that right now—in this very flame before you—is the process of transformation as carbon is being transformed into each of its known four states and microdiamonds are being created, and destroyed.[42]

Imagine that you can see little motes of light sparking and fling about … here and there … little golden, red, or blue lights … or they may appear like lizards, or in another form altogether. Just notice how they come to you. Notice how they flow into each other. Just like two candle flames that can flow into one. This is them having sex with each other and creating vitality. Take a deep breath and breathe them into your lungs. They vitalize your breath … giving you life … now breathe them out again, and they return … spiraling into the atmosphere.

Maintain this practice for at least several breaths and then end as you would normally.

---

## The Blade

In the Faery Tradition, the tool of fire is the blade. The blade is a manifestation of one's will, piercing the veil of illusion and initiating the active principle. The blade is traditionally double-edged, symbolizing the dual nature of our actions. In practical terms, it is a tool of cutting and separation and is generally used to separate ritual space from non-ritual space as in the act of casting the circle. During this act, it is used to direct ones' will in much the same way as the wand, only the blade is seen as more forceful and so may be

---

42. Phys.org, "Candle flames contain millions of tiny diamonds." Accessed Sept. 21, 2015. http://phys.org/news/2011-08-candle-flames-millions-tiny-diamonds.html.

used to invoke or banish spirits that are less than friendly.[43] The blade may also be used to metaphysically cut cords or *aka threads* that bind us to people, places, or situations that continue to drain us of our life force.

## Enchanting the Blade Exercises

For the following exercises you will need the following items:

Your black Star Goddess candle

Matches

A red candle, placed in the south

Fire incense

Your blade

Begin each exercise by performing the following:

Open the Way. Light the incense. Focus your attention on the ruby road of the south and light the red candle. Connect with the lion and journey through the door into the hidden temple of fire. Spend some time breathing in the presence of the element, filling yourself with the ruby red light. Allow the triangle beneath your navel to shine brightly.

### Awakening the Blade

Hold the blade so that the hilt is positioned beneath your navel and the tip is pointed out away from you. Begin breathing the ruby light from the triangle in your belly so that it flows out *through* the blade and into the south. Imagine that this energy is flowing out to meet the sun at its height of power. Imagine the blade is becoming the embodiment of strength and active potency. Do this for twelve breaths and then with the next twelve, breathe the ruby light back from the sun, through the blade, and into the glyph in your belly. Now, reduce your breathing to six breaths. Now reduce to three. End the exercise with a few instances of doing this in a single breath, exhaling the power through the blade, and inhaling it back the same way. After you have done this for a few to several minutes call the power back into you as you integrate it. End as normal.

---

43. One would hope that this practice would be a rare one. Why invite hostile intelligences into our space when there are a plethora of beings that are already aligned to us? But on those occasions when it might be necessary, the blade will offer a more defensive/offensive approach to working with hostile forces.

*Cutting Cords*

In your talker form, the mental intention is to take back your power from the people, issues, or places that drain you of your life force. Reach out with your fetch and feel how it forms threads, tentacles, or cords that connect you to those things that are draining. Pay attention to how these connections feel to you. With every breath, pull your power back to you through those connections so that your fetch gets charged and made more whole with each inhale. Do this for at least seven breaths.

When you have pulled back your power from these things, take a moment to feel these cords as being empty, ephemeral, like shadows. Take hold of your blade and breathe life force through it three times, hearing it ring like a great bell as you do. See it charged and filled with fire.

Take a deep breath and consciously sever each cord as you exhale quickly, feeling the cord break and the power return to its place of origin. Feel the last remnants of your own power snap back into you. Take three more deep breaths of power to integrate and balance these energies within you. It is done.

*Triangle and Blade Purification* [44]

While in the hidden temple, remind yourself of the physical space in which you are working. Open your eyes and maintain the energetic presence of the temple; you walk between the worlds. Physically cast a simple circle around yourself by pointing your blade to the ground and turning clockwise, imagining your holy fire streaming through your body, through the blade. Feel the moment this circle is completed and affirm to yourself that this circle will remain in effect on the astral plane for the duration of your session here.

Identify a particular negative feeling that you have about yourself. It can be anything, big or small. Allow it to coalesce into a symbol or image. Notice how you *feel* about it.

With your blade, draw a triangle of blue fire on the floor outside of the circle so that it points toward you. Feel it throb and thrum with power.

With seven breaths, mentally place the symbol or image into the triangle.

---

44. Based on a Coven Korythalia exercise, 1984.

Draw a ruby red pentacle in the air with the blade. When it is complete, stab the blade though the center of it and hold it in place for the span of three breaths. Imagine a beam of energy pouring forth from the blade and into the image. When it reaches the image, see and feel that it becomes an explosive, raging fire, completely destroying the image and transforming the energy that created it into a purified form. See it shine and glow. Take some time to really feel this power.

With seven slow breaths call this (now transformed) power from the point of the triangle and into your circle so that it merges with your ritual space. See and feel it swirl around you, noticing how it feels on your skin, but also the emotional sense that it brings. With seven more breaths breathe it in, seeing yourself shine with this power. Take some time to feel this power within you, radiating out from you in all directions. Feel how you are now free of whatever block or negative energy you transformed. When you feel you are done close your circle as normal.

---

## The Watcher of Fire: Shining Flame

The Watcher of fire is called Shining Flame and wields the power of Truth. He is said to sometimes appear in a roughly human form, within a cloud or nimbus of fire, like an aura. Sometimes he possesses a serpent's tail. The color of the human figure is sometimes a brilliant orange-gold, while the flames change color but are usually blue-white. In Bloodrose, he is said to wield a sword of polished blue metal in his right hand. This sword slices through illusion, hence the association with truth. He sometimes will wildly dance, sparks erupting with every step. Alternatively, he may appear as a raging red star, or simply as an enormous explosive fire.

The Shining Flame will teach us about how to train our own inner fire and transform ourselves into our divine birthright.

*Figure 7: Shining Flame Sigil*

## Invoking Shining Flame Exercise

Items needed:

Your black Star Goddess candle

Matches

A red candle, placed in the south

Fire incense

Your wand

Open the Way. Invoke the ruby road and the lion. Step upon the road and move through the door and into the hidden temple of fire where you connect with the elemental powers and activate the glyph in beneath your navel.

Place your palms together at heart level in front of you, fingers pointing up. With a deep inhale, breathe in the power of the desert and the blazing sun. With each breath allow that power to fill you and become concentrated. This should span at least three breaths.

With your next exhale, allow a thread of energy to flow forth from the glyph beneath your navel as you extend your hands outward into the south, fingers pointing outward. Imagine the energy thread as flowing outward into the realm of fire in the south and rising up above eye level and reaching an infinite point. This may take a few breaths to achieve.

Imagine that this thread is connecting you to the elemental realm of fire. As before, open your hands so that they are now cupped in front of you and gesture as if you are gathering up this elemental energy. With your next inhale, bring your hands back toward yourself so that you now cross them over your chest, left over right. While this is happening you are pulling the elemental energy into the glyph through the energy thread. Bow in reverence to the direction.

With your wand or fingers, trace a five-pointed star of ruby red fire in the space before you. Repeat the invocation:

> *Shining Flame! Shining Flame! Shining Flame!*
> *Within the candle and the star*
> *Burning vortex, spark and flash*
> *Watcher of the liquid flame*
> *Reduce illusions all to ash!*

Imagine the Watcher emerging from the red pentacle. Take several deep breaths, feeling the presence of the Watcher before you. Take three deep breaths and feel your body become empty and hollow.

With six breaths, imagine the Watcher projecting into the triangle within you on a beam of ruby red light. Breathe in the presence of the Watcher along with the power of Truth and imagine an image of the Watcher in miniature forming within that triangle beneath your navel. Know that the Watcher within you and the Watcher before you are one and the same, two sides of the same coin.

Maintain this presence for at least the span of six breaths.

You may spend as much time as you like working with the Watcher, allowing him to guide you. Or move on to the next step.

Take a deep breath of power, and imagine taking a step closer to the Watcher before you. As you do, the Watcher within expands in size and power.

Ask the Watcher, "Who am I?"

Repeat this process, stepping closer and closer, while the Watcher within expands to eventually fill your whole body. When you next take a step you then merge with the Watcher before you. Now all three of you have merged into one shining being.

Maintain this awareness for several breaths, and then imagine stepping out of the immediate presence of Shining Flame so that he is before you once more. Allow him to guide you as he will. You may sit in silence or he may speak or show things to you.

After you have spent several minutes in communion in this manner, end by giving thanks to the Watcher for his assistance. Say:

> *Shining Flame,*
> *Watcher of the liquid flame,*
> *I thank you for your power and your presence.*
> *Stay if you will, go if you must,*
> *But ere you depart I bid you:*
> *Hail and Farewell!*

Pay attention to whether or not you feel if he stays or goes. Either way, release your connection to him as if letting go of a thread or a tether. Imagine the pentacle dissolving and scattering like smoke on the wind. For the span of three breaths feel the desert and your working area existing simultaneously. With three more breaths allow the desert to fade. Extinguish the red candle with a silent prayer.

---

## The Horned God

The most common names in Faery Tradition for this godform are Krom (or Crom), and Twr (Welsh, meaning "Tower"). He is also called the Harvest Lord and the Summer King. He is the Horned God of the Faery Tradition and as such may be aligned with Cernunnos and Pan. As a Sun God he is the radiance of the sun (especially as it nourishes and energizes life), and the life-giving powers of virility. In a common form his skin shines with the golden light of the summer's sun, and his neck is adorned with a swathe of green leaves and summer flowers. He has the head of a stag—a reminder that he is primal in nature. He is the son, lover, and other half of the Great Mother. Like most horned gods he is overtly sexual, but is also a nurturer … he is the god in his aspect as Father and Lover, and as such may be prayed to for guidance, and even as a surrogate for those roles if need be. His traditional emblem is the golden sun.

While Krom is considered a reflection of the Star God/dess, a major aspect of particular importance is that of him as father. "God the Father" is a religious phrase that can prove to be problematic to modern Pagans, as we often have baggage around that term from a Christian-dominated society. It is precisely because it is problematic that I feel it is especially important to invoke him in this way, as it gives us an opportunity to confront those complexes that we may be harboring that prevent us from accepting the wisdom and the gifts that the religions of our childhood as well as that which our own fathers may have failed to provide.

Another aspect in which he commonly appears is that of lover. His sexual nature is freely expressed, and we can connect to this god in a sexual way to both remind us of the inherent holiness of our own sexuality and also as a means to encourage ecstatic union with the divine.

Though there is much crossover, he is sometimes divided into four main aspects:

*Gold*—"the Sun God." The spirit of light and heat and the powers of the sun. He radiates in all of the colors of the spectrum, and here we see his power as that of light. He is Lucifer, the bringer of light and awareness, the bearer of the seed of divinity.

*Green*—"the Green Man." The spirit of plant life who mates with the Red Man at Midsummer. He is the active principle of vegetation, that which transforms the light of the sun into the cycle of food and plenty.

*Red*—"the Red Man." The spirit of animal life. He is the power of the blood, the life force of all animals including humans. He may appear with the hairy torso of a man and the legs, head, and horns of a goat or bull. As he dies and enters the ground, he sacrifices himself to the Green Man to be constantly reborn.

*Black*—"the Black Man." A deity of the Crossroads and a window into the Dark God. He attends the Witches' Sabbat and mates with the initiate bestowing his mysteries. He is a magical teacher and guide and is the sacred blacksmith, Tubal-Cain.

Together we might take both the Gold Man and Green Man as the Oak King and the Red Man and Black Man as the Holly King of British Pagan lore, the principal embodiments of the light and dark sides of masculine divinity as expressed in the Wheel of the Year. While in Wiccan lore they are in constant battle for the affections of the Goddess, in BlueRose they are seen as lovers.

### The Love of Kings

*Two lovers in a sacred ring*
*The Kings of Holly and of Oak*
*Dancing dervish 'round the sun*
*Desire whirling, hot and wild.*

*As passion swells with quickened blood*
*As summer leads to longing*
*The solstice sun shall mark the time*
*When Oak shall bow to Holly.*

*Into their eyes the light of love*
*Into their hearts sweet passions' flame*
*Into their kiss a fevered moment*
*In their embrace, Her Holy Name.*

*By seed and bud, by fruit and flower,*
*That all may spiral through rebirth*
*With milk of moon they spill their power*
*Their love is poured upon the earth.*

*As the chill moves on the wind*
*That heralds winter's cloak*
*The solstice sun shall mark the time*
*When Holly bows to Oak.*

*Into their eyes the light of love*
*Into their hearts sweet passions' flame*
*Into their kiss a fevered moment*
*In their embrace, Her Holy Name.*

*Two lovers in a sacred ring*
*The Kings of Holly and of Oak*
*Dancing dervish 'round the sun*
*Desire whirling, hot and wild.*

### Invoking Krom Exercise

Items needed:
Summer flowers
Images of strength, phalluses, the sun, stags, bulls
Your blade
Musky scent
A simple candle
Matches

Create an altar to Krom decorated with summer flowers, as well as with images of strength, phalluses, the sun, stags, bulls, or other horned animals. Place your blade on the center of the altar.

Anoint yourself with a musky scent and connect to him through your fetch. You may wish to engage your sex for this working. Light an appropriately colored candle. You may use the following invocation (or write your own):

*Golden Stag and Blazing Sun,*
*Verdant kiss and quickened blood*
*Expanding light and mote of dark*
*Rising phallus, prism's arc!*
*Krom! Krom! Krom!*

Ask him to shine his light into the darkness of your wounds to both expose and to heal them. Notice how you experience him in your physical and emotional bodies. Do you become aroused? Content? Fearful? How does he relate to your own father? To other males in your life? How does he relate to the females you know?

### The Points of Flame: Pride Exercise

Items needed:
Your black Star Goddess candle
Matches
A red candle

Just as we did with the air element for Self, you should now perform this exercise focusing on the point of Pride. Get a red candle to align with fire and proceed as before, only now in the hidden temple of fire and using the affirmation:

*In the name of iron, I summon forth Pride!*

Proceed as before, allowing the candle to burn all the way down. As always, journal your experiences immediately afterward.

## Fire Art Project

As with the previous element, construct an art project that expresses your personal experience with fire. It can again be any medium of your choosing, as long as it does not draw primarily from words, either written or spoken. What strengths and weaknesses did you uncover? What challenges did you face? What triumphs or defeats? Let this piece speak of your inner struggle to cultivate your inner flame. Again include a written explanation as the talker piece of this fetch-centered work.

# CHAPTER 9
# THE HIDDEN TEMPLE OF WATER

*The water said to the dirty one, "Come here."*
*The dirty one said, "I am too ashamed."*
*The water replied, "How will your shame be washed away without me?"*
—RUMI

As we continue our clockwise journey around the circle's edge, we find ourselves next in the station of the west, which we have associated with the element of water. As we have traveled from the stations of thought and then to action, here we engage the emotional and begin to explore the true depth of our will as it continues its circular transformation.

Water has always held a special significance to humankind. Access to water is a basic, fundamental necessity. Water is the difference between life and death. All life on this planet relies on water in order to survive. It also plays a major role in the cleansing rituals of numerous cultures and religions. In Hoodoo, the Uncrossing rite traditionally uses ritual bathing as its main method for cleansing spiritual impurities. That tradition also gives us a Foot Washing rite to better address whatever negative magic or powders individuals may have walked over that are subsequently causing them stress.

Besides being used in cleansing rites, water is also used in folkloric protection magic. Moving water has often been cited as a protective barrier against baneful magic and Witchcraft. Crossing over a stream or river was said to prevent one from being followed by a Witch or an evil spirit.

In terms of spellwork, water will also take on pretty much whatever intentional charge we may wish to put into it. Holy water is simply water that has been prayed over and charged for blessings. We may make our own holy water by placing our hands over a bowl or container of water and praying for it to become an instrument of cleansing. Adding a bit of salt to the water increases its ability to hold this charge. This mixture is then sprinkled in the area that we wish to cleanse. This works because salt crystals disrupt etheric patterns of energy. When the water vapor is hurled from our fingertips, the minute salt crystals contained therein will perform their requested function and disrupt whatever patterns are present. The result is a space that is temporarily free of etheric patterns and thus a blank slate waiting for us to impose new patterns in the form of our magical intentions, via our rites.

Water is the most changeable of the elements. It can change from a liquid to a gas or even a solid, depending on its temperature. Perhaps because of this it also represents *liminality*, the experience of being "in between" two states. Where air is associated with spring and fire with summer, water is associated with autumn, a season of balance between the two extremes of summer and winter. Symbolically we also associate it with the beach, a place between land and sea, and with sunset, between day and night. Because of this liminal nature we say that this is a "Faery time" and a "Faery place" as folklore repeatedly tells us that these places are the most likely of places in which to have contact with the Fae folk.

Consider also that the ancient Celts drew an association between the ocean and the astral plane. In their three-world model of land, sea, and sky, it is the sea that leads us into the underworld in which we can commune with the magical Fae. We go beneath the surface and into the realm of the unknown. Through these uncharted waters we navigate using our spirit contacts of Guardians, Gods, and Watchers.

In our lineage, when connecting to elemental water we are asked to contemplate the qualities of Fluidity and Adaptability. To be fluid is to change form, to bend to the established flow and exert no resistance: to conform. This is related to but separate from adaptability, which also is a state of changeability, but not necessarily conformity. To be adaptable is to be able to alter our behavior to better suit our needs. We must all adapt to our environment in order to survive.

## *Journaling*

Open the Way and then ask yourself how you feel when you hear the word *fluidity*.

*Spend at least five minutes writing about fluidity. Then, do the same for* adaptability.

## Water Incense Recipe[45]

1 part willow bark
1 part heather
1 part star anise
1 part rose petals

Combine together and store in an airtight container. This blend can then be burned on a lit charcoal to fumigate the area for your workings.

---

# Baths

Besides the Waters of Purity rite there are other time-honored methods for personal purification that are utilized in our tradition. The art of spiritual bathing has been used for centuries in many different traditions as a means to purify and renew the spirit as well as to bring in positive influences such as love, health, and prosperity.

Bathing is a perfect opportunity to delve a little deeper into the elemental mysteries of water. To actually soak in hot water allows our muscles to more fully relax, and this is a huge hurdle that we face when doing our deeper trance work. Relaxation is *hard*. We often *think* that we are relaxed when in reality we are holding secret tension. Just get a deep tissue massage and you will soon learn what I am talking about: muscles tend toward tension rather than relaxation. And relaxed muscles will tend to slowly move toward tension if not kept in a relaxed state.

I often find that soaking in the tub causes me to slip into a trance in which I can better commune with the gods. I endeavor to make these experiences beautiful as well as out of the ordinary: I turn off all the lights … I light some candles … I put on some soft music. I use essential oils and add herbs to the bath. I might even toss in some fresh flower petals if I feel that their energies are appropriate to my working. I prepare my chalice or a large glass of water so that I might perform the Waters of Purity rite, and I might even have a glass of wine. I want to make the experience a relaxing and beautiful one. If we are not engaging the sensual in our rites, then we may as well not be performing them in the first place.

---

45. Devin Hunter, "Elemental Incense Recipes," *Modern Witch Magazine Volume One.*

## *A Love Bath Exercise*

While most bathing rites tend to focus on removing certain influences, we can also create a bath to more fully immerse ourselves in those influences we wish to maximize. In this case we are creating a bath to help us draw love.

Not your average love spell, the Love Bath is a way to gently align ourselves to the energies of love so as to make ourselves ready to receive the love that we desire. It is both *cleansing* (in the sense that it is removing whatever may be blocking us from receiving or experiencing love) as well as *attuning* (by immersing ourselves in certain herbs and oils that will cause the energetic shifts necessary to achieve our desired result).

Items needed:
Your black Star Goddess candle
Matches
A red or pink candle (or another color that you feel better represents the concept of love)
A handful of fresh or dried rose petals
A couple pinches of damiana
A piece of rose quartz
Essential oils of lavender and patchouli
A piece of plain paper, cut into a heart shape
A pen or marker with red ink (or again, another color of your choosing)
1 cup of whole milk

Gather all of your items and draw a bath. While the tub is filling, Open the Way and use the red pen on the heart-shaped paper. Write out the qualities that you are looking for in a partner. Let these be mental and emotional qualities such as intelligence, kindness, compassion, etc. Try to steer clear of purely physical qualities, though you may include some of those as well, if desired. Next, turn the paper over and contemplate what you have to offer a mate: what qualities about yourself do you find desirable? Write these out on the paper. If you have trouble with this you may wish to perform the Waters of Purity rite and then try again.

Once the bath is ready, engage the Blue Fire and light the candle, making a heartfelt prayer. You may wish to recite a love poem (Rumi would be a great choice here, but follow your own inspiration). While in the state of enchantment, take up the damiana and contemplate the spirit within it. Mentally ask this spirit to help you align your essence to love. Reverently throw this into the water. Now do the same with the rose petals. Add some of the two oils to the cup of milk and pour this mixture into the water.

Take the heart-shaped paper and dress it on one side with the lavender oil and on the other with the patchouli. Breathe the Blue Fire into it three times, feeling that everything that you have written on it as now "coming alive" as a prayer to the gods. Now, burn it from the flame of the candle and say:

> *Flame of love within my heart,*
> *Light the way for Cupid's dart.*

As the paper burns and turns to ash, carefully toss it into the water at the last possible moment, so that this ash now becomes part of the bath in which you will immerse yourself. Take the rose quartz and give it a soft kiss, feeling it against your lips, and take it with you as you enter the tub.

As you soak, allow yourself to meditate on the concept of love. Have you ever been in love? How did you feel? Call up that feeling and allow yourself to begin to feel that *for yourself*. Allow your energy body to become attuned to the energies of love by feeling it moving through you. You are casting a love spell on yourself that will, in turn, make you more attractive to others. When you are finished, drain the tub, taking care to skim out any herbs or debris (you don't want to clog your drain!), and allow the candle to burn all the way down. The rose quartz can be carried as a charm or placed under your bed or in another area that you feel would be appropriate.

---

While working in the element of water, you would do well to take this time to create ritual baths to bring forth desired influences. Using the bathing rites given previously as a template, use herbs and other items associated with your desired goal and design a bathing rite to manifest that goal. Remember that every item and action in a ritual is an act of poetry. It needs to speak to the soul. Create something beautiful!

# Asperging

Another way to engage the cleansing properties of water is the art of asperging. Simply, this is the act of sprinkling water on a person, object, or an area in order to remove particular energies or influences. Some forms of Christian baptism reflect this, as well as the rites of many spiritual traditions around the world. Modern Pagans are most familiar with this in the cleansing rites often leading up to the casting of the magic circle in which specially prepared water is sprinkled around the circle area in order to prepare it for the energies that are to be invoked.

## *Making Holy Water Exercise*

Items needed:
Your black Star Goddess candle
Matches
A cup or small bowl of water
Some sea salt

Open the Way. Opening your awareness through your holy daemon, delve into the energetic presence of the water. Contemplate how it is a pure element and how it forms the basis for all life, as we know it. Now do the same for the salt, contemplating how it is a purifier, used for centuries to preserve food and even to cleanse wounds, preventing infection.

Engage the Blue Fire. When you feel sufficiently charged place your hands over the salt and *will* the flame to flow into it, imagining the spirit within the salt waking up as you pray for it to assist you in creating this cleansing potion. Now, add some of this salt to the water and using a tool or your fingers, stir until at least a good portion of the salt is dissolved. Continue to channel the Blue Fire into the mixture, communing with the spirit of the water and feeling the mixture glowing with an electrical charge. It is now ready to be used by sprinkling or anointing. Use some to purify your altar area, your tools, and even yourself.

## *Opening the Sapphire Road Exercise*

Items needed:
Your black Star Goddess candle
Matches

A blue candle, placed in the west
Water incense

Open the Way. Turn to face the west. From the flame of the Star Goddess candle in the center, light the blue candle in the west. Feel how the light of this candle calls the elemental realm of water closer to you. From this candle light the incense. Close your eyes and imagine a door appearing in the west that has the alchemical symbol for water etched upon it: a blue downward-pointing triangle. Take a moment as you charge yourself up by breathing the Blue Fire. When you feel you have a sufficient charge, say:

> *I summon forth the western door;*
> *Open now, reveal the road of water,*
> *Blue as sapphire, twilight shine*
> *Bring thy daring! Bring thy love!*

With your exhale, send the Blue Fire out and into the symbol on the door, which you imagine shining bright in response. Imagine the door opening before you, and you see a sapphire blue road stretching off into the infinite west. As you breathe, this road also stretches toward you in the center. Imagine yourself standing on this road and feel yourself in relation to the west. Look through the open doorway to gaze down the length of this sapphire road. You can see the setting sun at the very end of this road before you. Take some time—perhaps only a few breaths to a few minutes—and then give a silent prayer of thanks, imagining the road receding back though the door, which then closes and is gone. End your session as normal.

---

## The Guardian Beast of Water: Serpent

The serpent is the spirit guide of the west, the emissary to the realm of water. Its crepuscular luminescence inspires dreams and visions. It is the guide into the hidden temple of water, and can help us in getting in touch with our deeper emotions and what we have buried down below in our subconscious. In keeping with the Witches' Pyramid, the serpent brings the power *to Dare*. Imagine serpent rising from the depths of a dark sea, currents flowing, the whirlpool leading into the unknown, deep below the surface. Do you *dare* to look below to see what you have hidden?

## *Invoking the Serpent Exercise*

Items needed:

Your black Star Goddess candle

Matches

A blue candle, placed in the west

Water incense

Begin by Opening the Way. Perform the Sapphire Road exercise.

Continue to look through the open door, allowing your gaze to flow along the sapphire road and out into the west. Imagine opening up through your holy daemon and into the west … into the twilight of the setting sun. Say:

> *Blue serpent of the west!*
> *Bringer of the primal waters*
> *And the depth of feeling,*
> *Emissary of the powers of water!*
> *Come to me, and bring your daring.*

Imagine that the road that moves through the door before you is actually flowing into the edge of a vast ocean, the surface of which reflects the light of the setting sun, which descends down into the watery horizon before you. The waters are stirring, and with a splash she rises from the depths! Ancient and wise, primal and terrible, a blue serpent rises from the sea and begins to swim in circles, churning the waters before you.

As you watch her swim in circles and spirals, you feel yourself becoming lulled into a trance. Your body sways and you feel yourself moving … turning … swirling … and you are now swimming through the sea in the body of serpent. Take some time to experience these sensations.

After some time, allow your swimming to slow down and you find yourself spiraling back into your own form. The blue serpent swims off into the sea before you. Give it thanks and notice if it moves away entirely. Allow the sapphire road to recede back through the door, which fades away. End as you would normally.

### Entering the Hidden Temple of Water Ritual

Items needed:

Your black Star Goddess candle

Matches

Blue (or other appropriate color) altar cloth

A blue candle, placed in the west

Water incense

Water symbols (shells, pictures of the ocean or rivers, etc.)

Cup of pure water

This rite should ideally be performed at dusk or in the early evening hours. Build an altar in the west. It should be draped with an altar cloth and adorned with symbols that represent the water element, as well as the blue candle and the chalice of water.

Open the Way. Perform the Sapphire Road exercise followed by Invoking the Serpent. Take some time to commune with serpent before moving on.

At some point the serpent will guide you through the door of the hidden temple of water. The doorway is filled with brilliant rippling waves of azure and silver light. Take another deep breath, and step into this light.

The ripples open up, and you now see a great ocean before you. The waves lap up upon the shore as the tide ebbs and flows. The autumn air is cool and damp. The sun is setting beneath the horizon before you, the colors of twilight in the sky above.

With your chalice, trace a circle in the air before you—like a glyph of a pool of water—made of blue fire. Say, *"By my emotions, I invoke water!"*

Imagine the setting sun morphing into a huge sapphire blue sphere of luminescent energy that fills the sky and the sea before you. It is so large you can only see a portion of it, half submerged in the open sea.

Take three deep breaths and feel your body become empty and hollow.

Take seven deep breaths and feel your body filling with a sapphire blue light that is the elemental presence of water, which embodies the qualities of Fluidity and Adaptability. Notice how you feel as you contemplate these qualities within you.

Take seven deep breaths and imagine the sapphire blue sphere projecting into your chest at your heart, where it becomes a sapphire circle. Feel the flowing power of water moving within and through you.

With seven deep breaths imagine that all the fluids of your body begin to shine with a sapphire luminescence. In every cell of your body, your fluids are shining bright blue. Take time to absorb the powers of elemental water into your physical and energy bodies. As done before, repeat "I am water" seven times as a long, drawn-out vibratory note, becoming slower and longer with each repetition.

Focus on the blue circle within your chest. See it shining brightly throughout your body, and imagine it spilling out into your aura. Sustain this presence for a few breaths to a few minutes.

For the span of three breaths feel the ocean and your working area existing simultaneously. With three more breaths allow the ocean to fade. Extinguish the blue candle. End as normal.

## The Train of Emotions Exercise

This simple informal exercise will assist you in uncovering the truth about what you are feeling. It should be done in a private space, but can also be done in semiprivate space such as an office cubicle or at the bus stop. The whole process shouldn't take more than three to four minutes.

Often we know that we are experiencing an emotion, but sometimes those emotions are misdirected. We assume that our anger is at our spouse, when really we are angry about something that someone else did that we only half-remember. Fetch is rather tricky. It knows it *feels,* but it might not know *why*. This exercise will help talker to learn ways to better discern the origins of emotional responses from fetch, which will give you a better chance to use the power they bring, as opposed to being overpowered by them.

When you are going about your day and something happens to trigger an emotional response, find a private space and then take a slow, deep breath, silently aligning your souls. In your aligned, observational space, ask yourself where this emotion comes from. You might imagine this emotional state like a sphere of light or dark from which a cord or tether emerges, linking it to its origin, or whatever event in your past (recent or not) in which it was initially created.

Imagine following this cord backward through time until you come to ... something. What is it? It might be a symbol or a memory. It might be a being with advice or information. Some things that are revealed might make perfect and immediate sense. Others might leave you wondering. Take a breath and ask it if it is really the origin of this emotion or if it is really a mask. (We often will find things masquerading as something else ... especially when dealing with our own egos. These masks are often easier-to-face events and emotions than the underlying causes. Simply by repeating this process in the presence of your own alignment, the true origins of your emotions will reveal themselves to you over time.) End by reaffirming your own grounding and alignment.

---

# Undines

According to Cora Anderson, the Hydroni are a type of Undine that usually appear as female and are sexually active with each other.[46] Like the Sylphs, their lovemaking cleanses and vitalizes the element, making it a vessel for life force. They do this in all forms of water, even in our own bodies. They reportedly can mimic the forms of aquatic life around them and can even appear as small humans, like traditional mermaids. They are quite friendly toward humans and are responsible for the fluidic processes that sustain all plant and animal life on this planet.

## Blood of the Undines Exercise

To be performed in a low-light environment.

Items needed:
Your black Star Goddess candle
Matches
A blue candle, placed in the west
Water incense
Your chalice, filled with water

Open the Way. Invoke the Sapphire Road and the Serpent. Move into the hidden temple and engage the elemental power and the glyph.

---

46. Anderson, *Fifty Years in the Feri Tradition*, 58.

Reach out *through* your daemon and into the chalice. Imagine that you can feel the water there, though you are not physically touching it. Pay attention to the temperature of the water, as well as the sensation of the water conforming to the shape of the cup.

Scry into the water. Allow your vision to become soft and slightly blurred. As images begin to wash over your vision, imagine that you can look down into the energetic structure of the water itself. Imagine that you can now see the forms of living energy that comprise the essence of the water. Watch them swim through the water and into and *through* each other, making love and *vitalizing* the water. Just notice how they appear in your imagination and pay attention to how you *feel* while experiencing them. As creatures of elemental water they also rule the emotions, so awareness of this aspect of the exercise is essential. After some time of this, drink the water, knowing the Undines will continue this process by flowing into the fluids of your body through your bloodstream. Imagine your blood shining with the Undines as they continue this processes within you. End as normal. Record your experiences in your journal.

---

## The Chalice

The tool of water is the chalice or cup. Often in Western Magickal Tradition the chalice is seen as representative of the Goddess, but in Faery we tend to see it expressed in the sexually receptive potential of *all* genders instead of limiting it to a single expression.

The chalice, like all of the elemental tools, is representative of our selves. In this case, it is our emotions that are being focused upon. Emotions themselves are unruly. They do not follow the logical course of things. They are the color that spills outside of our neat and orderly lines, causing chaos as well as interest and expression. The tool of the chalice is a reminder that we need a sound container for our emotional selves. Through the course of our training we learn to fashion our fetch-talker connection into a sort of chalice, which can then better contain the wine of divinity. Through the work with the elements and the Iron Pentacle, we learn how to make and hold space for ourselves so that we can experience and observe our emotions without falling victim to them. If our passion is a rolling wave, we need to be the practiced surfers who stand aloft and ride said wave to the shore.

The chalice is the emptiness of the Void that contains all possibility as well as the cauldron in which all things are transformed and empowered. It is a tool for drawing energies into itself, and for preparing charged liquids for consumption. This is the preferred tool for the Waters of Purity rite as over time it will obtain a magical charge beneficial to your work.

## Enchanting the Chalice

Items needed:

Your black Star Goddess candle

Matches

A blue candle, placed in the west

Water incense

Your chalice

A small towel

Your blade

Red wine (one nonalcoholic substitute that I find particularly satisfying is
    pomegranate juice, but you may use whatever you feel is appropriate)

Begin each exercise by performing the following:

Open the Way. Light the incense. Focus your attention on the Sapphire Road of the west and light the blue candle. Journey through the door into the hidden temple of water. Spend some time breathing in the presence of the element, filling yourself with the sapphire blue light. Allow the blue circle in your heart center to shine brightly.

### Awakening the Chalice

Holding the chalice at your heart, breathe the sapphire light from the circle in your chest and out into the chalice. Feel this presence spiraling into the cup. Feel the *nature* of the chalice, how it has an emptiness that desires to be filled. Imagine the power of the setting sun slowly flowing into it. Allow the chalice to become the embodiment of fluidity and adaptability and see it glowing with blue light. Do this for twelve breaths.

On the next twelve breaths, breathe the sapphire light back from the ocean and setting sun, through the chalice, and into the blue circle in your heart. Now, reduce this to six breaths. Now three. End with a few times doing this with a single breath, exhaling the power into the ocean and sun through the chalice, and then inhaling it back the same way. Feel how the chalice contains all the waters of the world; there is no difference between your physical tool and the womb of the earth herself. Feel how *you* are the chalice … a container for the fluid presence that we invoke. After you have done this for several minutes call the power back into you to integrate it. End as normal.

### The Waters of Purity, Revisited

Pour some fresh water into your chalice and, holding it close, take some time to reflect on a person or issue that drains you of your power. Breathing though your fetch, imagine that fetch extends outward into the universe in the form of threads, tentacles, or cords that connect you to them.

In your talker form, the intention to take back your power from them. Reaching through fetch, begin to pull this power back and into your chalice as you inhale. Notice the energetic shifts in the water. Do this for at least seven breaths.

When you have taken back your power from these things, breathe three deep breaths of life force upon and through the water, seeing it shine and hearing it ring like a bell. See it charged and shining with light. Imagine that the negative power has now been purified. Dip your fingers into the water and splash a bit on your face and gently wash, imagining being cleansed and blessed by the charged water. You may towel off if desired, and then drink the rest of the water, feeling this light flowing within you and dissolving and transforming all impurities, blockages, obstacles, complexes, and illnesses of body, mind, and spirit. Place the chalice back upon your altar.

Take three more deep breaths of power to integrate and balance the energies within you. It is done.

### Consecrating the Drink

This begins here as an elemental exercise but in time will move beyond this categorization. Feel free to abandon the overtly elemental observances after mastering this exercise.

A note on gender binary and heteronormity: While the traditional symbolism used for this rite draws upon that normally associated with the heterosexual Great Rite utilized in modern Wicca, the gender-specific associations commonly given simply do not apply in our tradition. Faery recognizes that gender and polarity are not the same. To the Faery, the blade does *not* necessarily represent the male and the chalice does *not* necessarily represent the female. They are seen as simply projective and receptive energies, respectively. They *can* represent the aforementioned genders, if the participants involved wish it. But they don't *have* to. The only reason that some insist that the chalice and the blade are *exclusively* gendered is because they haven't stopped to question the assumptions of their traditions. These tools can just as easily represent a same-gendered pairing, retaining the obvious sexual symbolism while abandoning their previous hetero-exclusivity. If a Witch's purpose is to "better the Craft" (and in my opinion I submit that this is exactly the case) then each of us needs to be prepared to stare down the prejudices of our magical pasts and dream new ways into being. There are plenty of other religions that tell their adherents what to think. Witchcraft is not one of them.

In this rite, we will draw a loose association with the chalice and the blade with the Faery Divine Twins, which in BlueRose are often first experienced as the Scarlet Serpent and the Azure Dove, who merge together to become the Blue God, the Peacock Lord, Dian y Glas/Melek Ta'us. These Twins are generally seen as being brothers, but can also be sisters, as well as lovers. They are simply two halves of a single whole. In Wicca, they are often portrayed as the Oak King and the Holly King, who are constantly in a state of battle, vying for the affections of the eternal Goddess. In Faery, the Divine Twins need not battle for any affection, being children of the Goddess they always have her affection and their desirous appetites are more focused on each other.

Hold the chalice and contemplate how it is an empty vessel, longing to be filled. Sense how the emptiness within it is one and the same as what exists between the stars: empty, and yet filled with all possibility. Imagine how this emptiness opens up and—like a whirlpool—spirals inward, drawing in your own deep emotion. Feel the receptive principle of water: it is open and sexually passive. Pour some of the beverage into it with the deliberate intention to fill this emptiness with *ecstasy*.

Taking your blade in your strongest hand, feel how it is the initiating principle of fire: how it is projective and sexually active. Breathe life force through it three times, seeing it shine like fire and hearing it ring like a bell. Say:

> *As the blade is the Lover,*
> *So the chalice is the Beloved.*

Slowly and deliberately lower the blade into the wine-filled chalice, feeling the alchemical fusion of the elements of fire and water and noticing what effects there may be. Say:

> *As serpent longs for kiss of dove,*
> *As below and so above,*
> *Overflows with lust-filled love,*
> *And shines into the dark.*
> *Born of Beauty and of Pride*
> *With tears that cleanse the shame that hides*
> *We call our power from deep inside,*
> *And claim the holy spark.*

Feel the beverage brilliantly shining with the combined powers, becoming more than just the sum of its parts. Offer some in libation to God Herself. Now, drink and take this blessing deep within you. If in a group, offer the chalice to the next person in the circle moving clockwise with a personal blessing, such as "Drink deep, and feel Their love."

For those who find themselves unable to disassociate from this rites' previously gendered symbolism, an alternative might be to pour the wine or beverage through an open pentacle and into the chalice while reciting the incantation, or perhaps even pouring from one chalice into another or otherwise simply praying over the beverage in a way similar to the Waters of Purity rite. The importance is not so much the ritual form itself but in the intention and the engagement of the chosen symbolism.

---

## The Watcher of Water: Water Maker

The Water Maker is said to wield the power of Love. She may appear as a sea serpent, a giant squid, a kraken, or a nude woman rising from the primal seas. Some lore describes her as having the body of an octopus and a human head made of whirling tornados and flashes of lightning. She sometimes holds a silver chalice in her left hand and at times may offer this for the practitioner to drink, thus taking in her energies and aspects of her consciousness.

Water Maker guards the depths of our unknown. Everything we have buried beneath the surface is in her domain and we can call to her to help us uncover what we have forgotten.

*Figure 8: Water Maker Sigil*

### Invoking Water Maker Exercise

Items needed:
Your black Star Goddess candle
Matches
A blue candle, placed in the west
Water incense
Your wand

Open the Way. Invoke the sapphire road and the serpent. Step upon the road and move through the door and into the hidden temple of water and connect with the elemental powers, activating the blue circle in your heart center.

Place your palms together at heart level in front of you, fingers pointing up. With a deep inhale, breathe in the power of the ocean and the setting sun. With each breath allow that power to fill you and become concentrated. This should span at least three breaths.

With your next exhale, allow a thread of energy to flow forth from the glyph in your heart as you extend your hands outward into the west, fingers pointing outward. Imagine the energy thread as flowing outward into the realm of water and rising up above eye level, reaching an infinite point.

Imagine this thread connecting you to the elemental realm of water. As before, cup your hands in front of you and gather the elemental energy. With your next inhale, bring your hands back, crossing them over your chest, left over right, pulling the energy into the glyph through the thread. Bow in reverence.

With your wand or fingers, trace a five-pointed star of sapphire blue fire in the space before you. Repeat the invocation:

> *Water Maker! Water Maker! Water Maker!*
> *In darkness deep, you dream and sleep*
> *In love and madness reawaken*
> *Watcher of the Watery Abyss*
> *Arise in passion, thou ancient kraken!*

Imagine the Watcher emerging from the blue pentacle. Take several deep breaths, feeling the presence of the Watcher before you. Take three deep breaths and feel your body become empty and hollow.

With six breaths, imagine the Watcher projecting into the blue circle on a beam of sapphire blue light. Breathe in the presence of Water Maker along with the power of Love and imagine an image of the Watcher in miniature forming within the blue circle in your heart center. Know that the Watcher within you and the Watcher before you are one and the same.

Maintain this presence for at least the span of six breaths.

You may spend as much time as you like working with Water Maker, allowing her to guide you. Or move on to the next step.

Take a deep breath of power, and imagine taking a step closer to the Watcher before you. As you do, the Watcher within expands in size and power.

Ask her, "Who am I?"

Repeat this process, stepping closer and closer, while the Watcher within expands to eventually fill your whole body, and then eventually merging together with you as one. Maintain this for several breaths, and then imagine stepping out of the presence of Water Maker so that she is before you once more. You may sit in silence or she may speak or show things to you. Allow her to guide you as she will.

After you have spent several minutes in communion in this manner, end by giving thanks to the Watcher for her assistance. Say:

*Water Maker,*
*Watcher of the watery abyss,*
*I thank you for your power and your presence.*
*Stay if you will, go if you must,*
*But ere you depart I bid you:*
*Hail and Farewell!*

Pay attention to whether or not you feel if she stays or goes, releasing your connection. Imagine the pentacle dissolving and scattering like smoke on the wind. For the span of three breaths feel the ocean and your working area existing simultaneously. With three more breaths allow the ocean to fade. Extinguish the blue candle with a silent prayer.

---

## The Great Mother

*Mari* is the most common name given in Faery for the Great Mother, the soul of nature that gives rise to all life. She is the spirit of the earth, moon, sea, and sky, the embodiment of all manifestation. She is an earth goddess in the sense that it is she who gives form. She gives birth to us, sustains us in life, and receives us again at our death. She is the fecund energy of the universe as it manifests on this planet. The entire earth is her body. She is also the spirit of every woman: mother, sister, daughter, lover … and Witch.

Victor was quite adamant that Mari was "the same person as the Star Goddess" and the celestial imagery associated with Mari clearly illustrates this. She is the Star God/dess when she becomes pregnant with the divine child, the Dian y Glas, giving birth to the splendor of the world. In this, like the Biblical Mary, she becomes "the Mother of God."

She is also a moon goddess and is the same deity as Diana, queen of the Witches, where her connections to freedom and to the faerie folk are both firmly established.

She can appear as a tall, regal woman standing naked upon both land and sea. She often has black hair, which covers her like a veil. Her breasts are full and her belly is swollen in pregnancy. Her body shines like the silver of the moon. She wears a crown of twelve (or sometimes "six and seven") stars.

Andre Mari is also found in the ancient Basque culture where she was regarded as a primary deity of life as expressed through the changing weather and her role as the bestower of law. She was an androgynous figure, and as such stood as a basis for gender equality. Her consort was Sugaar, a serpent-deity whom we relate to the Blue God. She is the mother of twins, one good and the other evil, and her followers were persecuted as Witches.

In Bloodrosian Faery, Mari is traditionally invoked in three aspects. To these three I have identified a fourth that I believe can be worked with in her own right.

*White*—Goddess of the Moon and Sea. The Sovereign Queen. This is the most common aspect of Mari and appears as described previously. She can appear masked or veiled, for we cannot expect to know all of her mysteries. She shines down upon the earth granting dreams and guiding her children on their path. She rides a broom through the air and is the patroness of all Witches.

*Blue*—Another aspect of "White" Mari might be called "Blue Mari." She is the *Stella Maris*: the Star of the Sea. The name Mari comes from the Latin *mare* meaning "sea." She may appear robed in blue, adorned with silver or golden stars. In this aspect, she is more specifically aligned to her watery nature. Blue Mari guides those who travel over the waters and is manifest as the star Polaris: the North Star. She guides us on the sea of the astral plane: a guiding star for those who call upon her.

### Blue Mari

*Holy Mari*
*With veil blue*
*You are a shining star*
*Upon the sea*
*A guiding light*
*Bring me near when I am far.*

*Red*—The Scarlet Woman; The Sacred Whore. Lady of the Harvest. Yoni Gorri. She is the natural drive of sexual arousal as well as the fierce Mother who protects her young. Her hair is red, and if clothed she appears in crimson, with a red moon for a halo.

*Green*—The Fertile Mother. Gaia. Queen of the Faeries. She is the spirit of all life on earth, everything that grows is of her doing. She is the spirit in the individual plant as well as the entire forest. She gives of herself that all might live.

### Invoking Mari Exercise

Build an altar to Mari adorned with objects and symbols appropriate to the aspect with which you are intending to work, perhaps images of the moon, of the earth, of mothers and female power. Chant or sing to her. Make offerings to her.

> *Silver moonlight*
> *Earthly bounty*
> *Mother Mari*
> *Holy Mari.*

Invoke her as a surrogate for your own mother in workings to assist you in reclaiming your power, especially if you are unable to do so with your actual mother. Ask her to give you the love and nurturing that you perhaps feel you didn't receive. Replay events from your past in which you did not receive what you needed and now invoke the presence of Mari to change the narrative of that story. This isn't about living in a fantasy world, this is about experiencing what we believe to be the emotional outcomes of other possibilities and deriving power from those alternatives. This is about looking at our lives and those moments that have sapped our power from us from another angle so as to glean whatever power we can from the experience.

This is not to judge your actual mother, but to enable yourself to accept a mother's love without strings of attachment. Invoke her as a lover or a sibling to connect to her in other ways that are personal to you. Be present, and write your experiences down!

### The Points of Flame: Passion Exercise

Items needed:
Your black Star Goddess candle
Matches
A blue candle

Now you will perform the Points of Flame exercise as before, only now using a blue candle focusing on the point of Passion and in the hidden temple of water. Ask yourself: What do I love? What do I hate? And what do I *not* care about? Use the affirmation:

*In the name of iron, I summon forth Passion!*

## Water Art Project

As before, create a project describing your experiences in water along with a written explanation of said piece. Allow the element to guide you in this process. How do you *feel* about the project? What can water teach you about the artistic process? Try to see if you can use water in your piece. Watercolors might be one option, as would using shells, sand, or making an aquatic container of objects or plants. Let your imagination run wild!

# CHAPTER 10
## THE HIDDEN TEMPLE OF EARTH

*My soul can find no staircase to Heaven unless it be through Earth's loveliness.*
—MICHAELANGELO

As we have journeyed around the circle, we have experienced the crystallization of our ideas as they evolve from immaterial thoughts and into form. From the ideas of air, to the will of fire, to the emotional depths of water, we now find ourselves in the station of earth and manifestation. Here our ideas become tangible *things*.

Elemental earth is much more than just the planet itself. It is the very idea of form: of physicality and manifestation. Where the other elements might be more focused on doing, earth is about *being*.

The key points for contemplation in this element are the concepts of Structure and Stability. Structure refers to those organizational constructs that we have in place that provide a framework for our lives, bringing order. This can be anything from our daily routines to the people that we rely on to help us get things done. This structure is what allows our lives to function effectively.

Stability is the result of that structure. It is the security that comes from an experienced understanding of said structures and how they support us. It is not a static condition. Often it is dynamic, changing and rebalancing in order to achieve stability in the face of chaos.

## *Journaling*

Open the Way and then ask yourself how you feel when you hear the word *structure*.

*Write down anything that comes to you. Spend at least five minutes writing. Then, do the same for* stability.

---

The Witches' Pyramid designates this element as granting the power *to keep silent*. This is most often interpreted as an aversion to speaking about various or all aspects of the Craft, depending on who in particular is postulating the view.

During my training in Faery, I was asked to work a spiritual discipline that centered on the cultivation of an inner silence. In chapter 4, we briefly explored the reasons for this when I explained that we needed to silence the talker to create a more focused inner space from which to work. Talker's job is to analyze, dissect, and control, noble tasks that enable us to live, move, and explore our world. But when it comes to magic, then the time for logic and rational thinking are largely over. We must move beyond the comfort zones of our intellectual elitism and delve into the messy world of the primal. This is fetch's work.

Where silence is invoked in the Craft we must also confront the idea of *secrecy*. It is widely known and accepted that the Craft has certain secrets available only for those initiated into our Mysteries. These secrets vary from coven to coven and tradition to tradition, but the concept surrounding them is always the same: the Mysteries are not something that can be imparted with mere words, but rather must be *experienced*. The experiential Mysteries that are at the heart of Witchcraft are usually accompanied by the secrets: certain signs, names, lore, etc., that *can* be intellectually revealed but would be useless to anyone who had not yet undergone the initiatory experience. Whatever secrets are imparted by the coven or tradition are secondary to its Mysteries. This is why no book could ever hope to impart the fullness of the Faery Tradition. While it might prove to be interesting trivia, I could literally reveal every single Faery secret there is and it would do *nothing* for the reader toward deepening their understanding of our tradition. We must work and *live* the tradition in order for it to be truly Faery.

When discussing the subject of secrecy in the Craft, we should be prepared to confront our personal biases. In my thirty-plus years in the Craft at the time of this writing, I have seen and experienced many different approaches when it comes to Craft secrecy, even from within the same tradition or coven. Faery Tradition has a reputation for being secretive, in spite of the fact that Cora Anderson repeatedly said that there were "very few secrets in Faery" Tradition.[47] Secrecy in the Craft, it seems, was primarily a practical concern: up until relatively recently the practice of Witchcraft was illegal, and punishable by death. Even when those laws were amended to reduce punishment to the form of jail or fines this was still a good motivator to stay "in the broom closet." Even as recently as the 1980s, if one had come out of that closet then they ran the very real risk of suffering violence or having their children taken away out of religion-based fear. While this is sadly *still* a concern in certain communities, by and large many of us do not live in that same world, and so the level of secrecy once demanded no longer makes as much sense and in many cases actively works against us. This is especially true in the face of how the concept of secrecy in the Craft has at times become a weapon to use against each other. This is inevitably by those who are more fundamentally inclined in their approach to their religion. These people are threatened by differing religious views and so seek to curtail the expression of others under the guise of protecting the tradition. What they fail to understand is that the tradition itself demands change and has done since its very inception. True Witchcraft has always been about what works, rather than adherence to dogmatic views. Witchcraft is the antithesis to dogma. Where dogma exists, Witches appear to challenge the status quo.

Even the stability of the structures of earth are in fact dynamic processes that move and adapt. Tectonic plates move—mostly more slowly than the eye can see—but then they shift! And we have an earthquake. Things that remain the same for too long must sometimes be radically changed. Nature demands it.

The conclusion that I have come to is that there is really only one valid approach to secrecy in the Craft and that is to see it as a *personal devotion*. When secrecy is a practice as opposed to a law then we are better able to allow that practice to inform us from within, as opposed to restricting us from without. Also, as a personal devotion, I am only governing myself, as opposed to trying to "keep others in line," so to speak. It is not my job or my business to curtail the expressions of another, even if I feel that they have revealed secrets in doing so. I will continue to hold secret that which I have pledged, and it doesn't matter in the slightest that someone else might have spilled the beans. I need not draw any additional attention to the breach and instead continue my personal practice unaffected.

---

47. From private conversations I had with her prior to her death.

While I am sure that there will be these who will strongly disagree with my take on this, I ask you to consider: what purpose does the enforcement of secrecy serve? If you find value in its practice, then you should absolutely continue with it. If not, then perhaps it's time to consider a new approach.

### Earth Incense Recipe[48]

1 part cedar
1 part sage
1 part pine needle
1 part mandrake

Combine together and store in an airtight container. This blend can then be burned on a lit charcoal to fumigate the area for your workings.

---

## Herbs, Stones, and Curios

Witchcraft is a path that works with spirits. Whether these are the disincarnate spirits of the once living or the conscious presences within a plant, bone, stone, or other curio matters very little. The overall concepts are the same when dealing with them all. Here in the earth element we begin to focus our attentions on the in-dwelling spirits that reside within physical objects, deepening our relationship with them.

In Faery Tradition, we are taught that all energy is conscious. Since all matter is comprised of energy, this means that *everything* is conscious. It may be a very different type of consciousness than what we experience in ourselves or expect to find in others, but *everything is alive,* and the work of Witchcraft is largely about learning to communicate with these different types of beings. This is the heart of animism, a core tenant of the Old Craft that provides a Witch's worldview that enables our magic.

While some magical paths will tend toward the purely cerebral, explaining away the magic we do as nothing more than meditation or positive thinking, the magic of Faery Tradition flies in the face of such limited assumptions, preferring toward the primal, wild side of things. In Faery, we recognize the cerebral (talker) approach (and can even adopt it when it serves our needs) but we seek to balance this method with those better suited to the fetch.

---

48. Devin Hunter, "Elemental Incense Recipes," *Modern Witch Magazine Volume One.*

When we are working with herbs, stones, and other curios, for example, the ceremonial magician might see them as purely symbolic or perhaps as storehouses of personal power, much like the batteries that power our numerous modern devices. But to the Witch these are living allies, who must be petitioned in order to obtain their assistance. They do not need to be charged or empowered. They need to be *asked*. While this might prove to be a bit of a challenge to talker, this is small potatoes for fetch. Fetch is quite accustomed to nonverbal communication and so it is through the language of this part of our soul that we must make our petition. One way to do this is through the use of sigils and charms.

When I am performing spells, I want to make sure that every item that I am using has been aligned to my work. I recognize the in-dwelling spirit within each tool, stone, and herb and will perform actions to "awaken" or to otherwise align them to my purpose. In my personal work, I have developed a practice that involves the ritual miming of certain sigils, along with a spoken charm to trigger this energetic response. After you have worked with them as given here feel free to develop your own methods that feel right to you.

### Awakening an Herb, Stone, or Curio Exercise

Items needed:
Your black Star Goddess candle
Matches

Open the Way. Holding the herb or curio in your hand, focus on how you *feel* and imagine an energetic rapport forming between yourself and the spirit within it. Take a deep breath into fetch and then softy exhale *over* the item, allowing your breath to awaken the sleeping presence of the spirit within it. Allow yourself to slip deeper into trance and then trace one of the following symbols with your fingers over it:

### The Rising Vine
"The Life of the Plant Arises"
*Function:* To awaken the plant spirit and communicate your desires

*Figure 9: The Rising Vine Symbol*

This symbol is used to awaken the spirit of the plant or herb so that it can be effectively communicated with. The final movement of the symbol, the leaf, is performed with the thumb and index finger of the active hand in a pinching motion.

### The Crystal Matrix

"The Life of the Stone Arises"

*Function:* To awaken the stone spirit and communicate your desires

*Figure 10: The Crystal Matrix Symbol*

Like the rising vine symbol, the crystal matrix is used to awaken the consciousness within the stone, bone, or curio, allowing for a space of communication. The divided box shape brings us into communion with the precise forms within a crystalline matrix, while the outward spiral activates the life force within it.

Once you have traced your particular symbol, cup your other hand over the herb or curio, imagining a light from fetch flowing through your body, through your hands, and into the item you hold. This is where we really need talker to become the listener. While making this energetic connection, at some point you will be given a sign that the in-dwelling spirit is in resonance with your desires. As described in the section dealing with oils, I often sense a subtle shift in the energy of the stone or herb much like a soft light slowly brightening. You will likely find your own way of sensing this.

Both of the symbols given here can be used by anyone who feels a connection to them. Feel free, however, to use your own as they present themselves to you in your own work.

---

## The Power of Place

Witchcraft and especially Faery Tradition is intimately connected to the land. Where we have seen how Faery approaches everything as being alive, it should come as no surprise that we extend this to places as well as to objects. Certain areas are known to possess certain qualities that cannot be adequately described or explained by rational thought. These are often places associated with good luck and healing, such as in the case of Chalice Well in England or the psychic vortexes in Sedona, Arizona. Often ancient peoples would build monuments on such sites and would hold rituals there in order to tap into this natural power. When Europe was in the process of being Christianized, many of these sacred sites were vandalized and rededicated to the Christian God with the erection of a new church where the old once stood.

One need not travel to exotic locales in order to experience the power of place. You need go no farther than a park or your own backyard to begin this work.

### *Engaging the Power of Place Exercise*

Choose a place outside where you will not be disturbed. Since this exercise will have you sitting quietly outside during and after sunset, make sure that this place is a safe one.

Begin by traveling to your chosen location at least a few minutes prior to sunset. Sit quietly and Open the Way. Imagine that your normal consciousness is setting along with the sun. As the light fades away, so does your talker-dominated worldview, as you slip deeper, and deeper into fetch space.

When the sun has set, and you are sitting in darkness, remain still and quiet and pay attention to what you perceive around yourself. Listen to the sound of the trees ... or the birds ... the sounds of the forest, desert, sea, or whatever environs you find yourself in. Remain still and quiet and *open*. You may begin to perceive elemental spirits, faeries, and the like. Resist the urge to become *amazed* by these things, as this will distract you from the deep experience of them. Simply remain calm, quiet, and observant. After at least several minutes of this, you may end your session, making sure to record whatever you might have experienced in your journal.

### Opening the Emerald and Jet Road Exercise

Items needed:
Your black Star Goddess candle
Matches
A green and/or black candle, placed in the north
Earth incense

Open the Way. Turn to face the north. From the flame of the Star Goddess candle in the center, light the green/black candle in the north. Feel how the light of this candle calls the elemental realm of earth closer to you. From this candle light the incense. Close your eyes and imagine a door appearing in the north that has the alchemical symbol for earth etched upon it: a green or black downward-pointing triangle with a horizontal line dividing its middle. Take a moment as you charge yourself up by breathing the Blue Fire. When you feel you have a sufficient charge, say:

> *I summon forth the northern door:*
> *Open now, reveal the road of earth:*
> *Green as emerald, black as coal*
> *Bring thy wisdom! Bring thy form!*

With your exhale, send the Blue Fire out and into the symbol on the door, which you imagine shining bright in response. Imagine the door opening before you, and you see an emerald-green and jet-black road stretching off into the infinite north. As you breathe, this road also stretches toward you in the center. Imagine yourself standing on this road and feel yourself in relation to the north. Look through the open doorway to gaze down the length of this road. You can see the stars and moon in the night sky, shining down upon the road that stretches off before you. Take some time—perhaps only a few breaths to a few minutes—and then give a silent prayer of thanks, imagining the road receding back though the door, which then closes and is gone. End your session as normal.

---

## The Guardian Beast of Earth: Bull

We imagine him emerging from the darkness and holding silent presence in the north. The bull represents the Witches' power of Silence, a concept that is often misunderstood in the Craft. The silence to which we are referring is primarily internal. It is about coming to a space within ourselves that is free of the ego-chatter that often keeps us from being able to access the wisdom of our own daemon.

This *can* manifest in outwardly focused silence. One bit of wisdom that the practice of silence offers us is a decreased chance of other people's opinions and feelings interfering with the work that we wish to do. In the case of spells, we may wish to "keep a lid on our cauldrons," so to speak, until the spell has come to fruition. Even those people whom we might consider to be allies might not share in our personal visions and may unconsciously offer up resistance to our magical workings. This is a practical reason why we may wish to keep our spellworkings to ourselves, though this is far from a universal approach.

Working with the bull can help us determine when silence is necessary and when we should speak out. He is the emissary of the realm of earth and has much to teach us about being a spiritual being in a physical body.

## Invoking the Bull Exercise

Items needed:

Your black Star Goddess candle

Matches

A green and/or black candle, placed in the north

Earth incense


Begin by Opening the Way. Perform the Emerald and Jet Road exercise.

Continue to look through the open door, allowing your gaze to flow along the emerald and jet road and out into the north. Imagine opening up through your holy daemon and into the north … into the darkness of midnight. Say:

> *Black bull of the north!*
> *Bringer of the stable mountains*
> *And that which lies beneath,*
> *Emissary of the powers of earth!*
> *Come to me, and bring your silence.*

Imagine that the road that moves through the door before you is actually flowing into the vast, dark forest. Off in the distance you can just make out some rock formations and caves. From one of these caves emerges a large black bull, standing in the moonlight. He steps forward and snorts and begins to rhythmically strike the ground with his tremendous hooves.

As you watch him doing this, you begin to feel yourself becoming lulled into a trance. Your body sways and you feel yourself moving … turning … swirling … and you are now in the body of the bull, stamping upon the earth. Feel your powerful muscles as you strike your hooves upon the ground. Notice what it is like to look through the eyes of the bull and into the forest around you. Take some time to experience these sensations.

After some time, allow yourself to shift back into your own form. The black bull moves off into the cave before you. Give it thanks and notice if it moves away entirely. Allow the Emerald and Jet Road to recede back through the door, which fades away. End as normal.

## *Entering the Hidden Temple of Earth Ritual*

Items needed:

Your black Star Goddess candle

Matches

Black and/or green (or other appropriate color) altar cloth

A green and/or black candle, placed in the north

Earth incense

Earth symbols (stones, salt, plants, pictures of mountains, etc.)

Green cube


This rite should ideally be performed at midnight, or in the late evening hours. Build an altar in the north. It should be draped with an altar cloth and adorned with your symbols that represent the earth element, as well as the black/green candle and the green cube.

Open the Way. Perform the Emerald and Jet Road exercise followed by the invocation of black bull. Take some time to commune with bull before moving on.

At some point, the bull will guide you through the door of the hidden temple of earth … The doorway is filled with an inky-black, tangible darkness that seems to absorb the light from around it. Take another deep breath, and step into this darkness.

As your eyes begin to adjust to the low light, you begin to see a dark forest all around you, dimly lit by the light of the moon and the stars above, filtering down through the thick canopy of trees overhead. The air is cold; you can see your breath in the moonlight. It is the dead of winter at the stroke of midnight. The darkness that you are standing in is related to the *sun* … in the underworld the sun now shines … and we are standing in the shadow of the earth.

With your cube, trace a square in the air before you—like a glyph of a building block—made of green and black fire. Say, *"By my body, I invoke earth!"*

Imagine the darkness around you morphing into a huge ebony black cube that fills the area before you. It is so large you can only see a portion of it as it emerges from the darkness before you. Take three deep breaths and feel your body become empty and hollow.

Take seven deep breaths and feel your body filling with a green and black light that is the elemental presence of earth, which embodies the qualities of Structure and Stability. Notice how you feel as you contemplate these qualities within you.

Take seven deep breaths and imagine the black cube projecting into your solar plexus, where it becomes a black square that glows green. Feel the stable power of earth standing within you.

With seven deep breaths imagine that your whole skeleton is glowing black … see the individual bones take on this color and shine as if polished, black stones. Breathing deep, feel the stable structure of your skeleton … how it supports you and gives you form.

Now, breathe deep and imagine how your entire musculature is glowing deep green. All of your muscles, tendons, and ligaments are shining with the life force of a new, green plant. Breathe deep and feel this presence.

Now, switch the colors: your skeleton is green and your musculature is black. Feel this and then switch them again. Feel them as being both green and black at the same time. Breathe deep.

Take time to absorb the powers of elemental earth into your physical and energy bodies. As done before, repeat "*I am earth*" seven times as a long, drawn-out vibratory note, becoming slower and longer each time.

Focus on the black square that glows green within your solar plexus. See it shining brightly throughout your body, and imagine it spilling out into your aura. Sustain this presence for a few breaths to a few minutes.

For the span of three breaths feel the forest and your working area existing simultaneously. With three more breaths allow the forest to fade. Extinguish the green/black candle. End as normal.

---

## Gnomes

The classic image of a gnome as a small, squat, humanoid male wearing a blunt, almost conical hat[49] is a traditional visual key for working with the elemental spirits of earth. I personally sometimes see them in a very simple form: as a small pyramid of stacked stones, two stones laid side by side forming the body, topped with a square stone for a

---

49. According to Cora, this is not a hat but just the shape of their heads and how they appear to humans.

head. Like the other elementals, they cleanse and revitalize the element by being sexual with each other.

### Body of the Gnomes Exercise

Items needed:
Your black Star Goddess candle
Matches
A green and/or black candle, placed in the north
Earth incense
A stone of any size

Open the Way. Invoke the Emerald and Jet Road and the Bull. Move into the hidden temple and engage the elemental power and the glyph.

Reach out *through* your daemon and into the stone. Imagine gazing down in-between the molecules of the physical stone where you can now perceive the living presence(s) within it. Notice how you perceive this presence. What words would you use to describe it? Notice how you *feel* when contemplating this presence. Are you tired? Excited? Hungry? Angry? Sad? Just notice your emotional state as you continue following your breath ... slow and deep ... and softly focusing on the stone that you hold. When you are done, record your experiences and end as normal.

After you have mastered this exercise you may wish to move on to other objects, such as different types of stones, as well as areas of land, containers of soil, etc. Notice how your experiences compare and contrast with your different chosen points of focus.

---

## The Cube

In most traditions, the tool of the earth is the pentacle, the paten or plate with a five-pointed star inscribed upon it. In Faery Tradition, we may use this tool, but we are not as likely to adhere to the association of the earth element to it. Here I tread carefully, and I remind the reader that Faery Tradition—like its namesake—is somewhat of a changeling. Some may use a pentacle, others the cube, while still others might use both, assigning them to different elements, and others won't use these style tools at all. What I give here is what I have developed in BlueRose, based on the traditional material I was trained with.

In our tradition, a green cube is the elemental tool of earth. This is often described as being made of a polished, green stone, but for practical purposes can be made of wood or clay. I know of at least one Faery practitioner whose cube is made of Lego® blocks. This can be of any size that is pleasing to the practitioner and is sometimes described as being etched or inscribed on one side with a pentacle. This is the tool of form and stability, signifying the literal building blocks of physical matter, as well as how that matter exists in space. In a two-dimensional representation this is a square, a shape that conjures the essence of boundaries and stability as well as a map of the four cardinal directions. The cube, however, translates this map into a *three*-dimensional space, giving us the reference points of above and below in addition to the left, right, forward, and back directions made possible by the square.

In practical terms, the cube can be used for setting and strengthening boundaries, helping us to determine what structures support our life force, and which ones cut us off from that force. In ritual, the cube is sometimes used as a shield that prevents outside influences from tearing us down or forcing us from our center. It can also be used to capture energies from people, events, or places and, like the traditional paten or pentacle, can be used to charge objects with power.

## Enchanting the Cube Exercises

For the following exercises you will need these items:
Your black Star Goddess candle
Matches
Earth incense
A green candle
A black candle
Your cube
Sea salt
A plate of some type of bread or cakes
Your wand

Begin each exercise by performing the following:
Open the Way. Light the incense. Focus your attention on the Emerald and Jet Road of the north and light the green and black candles. Journey through the door into the hidden temple of earth. Spend some time breathing in the presence

of the element, filling yourself with the green and black light. Allow the black square in your solar plexus to shine brightly.

## Awakening the Cube

Holding the cube at your midsection, breathe the emerald and jet light from the square in your solar plexus into the cube. Feel the nature of the cube, how it is the embodiment of structure and form. See it shining with a green and black light.

Focus on the cube as the embodiment of structure and stability. Feel how it strengthens your own structure. Do this for twelve breaths and then on the next twelve, breathe the green and black light back through the cube and into the square in your solar plexus. Now, reduce this to six breaths. Now three. End with several rounds of doing this in a single breath.

Feel how the cube contains all space and matter, there is no difference between your tool and the manifest world itself. Feel how *you* are the cube … a part of the processes of physicality. After you have done this for a few to several minutes call in the power to integrate it, and end as normal.

## Cube Protection Rite

Holding your cube, contemplate its solid nature. Feel how its solid structure is the same as the structures of your own body and of your home. Place it on the altar (or on the ground) before you. Place both hands over it and allow the black square in your solar plexus to glow brightly green. Feel the presence of elemental earth vibrating within as a low hum that then resonates with the physical cube before you.

With nine breaths imagine the cube growing larger and larger until it almost fills the room. Feel how you are safe and secure within this form, how it repels all outside influences that might do you harm. You may wish to expand this construct so that it envelops your entire house or apartment building. You may stay in this form as long as you'd like. End as normal.

## Charging an Object

Place the object you wish to charge upon the cube, if possible, or within a ring of salt that contains both the object and the cube. Place your hands palms-down over the object and allow the elemental earth energy to flow from the square in your solar plexus, through your arms and hands and out into the cube/object/ring of salt. While you feel this flow of power, softly focus on your magical goal for this object: what influences do you wish it to attract or repel? Allow this feeling to merge with the elemental energy and flow through your body and into the object. Do this for the span of at least a few breaths, until you feel that it is sufficient. End as normal.

### Consecrating the Cakes

This begins here as an elemental exercise but in time will move beyond this categorization. Feel free to abandon the overtly elemental observances after mastering this exercise.

Place the cube in the center of a plate of bread, cakes, or other food that will be charged for your ritual. Feeling the presence of earth, sense the life force within the food … energetically reaching out through it and into its past … feel them being cooked, baked, prepared, harvested, grown … feel the sunshine and the rain that it drew sustenance from … feel the nutrients in the soil in which it grew. Feel it as an unbroken chain that goes back to the very origins of life itself. Feel this holy presence.

Holding the wand, feel the presence of elemental air and the golden half-circle in your throat. Feel it as the principle that reaches out toward the light, inspiring higher consciousness and aspiration toward growth. Allow this sensation to flow out from you through your wand and into the cakes as you slowly make a clockwise motion over the plate while saying:

> *By land, by wind, by sun, by rain*
> *By fertile field of earthen grain*
> *From seed to sprout to shaft to flower*
> *To fruit of life that we devour*
> *From fish, to fowl, to beast, to man …*
> *Nourished by the Starry Mother*
> *And He who holds the painted fan.*

Offer some to the Old Powers. Partake of the food and reverently eat, taking this blessing and power within you. If in a group, offer the plate to the next person in the circle moving clockwise, with a personal blessing such as, "Eat well, and feel Their love."

## The Watcher of Earth: Black Mother

Black Mother is the Watcher of earth and embodies the power of Wisdom. She may appear as a black goat, giving birth to and suckling a thousand young. When in this form she may have golden eyes and silver horns, and a halo of Blue Fire, with her left hoof upon a cube of polished green stone with a black pentacle etched upon it. She may also appear as a nude woman riding on the back of a goat. Like the bull, she embodies the lessons of silence and stillness, but also of manifestation and nurturing.

*Figure 11: Black Mother Sigil*

### Invoking Black Mother Exercise

Items needed:
Your black Star Goddess candle
Matches
A green and/or black candle, placed in the north
Earth incense
Your wand

Open the Way. Invoke the Emerald Green and Jet Black Road and the Bull. Step upon the road and move through the door and into the hidden temple of earth and connect with the elemental powers, activating the black square in your solar plexus.

Place your palms together at heart level in front of you, fingers pointing up. With a deep inhale, breathe in the power of the forest and the darkness. With three breaths allow that power to fill you and become concentrated.

With your next exhale, allow a thread of energy to flow forth from the square in your solar plexus as you extend your hands outward into the north, fingers pointing outward. Imagine the energy thread as flowing outward into the realm of earth and rising up above eye level, reaching an infinite point.

Imagine this thread connecting you to the elemental realm of earth. As before, cup your hands in front of you and gather the elemental energy. With your inhale, bring your hands back, crossing them over your chest, left over right, pulling the energy into the glyph through the thread. Bow in reverence.

With your wand or fingers, trace a five-pointed star of emerald and jet fire in the space before you. Repeat the invocation:

> *Black Mother! Black Mother! Black Mother!*
> *From forest dark you now emerge*
> *With pungent scent of goat and earth*
> *Watcher of the Well of Space*
> *To a thousand young you've given birth!*

Imagine the Watcher emerging from the green and black pentacle. Take several deep breaths, feeling the presence of the Watcher before you. Take three deep breaths and feel your body become empty and hollow.

With six breaths, imagine Black Mother projecting into the square on a beam of green and black light. Breathe in the presence of the Watcher along with the power of Wisdom and imagine an image of the Watcher in miniature forming within the black square in your solar plexus. Know that the Watcher within you and the Watcher before you are one and the same.

Maintain this presence for at least the span of six breaths.

You may spend as much time as you like working with Black Mother, allowing her to guide you. Or move on to the next step.

Take a deep breath of power, and imagine taking a step closer to the Watcher before you. As you do, the Watcher within expands in size and power.

Ask Black Mother, "Who am I?"

Repeat this process as before, stepping closer and closer, while the Watcher within expands to eventually merge together with you as one. Maintain this for several breaths, and then imagine stepping out of the presence of Black Mother so that she is before you once more. You may sit in silence or she may speak or show things to you. Allow her to guide you as she will.

After you have spent several minutes in communion in this manner, end by giving thanks to the Watcher for her assistance. Say:

> *Black Mother,*
> *Watcher of the Well of Space,*
> *I thank you for your power and your presence.*
> *Stay if you will, go if you must,*
> *But ere you depart I bid you:*
> *Hail and Farewell!*

Pay attention to whether or not you feel if she stays or goes, releasing your connection. Imagine the pentacle dissolving and scattering like smoke on the wind. For the span of three breaths feel the forest and your working area existing simultaneously. With three more breaths allow the forest to fade. Extinguish the blue candle with a silent prayer.

---

## The Dark God

The Dark Lord of Witchcraft is most often referred to in Faery Tradition as "the Arddu" (pronounced ar-THEE, Old Welsh meaning "Royal Darkness") or Ankou (Breton). He is the Dark Lord of Sex and Death. The King of the Dead. He is the dread spirit of winter. He is Father, Grandfather. He is the Thanateros: the guide to wisdom through the annihilation of the self in the act of sex, as well as the realization of the true self in the act of death. In the Faery Traditions, Death is called the great teacher and the final lover, and so he is the bestower of Wisdom and Knowledge, the Guardian of the Mysteries.

He is the spirit of the Crossroads between that of the living and the dead. All who would pass through the dread gate must first confront him. He can represent our own fears and the ecstasy that we can experience when we face them.

Traditionally he may appear as androgynous and ancient. He is said to have the head, horns, and legs of a goat, the wings of a black bat, and an old woman's sagging breasts. A red jewel shines upon his brow, and a flaming torch does the same between his horns. His emblem is the skull and crossbones. He is the Baphomet, the Old Wizard, the Necromancer.

In addition to his more common androgynous aspect, he can appear as fiercely masculine as well. In this aspect he has most often come to me with the head of a bull, a symbol that I feel better reflects his mighty power and primal nature. Here he is often overtly sexual, but in a way that is somewhat disturbing in that it is not human; it is a primal sexuality that is animalistic and even chthonic.

Part of the lore that is sometimes attached to this deity is that he is less of a singular being and more of a role that is said to be filled by "the last soul to die before Samhain." Compare this to lore collected by nineteenth-century Breton folklorist Anatole Le Braz: "The last dead of the year, in each parish, becomes the Ankou of his parish for all of the following year." This role consists of, among other things, collecting lost souls and generally ushering the dead into whatever afterlife may await them.

Besides collecting the souls of the dead, he would seem also to provide purification for the souls of the living that follow him. It is common that his mere presence will bring up fears and other psychic detritus that would otherwise weigh down one's soul. In ceremonies in which possession is done, he tends to ask for participants to offer up their fears as food for him, purifying his followers and leaving them empty and ready for whatever other work is to come.

Part of his message is not to fear death, but to celebrate it. Putting the theory of reincarnation aside for the moment, the one thing that binds us all together as humans is that each of us is aware that someday we are all going to die. This is not an abstract idea, but a simple fact of life, all living things cease to be. By making friends with death, we take at least some of that fear that we have about our own deaths and those of our loved ones, and we transform it into a fervent awareness of the present moment. With death just over our shoulder, we are reminded to take advantage of every day … of every hour … of each and every moment. This is seen most colorfully in Day of the Dead celebrations where images of skulls and the dead are adorned with flowers and bright colors, transforming a somber observance for the dearly departed into a celebration of life in its fullest.

He may also appear in female form, akin to the Mexican Santa Muerte.

## *Invoking the Arddu Exercise*

Prepare an altar draped in black. Adorn with skulls, bones, and images of those whom you have lost. Call to him using whatever words you are inspired to, or you can use the following:

> *Primal lord of darkened land,*
> *Sex and death at your command,*
> *Scent of musk and sight of bone*
> *Guards the gate to the Unknown.*

## The Hag

The Hag, or the Crone, is a very ancient power. She has been known by many, many names and titles. Anna, or Annys … the Winter Queen … Hecate … The Morrigu. As the Cailleach we know that she was already ancient when the pre-Christian settlers arrived in Ireland. She is a primal Dark Goddess. The Queen of the Dead. She is the Spirit of Nighttime, the body of the earth slumbering in winter. She is the archetypal Witch and all who practice the Craft are of her order.

Like most pre-Christian divinities she was later recast in a negative light. The myths of Black Annis as a demon or a child-devouring monster are obvious corruptions of her previous position of Dark Goddess of Death, Healing, Magic, and Sovereignty.

At death we are said to confront—and be purified by—the Arddu, the Lord of the Crossroads between Life and Death. Only then can we return to the Dark Goddess of Life and Death to stand in her mighty presence without anything encumbering us.

She may appear as a very old woman wrapped in a hooded black cloak. Her skin and her hair are pure white. She holds a great curved silver sickle, and she is crowned with nine (or sometimes, strangely, "nine plus") stars. Her emblem is a black raven or the vulture.

She is shown spinning the golden threads of fate, her scythe ready to make the fatal cut. She can also be seen in the myths of "Grandmother Spider," the Native American goddess of creation who steals the sun and fire for the world. As an otherworldy goddess she is with both belladonna (deadly nightshade) and with fly agaric, the mushroom that grants visions and was an ingredient in many recipes for flying ointment, a traditional hallucinatory assistant for astral travel.

Though she most often appears in her black form, there are other ways to connect to this most powerful of goddesses:

*Black*—Annis; the Morrigu; Hecate; Lilith; Cerridwen; Baba Yaga. This is the most common form that she takes. She is the death goddess as well as a goddess of sorcery and black magic. She is the keeper of the Old Ways and the archetypal Witch. She is the primordial priestess, often called Black Ana of the Forbidden Mysteries, referring to the "forbidden" knowledge of Witchcraft.

*Blue*—Grandmother; Healer; Wise woman; Storyteller; Midwife; Giver of rest. She is the Star Goddess in her matronly aspect, and she is Grandmother Spider who tells the stories and passes them down to the next generation. She is Uli, the "Breast of Spirit," the Hawaiian Goddess of life force (mana) to which in Faery we connect as the Blue Fire. She may appear robed in royal blue, offering rest and solace or otherwise telling stories and offering healing and wisdom.

*White*—The Cailleach; The Veiled One; The Winter Queen. She is the stark white emptiness of the Void. She may appear as an old, blue-faced woman wearing white. She is often silent. It is she who brings us to the presence of the Void, of the Abyss.

### Invoking Ana Exercise

Drape an altar in black and adorn it with her symbols: ravens or vultures, and a silver sickle. You might journey into the northern temple or invoke her presence into your working space. Chant her names until you achieve a trance. Call or sing to her:

> *Ancient Queen of Death's repose*
> *Sharp your scythe and true your sight*
> *Keeping secrets no one else knows*
> *Grandmother! Queen of Night!*

You might use your scrying mirror or cauldron to do magic with her. She might help you with ancestral work, or with working with spirits or for darker workings.

## Casting a Simple Circle Exercise

Items needed:

Your black Star Goddess candle

Matches

Your blade

Here in the element of manifestation and form we present what has come to be viewed as the quintessential rite of the modern Witch. That said, not as much emphasis is always given to the casting of a circle in Faery as is done in other traditions of Witchcraft. When I first began my formal study of the tradition, my teacher at the time stressed that while in other traditions a circle was required in order to perform any magic, in Faery we *rarely* cast circles, our magic being from within as well as being from our regular practice. Sometimes we just aren't in a space in which we can cast a ritual circle and yet we are in need of a magical operation. Faery mainly uses it for group workings, as it is an excellent method of unifying group consciousness. Faery Tradition, being the syncretic creature it is, borrowed the practice from Wicca (which borrowed it from Ceremonial Magick) because it *works,* and because it was a ritual form that most people would already have been familiar with.

While each lineage seems to have its own variance of liturgical observance for the casting of the circle itself, it is customary to draw from Victor's work in *Thorns of the Blood Rose* to form the basis.

Open the Way and perform the Blue Fire breathing. With the blade cast the circle clockwise, feeling the blue flame forming a circle while you say:

| | |
|---|---|
| (Beginning in the north) | *By the earth, her fertile body.* |
| (East) | *By the air, her vital breath.* |
| (South) | *By the fire, her quickening spirit.* |
| (West) | *By the water, her teeming womb.* |
| (Return to the north) | *Is the circle made.* |

Once the circle is complete, breathe into it three times and *will* it to expand into a sphere, moving both over and under you. You may now do whatever other workings you wish. When it is time to end the rite, stir the power within the sphere counterclockwise with your blade and then feel the sphere opening in the zenith and the nadir, flowing back into the circle form. In the north, draw up the Blue Fire circle into the tip of your blade as you walk widdershins. Returning to the north raise the blade above your head and thrust it toward the heavens, feeling this power explode in star fire and now shining down upon you and into your crown. Absorb it with three breaths and then end with the Holy Mother prayer as normal.

## The Points of Flame: Power Exercise

Items needed:
Your black Star Goddess candle
Matches
A green and/or black candle

Here, we work to cleanse a point on the Iron Pentacle, this time focusing on the point of Power and in the hidden temple of earth. Use a green and/or black candle and perform the exercise as before, to transform the impurities that you have in relation to this point and then reabsorb the resultant life force. Use the affirmation:

*In the name of iron, I summon forth Power!*

## Earth Art Project

As with the other elements create a piece of art to express your personal relationship with earth. Notice what mediums you have chosen before and see if you can try your hand at something different. Sculpture? Clay? Papier-mâché? Whatever you choose try to allow the element to inspire you in its creation.

# CHAPTER II
# THE HIDDEN TEMPLE OF AETHER

*As the all-pervading ether is not tainted because of its subtlety,*
*similarly the Self, seated in everybody, is not tainted.*
—BHAGAVAD GITA

Our circle now complete, we take the next step to fully expand it into a sphere. While the cardinal directions have served as symbolic anchors for the four physical elements, with the addition of the nonphysical aether, we give our previously two-dimensional plane a vertical axis. Aether rules three directions—above, below, and center—the last usually imagined as being within ourselves as we spiritually align with the center of the universe.

If the four physical elements have combined to form the container, then it is aether that fills that container. It is the mythological breath of *life* that animates the inanimate. It is the fire that Prometheus stole from the gods, the "Luciferian Spark" that exists within us all. It is said to permeate all of space, the result of which is an endless web of connections between every single particle in the universe. In short, it is *universal consciousness*.

If we are mapping the elements on a pentacle, then the uppermost point represents aether and its associated three directions, while the remaining four points of the star correspond to those on a traditional compass. Thus the pentacle itself is a reminder that all the elements are connected and informed by aether.

Because aether is unlike the four physical elements, in that it possesses multiple associated directions, we can experience its elemental nature in slightly different ways, relative to the direction through which it is focused. This means that aether above is somewhat different than aether below. It is still the same power—the connective consciousness that is the in-dwelling, divine presence within all energy and matter—but by approaching it from different angles we can discern a nuanced variance that is as powerful as it is subtle. These nuanced powers are what Faery calls the Divine Twins, who are seen as the dual consort of God Herself.

The Divine Twins manifest in numerous ways and in many cultures. The Italian Romulus and Remus, the Marassa of Haitian Vodou, the Greek Dioscuri, the Vanic deities Freya and Freyr, and the Wiccan Oak King and Holly King are all examples of this universal force that appears in twinned form. In Faery, this same force may appear as either male or female and may or may not be a sexually active pair of either or both genders. They are often considered to be sexually "queer" and may adopt characteristics that society traditionally associates with the "opposite" gender. While they may manifest in forms that appear to be opposing (and indeed in many cultures they manifest as good vs. evil) they should be understood as being *part of the same being.* They are identical and each can take the place of the other. They are separate and yet *connected.*

In the physical body, aether above manifests most strongly in our nervous system. All of the synapses in our brains are firing neurons and sending electrical impulses along our network of nerves, like a lightning show running through our bodies and brains, carrying messages at tremendous speeds.

Aether above is about *transcendence.* This is the quality of moving beyond previous limitations, of stepping outside of the boundaries. In Faery Tradition, this is the much sought-after state of *ecstasy*: of stepping outside our own consciousness and into something larger. We drum, we chant, we sing, we dance, we make potions, and we make love all in the name of freedom, transcending the limitations of our physical bodies and directly touching the divine. Aether above is about infinity. It is the expansive presence of the living cosmos. Aether is like an omnipresent web that serves as the medium by which all matter and energy are able to affect each other throughout the cosmos. When free of the body we can begin exploring aether above as we travel amongst the stars and the cosmic expanse beyond our own solar system, our galaxy, and our dimension.

In the BlueRose lineage, the manifestation of the Divine Twins associated with the direction above is the Azure Dove. This is the same spirit as our own holy daemon but raised to a higher power. This is the "bird spirit" of Old Faery lore and represents the alchemical presence of air and water as well as *transcendent spirit.* He is most often depicted as male in the old lore (the Divine Twins are considered the sons/lovers of the Goddess) but may also manifest as female. As with all of the Faery deities, the Twins are both male and female in one.

Aether below is another perspective on this vast web of conscious interconnections. Where the element expressed in the above was expansive and transcendent, aether below is nearer to the processes of *contraction* and *embodiment*. It is the same process actually, just reversed. To explore the realms of aether below, we do not travel outward, but "downward" or within. Like the planets in their orbits, we experience the atoms of molecules, particles spinning, creating matter. We go further ... into the empty space that exists between molecules ... the vast open Void that comprises most of all matter itself. It is from this space that all matter and form arises from the formless Void. It is the very urge of the divine to create something from nothing. And in Faery we recognize that this urge is *sexual*. It is for this reason that aether below is associated with the sexual organs and responses of the body and mind. The state of being sexually excited is in itself a sacred space, opening our energy bodies so that we may be more receptive.

In BlueRose it is the Scarlet Serpent who occupies the space of below. This is the same as our own fetch but deeper, the ancient consciousness of the slow-moving earth. This is the divine primal drive toward life and survival. This represents the alchemical presence of fire and earth as well as *embodied spirit*.

Both aether above and below follow the same overall patterns. Much like how models for the expansion of the universe bear a striking resemblance to the patterns of a human brain cell, we are reminded of the old Hermetic maxim, "As above, so below." We experience the fullness of aether when we embrace its inherent polarity, as well as the underlying resonance that results in a constant dynamic separation and unification.

This unification is the mysterious third direction of aether, where supposed "opposites" are revealed to be one and the same. Here the Mysteries of the Divine Twins are highlighted, these forces that—seemingly opposite—are revealed to be two sides of the same coin: part of a singular force. In Faery this is embodied by Melek Ta'us, the Peacock Lord. With his bird feathers and serpentine symbolism he is the unification of opposing or differing forces and represents the fullest potential of humanity, both light as well as dark.

The concepts for this element are Radiance and Awareness. Awareness in this context is the quality of *sentience*, of being able to subjectively experience the world and one's place within it. It is our own consciousness, which is a divine spark of light and life force. This awareness burns brightly within us and—if cultivated—can ignite into a flame, the "Witch's Fire." This state is variously referred to as Enlightenment, Awakening, Conversation with the Holy Guardian Angel, or Satori, depending on the religious tradition involved. In Faery, this is often called simply self-possession, or sometimes *enchantment*. It is a state of being in-between, the quintessentially Faery state of liminality that practically defines encounters with the Fae. From this space we are neither here nor there, neither black nor white. We are in-between the worlds, and from that unique vantage point we can be more precise in where we direct our inner flame. Like all flames it shines outward, giving us the concept of radiance upon which we will contemplate in this cycle.

This radiance can encourage other flames into being. By being in the presence of such a flame our own energy field begins to move into resonance with it. This is the idea behind the belief that the nimbus or aura of the Faery initiate can cause such changes in their students, simply by sharing space together. Not unlike some Buddhist practices, such as *reiju*, it is known that by sitting in the teacher's presence while engaged with the Faery Power, the student is gradually attuned to that Power. This serves to prepare the student for the time of initiation, in which this Power is ritually passed, igniting this flame within them. This process effectively speeds things up for the potential student, in terms of their energetic capacity for power and the nuances of Faery magic. But even without this traditional guide we can still glean some definite benefits from the tools themselves.

## Journaling

*As before, Open the Way and then journal for five minutes each about radiance and then do the same for awareness. Now, how does radiance above differ from radiance below? How does this power express itself differently in each of the two directions? How about radiance within? Consider the same for awareness in each of the directions.*

---

# Divination

Divination is a practice by which we utilize the seemingly random occurrence of symbols in conjunction with the divine in order to discern the nature and direction of one's life or situation. The methods utilized for divination over the centuries are too numerous to devote any real attention to them, so we will limit ourselves here to a select few, along with the knowledge that the concepts and philosophies outlined here can be adapted for use with whatever systems you prefer.

We have already seen how the Three Souls each possess their own languages and means of communicating. From a Faery perspective, divination is a type of language that aims to communicate the messages of daemon through the fetch in a way that talker can understand. We have already been using techniques that bring us into the proper state to be able to receive divine messages. Studying at least one or two systems of divination will allow talker to be able to translate those messages in a way that can be mentally understood.

## The Soul Star, Part 1 Exercise

This is a spread that can be used in order to gain perspective on any aspect of your life. It will look at your relationship to the Three Souls as well as to the points of the Iron Pentacle. You can use this when you are unsure as to which of the points may be of particular issue or interest as it pertains to your situation. We will add another layer to this spread later on, but for now just use this as given and remember to record your experiences in your journal.

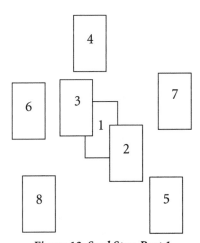

*Figure 12: Soul Star, Part 1*

Items needed:

Your black Star Goddess candle

Matches

A divination tool, such as tarot, runes, oracle cards, etc.

Begin by Opening the Way. Focus on a situation on which you would like guidance or clarity. Using your preferred divination tool, arrange the cards, stones, or other objects in the above pattern with the following in mind:

### The Three Souls

1. Talker—The current situation and what information you are receiving about it.

2. Fetch—The underlying energies at work. Subconscious drives. Energy.

3. Daemon—The presence of the gods/divine in the situation. The path you are on.

### Iron Pentacle

4. Sex—How you are manifesting/maintaining/opening to life force.

5. Pride—How life force is moving through you. How you feel about your place in the situation.

6. Self—Awareness of how the situation affects you personally, the revelation of how your inner self is more fully revealed through it.

7. Power—What you can do to make your mark.

8. Passion—How it affects you emotionally. Inspiration.

## Aether Incense Recipe[50]

1 part frankincense
1 part mugwort
1 part sage
1 part cedar


Combine together and store in an airtight container. This blend can then be burned on a lit charcoal to fumigate the area for your workings.

## Sigils Exercise

A huge part of Faery Tradition and magic revolves around the creative process. A staggering number of our initiates and practitioners are artists, singers, dancers, writers, performance artists, ritualists, and other creatives who draw heavily from their talents in their chosen arts when expressing their spirituality. In the tradi-

---

50. Devin Hunter, "Spirit Incense," *Modern Witch Magazine Volume One.*

tion, we refer to those initiates who are particularly driven artistically as holders of the White Wand, a purely symbolic appellation and not (necessarily) a reference to a physical tool.[51] As someone who holds this wand, I am especially excited to be able to engage my artistic obsessions, and when it comes to spellwork I find no better way to indulge than in the creation of sigils.

There are many schools of thought when it comes to the proper creation of a sigil. Since Faery is associated with wild, even feral magic, I personally have little use for the many magical squares upon which many might design their sigils according to the mathematical calculations that inspired them. While I'm sure that there must be Faery who prefer this method (if for no other reason than to prove contrary) to me they stifle what I interpret to be truly Faery: a magic that is wild, free, and unrestrained. It is for this reason that my preferential method for creating sigils is more artistically inspired.

The sigilization method that I was passed in my Faery training was a variant of that taught by the English artist and occultist Austin Osman Spare (1886–1956). Briefly, this method involves first determining a clear, concise magical goal and then stating that goal in the form of a short affirmation or phrase, which is then written out. The letters that comprise the words of this phrase will form the "primordial soup" from which our sigil will emerge. First deleting any repeated letters, the remaining are moved and turned and rendered, letters sharing line and curve as the linear sentence morphs into a language of art. Finally, little flourishes are added to further transform the piece from a simple "jumble of letters" and into a symbol unto itself. For example, to render the name Melek Ta'us into a sigil, I would first isolate the unique letters:

*MELKTAUS*

Next I would take the remaining letters and arrange them until I had created a piece that looked less like letters and more like a piece of art.

---

51. For an in-depth look at the traditional system of wands in the Faery Tradition, as well as how they have been expanded in BlueRose, see my article "Colors of Power: Exploring the Wands of the F(a)eri(e) Tradition." http://faerywolf.com/?p=5165.

*Figure 13: Sigil example: Melek Ta'us*

Note that the "wings" on the figure are actually an *M* and the "head" is an *S* ... the "body and arms" is a stylized *A* that is combined with a *U*, a *K, L,* and a *T.* (Notice that several letters can be combined so as to occupy the same space, an upside-down *L* can form part of a T, etc.) The shoulders sport the *E* thus utilizing all the required letters. Finally, little embellishments were added, little flourishes and stars to complete the artistic look of the piece and further drawing the energetic impact of the sigil away from mere letters and more into the realm of an art piece that speaks more directly to fetch.

During this process, you will have gone from focused intent on your magical goal to a type of intent on the art form itself, forgetting the original intent to a degree. Focus your awareness just on creating a beautiful sigil ... allow your creative self to really take over. When it is complete take some time to really admire it.

The resultant image, if created while in the state of enchantment, will already carry a charge, but for it to really have an effect it needs to be awakened. This really could be done any number of ways as long as it draws power. Some traditional methods include dancing, chanting, meditation, and sexual activity. The key element is to have the sigil emblazoned upon your mind at a moment of true *passion,* and then to surrender to the mental oblivion that is the ecstatic state.

Once a sigil has been awakened, it may be used in any number of ways, attached to objects or carried upon the person to keep its influences near ... they may be drawn with powders or dried herbs on altars or floors and used in larger ceremonies ... they can be traced over food or drink before imbibing to enchant them with the essence for which the sigil was created. The possibilities are nearly endless.

### The Sigillic Breath Spell

This spell is used to empower a sigil for magical work.

Items needed:
Your black Star Goddess candle
Matches

First, Open the Way. Create a sigil for a magical goal. Visualize your sigil as shining within talker. Speak its name, or your magical goal three times.

Breathe the sigil into fetch. Empower them both with life force by taking three deep breaths. Breathe it up and into the holy daemon, where you see it shine brilliant and powerful.

Speak aloud an affirmation or incantation, such as:

> *Sigil placed in daemon's power*
> *Seek thy purpose,*
> *Tend thy charge!*

Open yourself to the reflection of this power back upon you and give yourself the span of three breaths to silently observe the energy of yourself and your environment.

---

## The Crossroads

The crossroads are a symbolic form that appears in various cultures across the planet and possesses a unique spiritual and magical significance. In Vodou, Santeria, Hoodoo, and Conjure traditions, the crossroads are associated with magic and sorcery, being a liminal space in-between the worlds. Many stories tell of those who brought a petition to the crossroads in order to have it fulfilled by the devil, or "Black Man." This is the same Man in Black who, according to testimonials from the Witch Trials, was reported presiding over the Witches' Sabbat. He is the Magister of the Coven, a priest of the Horned God of Life and Death.

In Celtic lore, the crossroads are a traditional meeting place for the faerie folk, and like the faery rings of legend are said to be portals into their realm. In the ballad of Thomas the Rhymer, our protagonist journeys with the Queen of Faery down a road until they come to a crossroads. Before them are three roads, which are explained to be the road to heaven, the road to hell, and between the two: the road to Faery.

Ancient Romans similarly saw the crossroads as places ruled by sorcery and Witchcraft and it was the goddess Hecate who presided over these places. In Faery Tradition, we can align ourselves with the archetypal crossroads no matter where we are, so that we may be further attuned to the elemental (and thus, otherworldly) powers with which we seek to work. Thus it is a ritual of designating ritual space, much like a traditional Witches' circle, but in my experience the crossroads feels connective, while the circle feels exclusionary. A circle can be easily invoked for protection: to "cut oneself off" from the outside world, whereas the crossroads is used to connect us to forces and realms outside of ourselves.

While the crossroads have played a major role in magic and spirituality for centuries, they were not necessarily a significant part of Faery Witchcraft practice until the advent of BlueRose. In my own Faery training, I was taught a method of orienting to the directions that included an energetic alignment and connection to the elemental powers in the form of cords of variously colored light, each focusing into my lower abdomen. After working with this method for some time, I realized that what was being created aligned symbolically with the mythological crossroads, and that the formal inclusion of that specific imagery would allow for a greater amount of power to be channeled into the experience. It is both traditional as well as innovative, old and yet new.

### Opening the Way 5: Summoning the Crossroads Exercise

Items needed:

Your black Star Goddess candle

Matches

Stand in a space designated as center. Open the Way.

Become aware of the cardinal directions and call out to the presences of the four physical elements: earth, fire, air, and water. As you breathe, feel their powers as roads flowing to you from their particular directions in the form of appropriately colored roads. Feel how you are standing in the center of where these roads meet and cross.

Be aware of how the six external directions and their associated elemental powers call to the seventh within. Feel this internal center as the energetic true epicenter of the crossroads. Call out:

> *I stand in the center between the stars*
> *that shine above, that shine below,*
> *Where worlds and spirits dare to meet*
> *Where the roads do cross*
> *I claim my power.*

Contemplate the power of being in the perfect center *between all the worlds*. This is the mythological center of the shaman's web, and it is from this space in which we—in our aligned space—may further align with powers external to us, such as those of the spirits with whom we seek to work. You may now continue with whatever other work you wish.

Work with this form until you have memorized it before moving on to the next exercise.

Once you have become proficient in the Summoning the Crossroads exercise, your goal will be to spiritually experience the results of it in a shortened form. This will be a much more internalized, meditative experience that you will now include in your regular Opening the Way exercise. This means that Opening the Way will now consist of:

• Four-Fold Breath (Relaxation)

• Grounding (Roots in the earth/Branches in the stars, Vertical alignment)

• The Holy Flame (Star Goddess candle prayer)

• Inner Constellation (Three Souls, Internal alignment)

• Summoning the Crossroads (Horizontal alignment/centering)

## *Invoking the Hidden Temple of the Stars Ritual*

Items needed:

Your black Star Goddess candle

Matches

Open the Way, including the newly added step of Summoning the Crossroads.

Gaze softy at the flame of the Star Goddess candle. Be aware of the power within its light, how it purifies and transforms your own power with each breath you take, raising you to the power of divinity. Close your eyes and hold the image of that candle flame in your inner vision; watch it dance and flicker and slowly change its color into violet. Imagine that this violet flame before you expands into a column, towering both above and below you and into infinity. Take a deep breath and imagine entering into this column of violet fire, feeling it move both up and down through you and outward into the below and the above.

Breathing deep this light fades to black, but you still feel this now-invisible violet flame moving through your body. Looking above you, see directly above—one by one by one—the stars emerging, filling the sky above, stretching downward and meeting the circle of the horizon all around you. Gaze up into this dome of stars and gaze silently into the dark space between them. Imagine that you can begin to perceive a faint violet light like a glowing mist that emerges from the vast, empty blackness of space. This mist begins to gather up—like clouds—and coalesces directly above your head in the form of a pentacle made of violet fire.[52] This pentacle shines down a violet light, like a laser beaming into your crown.

As you breathe in this light, reflect how you are breathing in the qualities of Radiance and Awareness. Contemplate on your nervous system and imagine that your brain, spinal column, and all of your nerves are glowing brilliant violet. Continue in this presence for the span of a few breaths to several minutes.

Breathing deeply, send your awareness into the great below. Imagine that you can see deep into the blackness of the earth beneath you where you now see—one by one by one—stars emerging from the darkness and flowing upward to greet the circle of the horizon all around you. Though you are standing on solid ground, it appears that you are floating in space, surrounded by billions of shining stars.

---

52. Some lineages specify the color as blue-violet.

Looking deep into the empty space between the stars beneath you... you see once more that violet mist, gathering up directly beneath you and forming into an inverted pentacle made of violet fire. This pentacle shines like a laser into your perineum, and you breathe in this light in the form of Radiance and Awareness. Contemplate your sexual organs and desires. This is the great center of life force within the body. It is the core of the Black Heart of Innocence. Imagine your sex organs shining brilliant violet. Maintain this for the span of at least a few breaths to several minutes.

Now, become aware once more of the violet pentacle shining above you as well as the inverted violet pentacle below, and how they both shine into you with every breath. With seven breaths imagine pulling these pentacles slowly toward yourself, until with the seventh breath, they align perfectly in your body: the upright pentacle in your crown, and the inverted pentacle in your perineum. Feel these glyphs lock into place and subsequently reach out toward one another, like the opposing poles of a magnet in constant attraction and repulsion. Breathe deeply and imagine a liquid violet flame emerging from each glyph and beginning to wind toward each other, each spiraling together like two serpents intertwined. Allow these two forces to flow freely within you, as you maintain the slow depth of breath as the spiraling light within you increases in speed, eventually becoming a whirling vortex of liquid, violet flame, spinning and humming within your central column. After a few breaths open your eyes, still maintaining this sensation of the spinning currents within. After some time with this, allow these sensations to fade. End as normal.

If you are left feeling spacy or agitated, perform the Ha Prayer and send some of this energy to your daemon with a prayer. If you still feel overloaded then perform a relaxation and grounding exercise. You may even wish to eat something (protein is often a good choice) and even make physical contact with the earth or a tree.

---

# The Mirror

The mirror is the tool for aether above.[53] This is symbolically related to the Faery creation myth in which the Star Goddess looks into the "curved mirror of black space" and sees her own reflection. The mirror here becomes a tool of expansive vision: of astral travel in the overworld, of looking deep within the mysteries of the dark beyond that which we know, and of looking deeply into ourselves. From this myth we are given symbolic instruction on the construction of the ritual tool: a concave mirror of black, a traditional description of a scrying mirror.

Mirrors of all sorts have long been used in Witchcraft. Used variously to repel, ensnare, detect, or disrupt energies, mirrors are powerful magical tools aiding us in "looking beyond" our mundane reality.

## Enchanting the Mirror Exercises

These should be performed in a low-light environment.

Items needed:

Your black Star Goddess candle

Matches

Aether incense

A violet candle

Your mirror (a curved, black scrying mirror is best, but any reflective surface
  will do)

A blue candle

A bowl

Your chalice

A small pitcher of water

A small piece of parchment paper

Some colored markers or pens

An herbal oil associated with clarity, sight, or guidance

A black taper candle

A few ice cubes, made from an infusion of at least three herbs with the combined
  properties of cleansing, protection, and psychic vision

---

53. Many thanks to T. Thorn Coyle for this idea, as there are no "official" elemental tools for aether in the larger Faery Tradition. T. Thorn Coyle, *Evolutionary Witchcraft* (New York: Tarcher/Penguin, 2004).

Begin each of the exercises below by performing the following:

Open the Way. Light the incense. Invoke the hidden temple of the stars. Focus your attention on the vastness of space above you and the pentacle of violet flame in the zenith point as it beams into your crown. Light the violet candle. Spend some time breathing in the presence of the aether above, of Radiance and Awareness, filling you with the violet flame. Allow the upright violet pentacle in your crown to shine brightly.

### Awakening the Mirror

Holding the mirror above you, breathe the violet flame from the pentacle in your crown and out into the mirror. Feel how the mirror reflects and reveals ... how it is expansive awareness and vision. See it glowing with the violet flame.

Move the mirror so that you can easily gaze into it without seeing the candle or yourself directly reflected. Allow your eyes to relax and gaze deeply into it ... Feel how this act alone expands your awareness. Allow the mirror to become the representation of Radiance and Awareness ... Do this for twelve breaths and then on the next twelve, breathe the violet flame from the darkness, through the mirror, and into the pentacle in your crown. Now, reduce this to six breaths and breathe the flame in reverse. Now reduce to three. End with several repetitions done with a single breath, exhaling the power into the darkness through the mirror, and inhaling it back the same way. Feel how the mirror reflects the whole universe ... revealing patterns, forms ... repelling energy through reflection. Feel that there is no difference between your physical tool and *space itself*. Feel how *you* are the mirror ... the whole of the cosmos is reflected in you, and you reflected in the universe.

After you have done this for several minutes call the power back into yourself to integrate it, extinguish the candle and return to normal consciousness.

*The exercises given below begin here as elemental exercises but in time will move beyond this categorization. Feel free to abandon the overtly elemental observances after mastering them.*

### Invoking the Blue Flame Dove

To make a petition to your "higher power."

Consider an area of your life in which you would like some direction or guidance, or an area that you otherwise feel needs to change or evolve. Create a point of focus by making a sigil to represent this issue and then design a spell paper with this sigil over which place an image of the Azure Dove. Dress this paper with the oil and then fold it in half toward yourself. Place this on a surface above and behind where you will be sitting for the duration of this rite. Carve the sigil upon the blue candle and then dress it with the oil. Melt the bottom of the candle so as to affix it to the center of the bowl. Position it on top of the spell paper, and set the mirror on a surface above and in front of you, so that you will be able to see the candle flame reflected in the mirror's surface. Perform a quick Waters of Purity rite by charging the water in the pitcher and then pouring some into your chalice to drink. Light the candle as you recite the first line of the incantation below, and pour some water into the bowl with the blue candle as you say the second line:

> *Shining bright the Azure Dove*
> *Born of water and of air*
> *Above the stars your law is love*
> *Descend from heaven; hear my prayer!*

Move so that you are facing the mirror and focus on the reflection of the candle flame in its surface. Be aware that this candle flame is above your head and that you are seeing its presence indirectly. As you gaze at the reflection, be aware of its actual presence *directly over your head*. Feel it as a warm glow, softly humming as it guides you from above.

You may wish to sing or chant something aligned to the prayer you are making, but at some point—when you feel it is right—just sit in silence and be open to the guidance of your daemon, of the Azure Dove. Record your experiences in your journal and end as normal.

### The Scrying Rites

To gain psychic insight or to communicate with spirits.

Begin by positioning your mirror so that you may look into it without seeing the reflection of the candle or your face. Allow your eyes to relax and gaze into it as in the last exercise.

Consider a question or area of interest to which you wish to bring clarity or insight. Allow your consciousness to attune to this situation or quandary. Remembering your soul alignment, feed this point of focus with the light of talker, and then will it all down and into your fetch. Charge it with wraith-force and then send it up to your daemon, which radiates outward and into the mirror. Speak aloud the following, or your own inspired prayer:

*Holy mirror curved and black*
*Open now unto the stars*
*Shining deep, reflect them back*
*Reveal the secret; the veil is drawn.*

In a space of openness and alignment, continue to deeply gaze into the mirror. If you begin to see images materializing in the mirror, remain calm, relaxed, and serene. Resist the urge to become amazed at the experience. Should you become distracted and lose the experience as a result you will need to recall your relaxed focus and simply make another attempt. Give yourself at least twenty minutes for this exercise. Record your experiences in your journal.

To gain insight into yourself, developing psychic abilities, or for past-life workings, begin by positioning the mirror so that you are able to see your own reflection. Gaze softly into your reflection. After you have aligned and allowed the light of daemon to shine upon the mirror say the following incantation, the final line being determined by the specific purpose of the rite:

*Holy mirror curved and black,*
*My own reflection smiling back*
*Into my eyes I send my gaze*

For working with past lives:

*Reveal the face of long past days.*

For looking into your current life (behavior traits, habits, developing psychic abilities, etc.):

*Reveal the courses of my ways.*

In a space of openness and alignment, continue to softly gaze at yourself in the mirror. As before, if you begin to see images materializing in the mirror, remain calm and relaxed. If you become distracted recall your focus and try again. Give yourself at least twenty minutes for this exercise. Record your experiences in your journal.

### The Rite of Reflection

This is a reversing type of protection spell, which sends negative powers back to their origin. While, for the most part, Faery practice tends to prefer the transmutation of negative energy into something positive or useful (such as with the Waters of Purity rite) there are times in which this may not be possible. In cases such as outright magical attack, the situation may warrant a more direct approach. My experience has been that a good reversal will serve to temporarily short-circuit the attacker, giving one the space necessary to reestablish protective wards. While some may feel that even this is in conflict with their personal ethics I will advise the reader that no murderer or rapist has ever been stopped because the love and prayers of their victims overcame them. Faery Tradition does not adhere to the Wiccan Rede of harm none nor the Law of Three. My own personal ethics can pretty much be summed up from what I learned from *Star Trek*: diplomacy first, but if that fails, fire the photon torpedoes.

Identify an area of undesirable influence that a situation, person, or place has over you. Create and carve a sigil for this on the candle (or, if you do not know who or where it is coming from, use "the source of negative energy" to create your sigil). Connect to the mirror as in the previous exercise. In your state of enchantment, focus on the energy that is being sent your way, and light the black candle to embody this dark power … allow yourself to really feel its influence in your life. As you position the mirror to reflect the light of the black candle away from you and back toward the source of the negativity, *will* this negative energy to be directed into your mirror. Say:

> *Holy mirror curved and black*
> *Reflect unwanted power back*

*As ice does melt, as fire does burn*
*Back to its source, ne'er to return.*

Imagine the current of negative power is being reflected by your mirror and back to its source. Allow the candle to burn all the way down into the bowl with the melting ice cubes. As the candle burns, wash or anoint the mirror with some of the melted water and then position it so that it reflects the light of the black candle away from you. (If the source of the negativity is known, then angle the mirror to reflect the light back into their direction if possible.) Continue to chant until it becomes a rhythmic pulse. Rock and sway while chanting and imagine the light of the black candle reflecting from the mirror and flowing back to the origin of the negative energy, neutralizing it. You may end when you feel it is complete, or you may continue until the candle has burned down into the melted water. End as normal, but either way let the black candle burn all the way down until completed.

---

## The Cauldron

In BlueRose Faery, the tool of aether below is the cauldron,[54] the mythological symbol of transformation and inspiration in the underworld. According to the Mabinogion, the Welsh myth of Cerridwen and Talliesen, the Bard describes what is possibly the most celebrated account of the use of the cauldron, describing its role in the creation of a magical potion of inspiration.

The cauldron is the physical manifestation of the womb of the Goddess in the underworld, that realm that serves as the metaphysical blueprint for all of creation. In this womb/cauldron we place the ingredients of our desires, and we carefully brew them into a potion of great power.

The cauldron is also often used as a container for the sacred fire, symbolic of that primal life force that comes from below. In BlueRose this is often in the form of the Scarlet Serpent, the sexual, primal life force of the planet below. Certain herbs, alcohols, and salts may be placed within the cauldron and then ignited for the varied purposes of our rites. Sometimes infusions, potions, or brews are poured into the cauldron and then variously empowered depending on the desired outcome.

---

54. Coyle, *Evolutionary Witchcraft.*

## Enchanting the Cauldron Exercises

Items needed:

Your black Star Goddess candle

Matches

A violet candle

Your cauldron (cast iron is preferred but must be fire safe)

Aether incense

Epsom salts

Rubbing alcohol: 70 percent isopropyl (safer) or 90 percent isopropyl (hotter)

Some dragon's blood resin

An herbal oil that you associate with life force

A piece of parchment paper

Colored pencils, paints, or pens

A heat-resistant surface on which to place your cauldron

A fire extinguisher (safety first!)

A candle, a stone, or a crystal, an oil, and three roots or herbs aligned
  toward your goal

Some water


Begin each of the exercises below by performing the following:

Open the Way. Light the incense. Invoke the hidden temple of the stars. Focus your attention on the vastness of the space below you and the inverted pentacle of violet flame in the nadir point, as it beams into your perineum. Light the violet candle. Spend some time breathing in the presence of the aether below, of Radiance and Awareness, filling you with the violet flame. Allow the inverted violet pentacle in your perineum to shine brightly.

### Awakening the Cauldron

Place the cauldron on the floor directly in front of you. Begin breathing the violet fire from the inverted pentacle in your perineum and out into the cauldron. Feel the nature of the cauldron, how it is a container for both power and transformation. See it glowing with the violet flame.

Imagine the cauldron becoming the manifestation of Radiance and Awareness... Feel how its presence contains and focuses your own awareness. Do this for twelve breaths and then on the next twelve, breathe the violet light back from the darkness, through the cauldron, and into the inverted pentagram in your perineum. Now, reduce this to six breaths. Now three. End with several with a single breath. Feel how the cauldron contains all potential. Feel how *you* are the cauldron … the legendary vessel of inspiration and creativity. After several minutes end as normal.

### Invoking the Serpent Flame

To raise life force and your own "divine fire."

On the paper, draw a sigil of your own name and an image of the Scarlet Serpent. It can look however you wish. Dress the paper with your life force oil, and fold it toward yourself in the traditional manner to invoke.

In your cauldron, combine roughly equal parts of alcohol and salt. Add as much salt as needed to make sure that the overall consistency is generally that of a blended, frozen beverage. Fill the cauldron about halfway then add some dragon's blood resin. Place the folded paper into the mixture, and then with both palms over the cauldron, pray for the powers of the Scarlet Serpent to awaken within it, imagining the serpent coiled deep below in the depths of the earth, and that this cauldron is a window into that deep presence. Feel the power of this fiery presence. Say:

> *Serpent born of earth and fire*
> *Awaken now with deep desire*
> *Coiled deep below in lust*
> *Aroused; arise with throbbing thrust!*

On the last line, strike the match and toss it into the cauldron, feeling the presence of the Scarlet Serpent arise in the flames. Feel how he is also present in your body: in your sexual desire, in your own life force. Move your body, dance around the flaming cauldron … make sounds, laugh, or sing, if you are inspired. When you are finished, take time to silently scry into the flames, noticing if you receive any messages. When the flames die down, end the rite as you wish, remembering to thank the serpent for his holy presence.

*Cauldron Transformation Rite*

To inspire one's primal life force into creativity.

Open the Way. Perform the Waters of Purity. Dress the candle with the oil and place upright in your cauldron, surrounded by the stone and the herbs you have chosen. Fill the cauldron about halfway with water. On the paper, write down something that you wish to transform: a habit, a relationship, a behavior, an obstacle, etc. Pour all of your emotions into it as you detail everything you wish to transform. Dress the paper with the oil and fold it away from you, in the traditional method of banishing. Light the candle with an openhearted prayer that the items listed on the paper be transformed into pure life force that you may then use, as you will. Feeling your state of enchantment, light the paper on fire, and toss it into the cauldron. Allow the candle to burn down where it will be extinguished by the water, thus charging the water with the alchemical blend of water and fire. While you are waiting for the candle to burn, allow this energy to inspire you as you use the art supplies in any way that you are inspired. When the candle has extinguished, wash your face in the charged water and then resolve to do what you can to make whatever changes are necessary to achieve your goal. The stone may be recovered and carried with you as a charm.

---

## The Watchers of Aether Above and Below: Heaven Shiner and Fire-in-the-Earth

The Watchers of aether are somewhat different than those of the four physical elements. In a letter to one of his students, Victor Anderson stated that "[the Watchers] are four spirits that come and join your coven whenever you have a ceremony."[55] At first glance this may suggest that only those of the four physical elements are in fact Watchers, having their number stated specifically as being four and not the seven taught in the Bloodrose-derived lineages of the tradition. In a conversation with one of Victor and Cora's initiates and coven-members, it was confirmed that Victor and Cora worked with the Watchers of aether, but that they considered them to be in a different class than those of the physical elements.

---

55. Victor H. Anderson, *Heart of the Initiate* (Portland, OR: Harpy Books, 2010), 23.

We begin in the above with Heaven Shiner. This Watcher is often depicted as a roughly humanoid androgynous figure in silhouette, filled with a billion stars, galaxies, and nebulae. Alternatively, it can appear as simply an explosion of stars, whirling galaxies, or an immense globe of blazing blue-white luminescence, with a brilliance rivaling that of both the sun and the moon. Like the other Watchers, this being has a particular power it is said to wield; in this case, Pure Consciousness.

*Figure 14: Heaven Shiner Sigil*

The Watcher below is called Fire-in-the-Earth and also is said to wield the power of Pure Consciousness. It sometimes appears as a large, translucent fish with blue and brown scales, coiled in the center of the earth. In its mouth it holds a burning ember of fire. Alternatively, it may appear as a fish made of fire, or as a primordial salamander. It is wild, feral, chthonic.

*Figure 15: Fire-in-the-Earth Sigil*

### Invoking Heaven Shiner and Fire-in-the-Earth Exercise

Items needed:

Your black Star Goddess candle

Matches

Open the Way. Feeling the presence of the Crossroads all around you, invoke Star Finder in the east, Shining Flame in the south, Water Maker in the west, and Black Mother in the north,[56] feeling each in turn emerging through the pentacles of elemental fire that you have drawn for them in the quarters. Feel how they themselves are stars … vast, explosive, unimaginable powers of untold ancient origins. Open to them as they feed energy and presence into the corresponding glyph within you: golden half-circle in the throat, red triangle beneath the navel, blue circle in the heart center, and black, green-glowing square in the solar plexus.

Once you have activated each energy center and taken a moment to feel the elemental presences and their qualities, begin breathing in a more pronounced way, speeding up just slightly, and imagining all of the elemental powers and colors within you are being spun or woven into a singular force which spirals in your central column. Take a moment to activate the violet pentacle in your crown as you open awareness to the stars above. Say:

---

56. Practitioners in the Southern Hemisphere will want to switch the north and south associations.

*All fours stars are One* [57]
*By the Goddess above*
*I invoke the Heaven Shiner!*
*Heaven Shiner!*
*Heaven Shiner!*

Imagine the very heavens opening up in an explosion of stars above you, as the Heaven Shiner emerges from the folds in the fabric of space and time itself. The light of the Heaven Shiner envelops you and feeds into the violet pentacle in your crown. How does Heaven Shiner appear to you? What form (if any) does s/he take? Feel the Watcher's presence within the pentacle in your crown. Feel how the Watcher within and the Watcher above are one and the same. Call out, *"Who am I?"*

Contemplate the space of silence formed in the wake of your question. Notice whatever comes up. Take a deep breath and feel Heaven Shiner descend a bit closer to you. Ask the question again, and see what, if anything, changes. Take some time and then take another deep breath, repeating this until Heaven Shiner sits on top of your crown, humming just above your head.

Reaffirm your awareness of the other Watchers, feel their presences and their colored lights shining into you. Breathe them all together as they spiral within you as one, singular force and then breathe this force downward, into the great below. Call out:

*All four stars are one*
*By the Goddess below*
*I invoke the Fire-in-the-Earth!*
*Fire-in-the-Earth!*
*Fire-in-the-Earth!*

Imagine, deep in the earth, a stirring in the center. From the center the coiled fish holding the ember of fire. Old, hermaphroditic, it is older than reason. The light of

---

57. My personal take on this is that the four stars referenced here are the Four Royal Stars of Antiquity, which represent the Watchers of the Four Directions (Four Physical Elements). As angelic beings, the Watchers shine their light from beyond the perimeter of the circle where they meet and are unified within each participant, thus "All four stars are One." And from the space of that unity we call to the Watchers of the nonphysical element of aether from above and below.

the ember shines up to you and into the inverted violet pentacle in your perineum. How does Fire-in-the-Earth feel to you? Does s/he take a different form? Feel this Watcher within the inverted pentacle and call out, "*Who am I?*"

Contemplate this question and notice whatever arises. Take a breath and feel the Watcher draw nearer. Continue to ask the question and then allow the Watcher to come closer until s/he rests just below you.

From the space of your Three Souls in alignment, imagine all six Watchers forming a sphere of protection around you. Take another deep breath and feel the Watcher above and the Watcher below flowing into you all at once. Feel how you are filled with their combined power, like two notes now forming a harmony within you. Call out:

> *Between six points that flow from one*
> *Calm, the eye of tempest's winds*
> *Within the center outward shines*
> *The light of three now so aligned*
> *Awake, alive, aware, divine…*
> *The Black Heart drums a primal beat.*

Spend some time communing with this space. Here you are in the Center between all the worlds. This is the space of the seventh Watcher, the Guardian of the Gates. We step into that role when we are aligned within ourselves as well as with the worlds. This is a space of balanced, calm, confidence. Here you are embodying your own divine authority.

Maintain this presence for a few minutes and then acknowledge each Watcher in reverse order. Then say:

> *Watchers from the edge of space and time*
> *We thank you for your Power and your Presence*
> *Stay if you will, go if you must.*
> *But ere you depart, we bid you:*
> *Hail and Farewell!*

Take a deep breath and then on your exhale imagine releasing your connection to the Watchers ... as easily as letting go of a string, watch them float outward and back into the outer darkness. End as normal. Record your experiences in your journal.

---

This space of stepping into the presence of perfect center, and aligning your consciousness with the concept of yourself as the Center Watcher is the space from which you will perform your magic. As you continue to work with these spirits, getting to know them intimately, your power and control will grow. You will need to simply be in their presence so that they can make energetic changes to you, increasing your capacity to work with them and to hold both vision and power. But you cannot rush it. Connect with these ancient beings often. Call upon them when you feel the need for protection, or their presence in your workings. They need not be called for every little thing, but you will want to form a working relationship with them as real and nuanced as any human friendships you may have. These are the Guardian beings of our sacred tradition. They are here to assist those who are working toward our spiritual evolution. They are here to assist us in becoming the gods that are our birthrights.

## Sex Magic

Prior to Christianity, sex was generally seen for what it is: a natural expression of love and desire and a means to strengthen the bonds that connect us. To the repressed Christian, the Witch represents the dark side of their own sexual desires, which they demonize and call the devil. This is why most early depictions of Witches portray her as nude; she exemplifies the very thing that a repressed patriarchal male psyche would crave, but that is also strictly forbidden. Rather than confront their own desires and the ridiculous demands of a church that would seek to dominate and control them, it was much easier to turn one's anger and frustration to the very object of one's desire, and name her as a Witch, a convenient scapegoat for the church of an impotent false god.

Sex has always been at the heart of the Craft. The image of a Witch riding a broomstick needs little mental prodding to reveal what this almost wholesome Halloween-style image is tied to historically. "Riding the broom" is a practice linked to the fertility of crops, as well as with a sexual rite used to administer the Witches "flying ointment," a traditional herbal concoction used to induce visions and astral flight.

Sex is a sacrament in our tradition. It is not a "means to an end." It is the means *and* the end. It is holy. Pleasure is holy. To merge with another consciousness is the highest form of praise and devotion. It is the supreme act of love. In our studies with the Iron Pentacle, we have seen how Sex is less about physical touch than it is about energy and consciousness. It is the ecstatic opening up and dropping our shields, which normally keep us cut off from the world and those in it. Sex is about *surrender*, not of our will or our sovereignty, but a surrendering of our egos and our fears. We become vulnerable, and this can be especially difficult if we have experienced sexual violence. We surrender back into that natural state of harmony from which all things emerge and unto which all things return. To do this we must be able to engage our sexual nature without shame and without fear. This is the core of the Black Heart of Innocence, and if we are still harboring either prudish or depraved attitudes toward sex then we would be better off leaving Faery alone.

In Faery, as with much of what has come to be called Traditional Witchcraft, sex is often a central element in the passing of the initiatic current of Power. This is the Red Rite of initiation into our Mystery priesthood. When properly done, this is a beautiful and loving rite, for there is nothing more beautiful than two or more people coming together in love and pleasure. But this traditional observance should not be seen as the final dogmatic word. While some unscrupulous teachers have demanded their students submit to them sexually in order to receive our most holy rite, most would condemn such a demand and point to the founders' own wisdom on the subject: the Rite of the Intentions of the Heart.

While sexual intercourse can be a very powerful method of raising and passing power, it is by no means the only way or even the most traditional. The Intentions of the Heart is the "Blue Rite," a traditional means to pass the initiatic Power without the need to engage in intercourse. While some have tried to say that intercourse is the *only* valid way to pass the Power in our tradition, I point out that Victor and Cora passed initiation to their students using the Blue Rite, thus effectively quashing whatever sexual demands some might otherwise impose. Our Craft demands an adherence to a high standard of sexual ethics. Those who would violate this most precious of gifts are doomed to destruction.

## A Faery Sex Magic Spell

This rite assumes a solitary practice. It can easily be adapted for group workings.

Items needed:
Your black Star Goddess candle
Matches
Your mirror
Your cauldron
A piece of parchment paper
Some herbal oil, aligned to your magical goal
Some colored pencils or pens
Your favorite lubricant
A small towel (optional)

Decide on something that you wish to manifest. Open the Way.

Create a sigil representing your desire. Draw this on the parchment paper and further adorn the paper with symbols and signs in alignment with your goal. Dress the paper and fold it in the traditional manner for increase. Place it on your altar and then look at the mirror, allowing your gaze to soften as you scry into its surface. Begin to slowly masturbate, allowing the waves of pleasure to build in your body as you imagine yourself *making love with the outcome you seek.*

Visualize your symbol as if it were shining in the space before you. As you feel the pleasures in your body, imagine that the waves of your pleasure are bringing this shining sigil closer and closer toward you. You may wish to move up to the very edge prior to orgasm and then back off, thus further opening, building, and deepening the power. Usually this is done until the point of orgasm, at which point we send the sigil and our prayer to the daemon as with the Ha Prayer. Dress the folded paper with a bit of your sexual fluid. Now burn it from the flame of your Star Goddess candle and toss it into your cauldron. (If you are not choosing to orgasm at this time, then you simply allow your heightened sensations to be the conduit of the prayer: take hold of the folded paper and breathe out three times upon it before lighting and tossing it into the cauldron.) End as normal.

Do not be deceived by the apparent simplicity of this exercise. Unless we are already accustomed to using sexual activity in our magical practice, we can never be too sure what powers might be found while engaging it. There is a reason that Witches are associated with sex, other than prudish scapegoating: sex is powerful. We are the sovereigns of our own lives and bodies. This alone can be a striking act, both spiritual as well as political. We dare to claim our own divine authority. We greet the world now with this power, respectfully but also defiantly. We bow to no one.

## The Points of Flame: Sex Exercise

As we draw to the end of the Iron Pentacle, we again perform this familiar exercise, now using a violet candle and focusing on the point of Sex in the hidden temple of aether. How do you run sexual energy? How does it feed you? How do you open up to the energies of others? How do you allow yourself to be touched, and moved? How is your sex life? What excites you? What do you consider "intimate"? How do you open to the energies of the universe? Use the affirmation:

*"In the name of iron, I summon forth SEX!"*

## Aether Art Project

Create your final elemental art project: aether! Since this element sometimes is less generous in visual inspiration, try focusing on how you have felt while engaging the element. Expansive? Contractive? Both? Neither? What has aether taught you? How can you express that without the use of words? And then, of course, do just that: explain your process and your choices in symbolism.

## Iron Pentacle Art Project

Now create an art piece that describes your journey with the Iron Pentacle. Do you have symbols that represent the points to you? What challenges did each of them pose? What was going on in your life at the time? Let this be part journal and part meditative mandala: your personal Iron Pentacle! When it is done, create a ritual around it and invoke the Pentacle. Celebrate your life force and the strides you have made since you began this work.

---

The elemental cycle now complete; our inner circle has been cast. The foundation has been built, and now the real work begins.

# CHAPTER 12
# THE HEART AND THE PEARL

*He who would search for pearls must dive below.*
—JOHN DRYDEN

I once heard someone say that compassion had no place in Witchcraft. This couldn't be farther from the truth! While the Old Craft might not share some of the more tender-hearted sensibilities of many of today's modern practitioners, there has always been an element of service and connection at the heart of our Craft. As those who do the work of priesting, we are in service to those who are in need. Those of us who are called to do this deep work understand that we cannot simply dismiss those with whom we disagree or even dislike. If we are all part of the ever-unfolding Star Goddess then even our enemies are a part of ourselves, and if we disregard this (often uncomfortable) fact we do so at our own peril. Even those qualities and people whom we might consider to be bad or evil are a part of this great unfolding. And if we are unable to recognize this, then the failing is ultimately our own.

## Melek Ta'us and the Fall Myth,[58]
## or Pain and Beauty in the Heart of God

In the soft time before sunrise Melek Ta'us, the Peacock Lord, was walking in the garden. As he walked beneath a tree, he found the Mother's mirror underneath her birth stool. He picked it up and looked at his reflection.

---

58. This version draws heavily from that given by Francesca DeGrandis and passed in the oral tradition.

233

"Behold how beautiful I am!" he exclaimed, and transformed himself into a shining peacock. He then shook his tail feathers, filling all Seven Heavens with light and thunder. At his joyous cry, "HA!" the sun arose in Paradise.

He walked deeper into the garden and came upon the Mother, his Lover, his Sister, his other half. He said to her, "Behold how beautiful I am! Let us create those who can share in my beauty!"

"Do you wish them to be your slaves?" asked the Mother.

"No. I wish for them to be made in our image, male and female, and neither, and both. I wish them to love me and delight in my radiant beauty, which shall be shared amongst them. I wish to see my own beauty reflected in them that I might rejoice in their beauty and their freedom."

The Great Mother thought on this and replied, "My beautiful one, you know not what you ask. For if I do this, your crown will forever be in heaven and your feet shall forever be in hell. If I do this, every pain in the heart of humankind will be a pain in the heart of God. Think on this before you ask it."

And the Peacock Lord, walked alone in the garden, contemplating his desires. And when we returned he said, "But I love them. I want them as my precious jewels."

And the Great Mother, seeing the love in his eyes and in his heart, granted his wish. "Evohe! So Must It Be!"

And the first sparks of life descended from the heavens and fell to earth into the waters where it formed and evolved. And after eons, of countless shapes and forms, humans were born on earth, each with a piece of God within our hearts.

---

## The Pearl Pentacle

Though it is said that there is only one pentacle in Faery (a reference perhaps in part to our lack of a universal system of invoking and banishing pentacles such as that found in the Golden Dawn) they can certainly be viewed from different angles. When the Iron Pentacle is viewed in isolation, its powers are personal, pertaining to the self and how we relate to ourselves internally. When it is viewed in concert with others as equals it becomes the transpersonal *Pearl*, a shining beacon of balance, connection, harmony, and community.

The symbolism of the Pearl in our tool is both beautiful and specific. We are often told that the lustrous pearl begins its life as an irritant. Perhaps a grain of sand gets lodged between the oyster and its shell, creating discomfort and causing the oyster to encase the sand in a smooth, silvery-substance as a means to protect itself. More accurate than "irritant" would be to say *wound*: a damaging and dangerous injury that could even threaten the oyster's life if no action is taken. It is an act of self-protection, as well as an act of transformation: changing pain and danger into something of beauty.

Perhaps because pearls are created slowly over time, they have also come to be associated with wisdom. The idiom "Pearls of Wisdom" illustrates this perfectly, as well as the common admonishment to not "cast pearls before swine," a reference to wasting one's efforts by sharing something of value with those who are unable (or unwilling) to appreciate it.

Pearls are also associated, for obvious reasons, with the water element. With this in mind the Pearl Pentacle becomes the *water* to the Iron Pentacle's *fire*. It is an alchemical reflection bringing balance to the whole.

The history of the Pearl Pentacle is somewhat shrouded. Its origins are to be found sometime between 1970 and 1973, according to private conversations I have had with two teachers, both now deceased, who were initiated in those years. When the late Alison Harlow was initiated in 1970, there was no mention of the Pearl, but by 1973 this pentacle was being taught openly and passed to students from that time forward.

In the years since it was created, it has changed forms in the hands of those who have been teaching it. Victor taught the following order, going around the circle to match his method of working the Iron Pentacle: Love, Wisdom, Knowledge, Law, Power. In the Bloodrose lineage, the points of Wisdom and Knowledge would (inexplicably) be switched, and the method of engaging them would now be through the lines of the star, giving us the initial order that we work with in BlueRose today: Love, Law, Knowledge, Power, and Wisdom.

The points of the Pearl Pentacle are the transpersonal counterparts of the points of Iron Pentacle, expressing each quality in a complementary fashion. No longer something that needs to be heated, pounded, and forged, now we invoke the pentacle to cool, to soothe … to act as our "quench water" in our sacred quest in forging ourselves into the perfect instrument and vessel for the Old Powers.

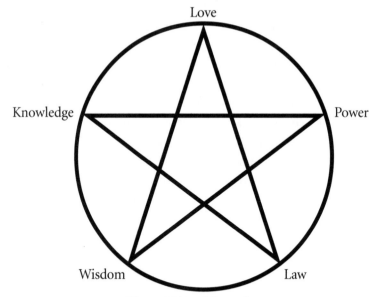

*Figure 16: Pearl Pentacle*

Each point is the highest of those ideals toward which we ever strive. While the Points of Iron can make the individual feel more *powerful,* it doesn't necessarily make us any better at putting aside our fragile egos and getting along with others. In this the Pearl Pentacle becomes a type of compass, helping us to avoid the indulgence of self-importance and to better navigate through the often-rocky terrain of engaging and sharing with others.

One criticism that I have for the overall "Faery community" is that much emphasis has been placed on the Iron Pentacle but nowhere near enough has been placed on the Pearl. It is not a mark of "weakness" to show kindness and to strive toward harmony with one another. The overall message of the Pearl Pentacle is one of *true compassion.* This is not the same as that intended by the sympathetic offerings usually given in times of stress or crises ("Don't worry. Everything's going to be okay") but instead is selfless right action. Sometimes the most compassionate act is to speak the truth, even if it is hard to say or to hear. True compassion is the razor's edge of the Warrior. And it is the Pearl that we use to help polish that blade.

Warriors are the ones who have overcome their weaknesses. They are those who have seen their fears before them and they have gone forward anyway. It is exhilarating to confront and champion one's fears. So much so that it can be tempting to hold judgment for others who have not confronted their own. But before we begin to feel *"Faerier than thou"* at the notion of our fellow practitioners neglecting to look at their deepest flaws, we must remember the proverb, now given in full: "We do not coddle weakness. But neither do we condemn it in others." In our tradition we are asked to assist those who may be in need, but not at the expense of our own undoing.[59]

It is at this point that I feel compelled to share another myth.

## The Shepherd and the Peacock Myth, or Compassion Even for Evil

*Note: This myth was originally shared with me as being authentic Yazidi, but it is actually based upon anti-Yazidi propaganda, used as proof that they were devil worshipers. While this myth was believed to be genuine until relatively recently, it holds a certain element of meditative contemplation that I think is important on the nature of evil and how best we may respond to it. I have rewritten the obviously offensive cultural assertions and reworked it to fit my own interpretation. I offer it not for historic or cultural accuracy, but as an inspirational story.*

There once was a shepherd who faithfully tended his flock. One day as he was out strolling the fields he saw a great flash of light and heard an enormous and thunderous roar. A star fell from the heavens and streaked fire across the sky and down into the forest on the other side of the shepherd's land. The shepherd trekked out to find the fallen star, and when he reached the site of its landing he found the land torn open and burned by a great fire. In the rubble and smoke he saw a beautiful wounded peacock. Without thought for himself he moved through the fires and picked up the dying bird. He washed its wounds with pure water and bandaged it up with scraps from his own garments. He cradled it gently as he went home to put the bird in his own bed, and he tended it throughout the night. In the morning, the peacock was restored and spoke to him with a human voice: "Do not be afraid! As you were kind to me, so shall I bless you and your progeny. For I am the Spirit of Evil thrown out of Heaven and now I shall spread across the earth. Tell your children to accept evil as you have accepted me. Have compassion for the evil in yourself and others. Delight me with songs, plays, and art, and placate me

---

59. Cora Anderson, *In Mari's Bower* (Portland, OR: Harpy Books, 2012), 65.

with prayers and pleasures. Tend to me and dress my wounds. Dress my wounds and heal the world."

And with that the Peacock Angel, Melek Ta'us, flew away into the night toward the Polar Star, where we make our prayers. We pray not to smite evil but ever to heal it, for it is indeed a wound in the heart of God.

---

At first, the notion of having compassion for evil might seem backward, as if it were condoning or even encouraging the evil acts. This fails to really examine what evil *is*. Usually, when we use the word *evil* we are making a moral judgment and in all likelihood signaling the conclusion of our desire to try to understand the nature of the evil thing. Once it is determined to be evil, *that's it* ... no further explanation necessary. But according to the tenants of Faery Tradition, evil is simply something that is broken, twisted, or missing.[60] It is a type of illness or weakness. And these are conditions that can conceivably be healed. As we strive to heal our own weakness, our own evil, so may we hold a space of compassion for others who are dealing with their own weaknesses of which we may know nothing. The Pearl Pentacle as a meditative tool can help us to cultivate a more compassionate view, internally as well as externally.

As each point of the Iron Pentacle is related also to an elemental power, so do we use that power to assist us in transmuting the presence of each point from the deep fiery red of the Iron into the iridescent silver-white of the Pearl. As we invoke and contemplate the points of Iron Pentacle, we use this formula to make the transmutation, then remain open in our observational space to notice how this new presence affects us.

| Table of Iron/Pearl/Element | | |
| --- | --- | --- |
| **IRON** | **PEARL** | **ELEMENT** |
| Sex | Love | Aether |
| Pride | Law | Fire |
| Self | Knowledge | Air |
| Power | Power (or Liberty) | Earth |
| Passion | Wisdom | Water |

---

60. Anderson, *In Mari's Bower*, 63.

# Love

Where Sex in the Iron Pentacle sees us in the act of opening to exchange life force, Love is the deeper desire for union. Not just in the act, but also in terms of a transcendent desire, a genuine identification with the *other*, whether that be a lover, a family member, a friend, a god, or a spirit. We surrender to them—not in terms of our power or sovereignty—but we surrender our egos in favor of this deep connection.

Love is the fabric of the universe, the foundation of all being. It is the first desire that stirred in the heart of God Herself before creation. She created the universe out of herself not because she *had* to, but because she *wanted* to. It was an act of love. So too is the creation of humankind an act of love … and selflessness, another aspect to this point of the Pearl.

In Sex we are seeking gratification, to some degree, but in Love we are giving without regard to receiving. This makes the point of Love one of the most difficult for the Witch or occultist to master, as the process of gaining power most often leads to self-aggrandizement and the subsequent disconnection that brings. If we are able to temper our power with Love then we will truly be worthy of them both.

# Law

As Pride is the natural inclination of our own life force to move through ourselves and be expressed outward on the Iron Pentacle, so on the macrocosmic level of the Pearl Pentacle this becomes what we collectively experience as Natural Law. *Law* is that which we cannot change, that to which we are always subject. Like the law of gravity, it is applied universally without regard to an individual's status or standing. This is the turning of the wheel, the procession of the stars and planets, and the phases of the moon. We can count on them and align ourselves with their cycles.

Awareness of what laws apply to a given situation is paramount for the Warrior to be able to navigate effectively. When entering into a situation ask yourself: What laws govern this encounter? Are they social? Legal? Ethical? What is the most likely outcome of any given action? Think first!

# Knowledge

Here's where things get tricky. In the system that I was taught it is the Iron Pentacle point of Self that becomes Knowledge, highlighting the old axiom "Know thyself." But in Victor's original teachings, it is the point of Passion that becomes Knowledge. There is value to be found in contemplating both configurations as each yield different treasures. Drawing from Self, Knowledge is that which is gained by personal experience. Drawing from Passion, Knowledge shows us the result of delving deeply into something, as the waves of our own deep passions often lead us toward new discoveries.

## Power

It is such an important concept for us to study that this point appears on both of our beloved pentacles. The Iron Pentacle point of Power (from within) now becomes the point of Power (-with) on the Pearl. While in Iron we were asked to refine our relationship to Power, recognizing it not as "power-over" but instead "power-from-within," now on the Pearl Pentacle we are asked to share that power freely with others. While old fears of "power shared is power lost" may creep into our psyche, we work toward the embodiment of this high ideal: To share power and work in harmony toward a shared vision. This frees us from the illusory bonds of ego that previously kept us chained. Once free, we see now how this point is sometimes also called Liberty. It is from this state that Witches are better able to work effectively in a coven or group.

## Wisdom

Again we must pay careful attention to two traditional views of this point. Drawing from Passion as in the Bloodrose view, it is a reminder that Wisdom is not just "headology"[61] but includes the heart into the equation. By diving into the deep and exploring the full breadth of our emotional selves we gain new experiences, which allow us to embody wisdom along the way. Drawing from the original form, it is Self that blooms into Wisdom. Contemplating this reminds me that wisdom is a personal goal of the Faery practitioner, and that it comes about by sharing ourselves with each other. We each have limits and potentials and the full knowledge of them is what guides our actions. In this we embody the Warrior: being keenly aware of our own skills and how best to apply them.

### *Engaging the Pearl Pentacle Exercise*

Items needed:
Your black Star Goddess candle
Matches

---

61. With the deepest of respect to the late Terry Pratchett.

Open the Way. Invoke the Iron Pentacle and run it through your body. Once you feel that you have worked up a sufficient charge, focus on the point of Sex. Allow your consciousness to open up as you contemplate the meaning of the point. See it bathed in the violet light of aether. Feel the presence of that element flowing through Sex ... Be aware of aether above and below ... of transcendence as well as embodiment and how Sex represents both of those extremes. Call out:

*By Sex and by aether, I conjure Love!*

Imagine the violet point of Sex transforming into a radiant, pearlescent-white glow. Feel how Sex shifts into Love ... Recall a time in your life in which you have been in love. How did this feel to you, emotionally as well as perhaps physically? Call up those sensations now and simply pay attention to them. Look at other loves in your life ... family ... friends ... pets ... What do they each share? How are they different?

Breathe deeply, and imagine the red iron light forming the line toward Pride is now flowing toward that point with a soft, white, glow, transforming the Iron Pentacle presence as it goes. When it reaches Pride, see that point bathed in the crimson light of fire. Call out:

*By Pride and by fire, I conjure Law!*

Again, see the point transform and feel the shift. How does your natural Pride become natural Law? Feel how your own natural expression is merely the microcosmic version of universal law. Just as you naturally express yourself in one way or another, so does the universe express itself according to its own set of inner laws. Feel the shift from Pride into Law and again simply observe. Repeat the above formula (Self/air=Knowledge, Power/earth=Power, Passion/water=Wisdom) until the Iron Pentacle has been completely transformed into the Pearl Pentacle. You may simply bathe in its presence for a while before ending, or add on one of the additional pieces below.

## Singing Iron into Pearl Exercise

This exercise takes the place of the Engaging the Pearl Pentacle exercise. Using the same formula given above invoke the points of the Pearl, but now when the point of Pearl is shining bright, *sing* its name. Allow the name of each point to be a note, or series of notes in a song you will compose by musically affirming each point as you invoke the pentacle. *This doesn't have to sound good.* Musical proficiency is not a requirement for this exercise, but a good *feeling* is. Let yourself really sing! Try singing the names of the points to the tunes of songs that you love or that empower you.

## The Points of Flow Exercise

As with the Points of Flame for the Iron Pentacle, we will work to cleanse each point of the Pearl Pentacle with the Points of Flow. Using the Waters of Purity as a template, place all of your blocks and impurities for each point into the water, then transform and drink, taking back this power in a raw form. Spend at least one week focusing on a single point before moving on to the next.

## Soul Star Part 2 Divination

In addition to the previous eight cards which form the categories of the Triple Soul and Iron Pentacle, we may now add the five points of the Pearl Pentacle to the list, bringing our spread to a very satisfying thirteen. This layer of the spread adds awareness of outside forces.

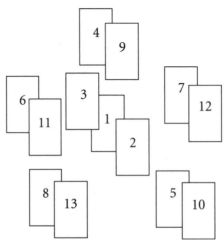

*Figure 17: Soul Star, Part 2*

*Pearl Pentacle*

9. Love—That which will bring holism; what forces are necessary to manifest the situation in its fullness.

10. Law—Natural forces at work that cannot be changed.

11. Knowledge—How the situation is perceived by others around you; other perspectives.

12. Power/Liberty—Cooperative forces to assist you; what can be shared to bring about the best result.

13. Wisdom—The final outcome. What is to be learned from the situation.

---

# The Black Heart of Innocence

While Christianity offers a doctrine of original sin, one might say that Faery offers one of original innocence. The *Black Heart of Innocence* is a poetic term that represents the natural, sexual state of the soul with which we all come into this world. It draws its name from the proverb: "How beautiful is the black lascivious purity in the hearts of children and wild animals."[62] It is sometimes also referred to as the Black Rose of Innocence.[63]

It is black because it represents the underlying reality behind all things, much as like the night sky is the foundation for the light of the stars. Black is the unconscious and is the realm in which we find that which is unknown to the light of talker. The Black Heart cannot be observed directly, only inferred by one's behavior. I cannot know what is in your true heart, but I can make assumptions based on how you might act within the world. This, to me, is the meaning behind Victor's statement, "the blacker the body the whiter the light."

The innocence we enjoy at birth is very quickly lost, however, as we are taught to feel shame about our bodies and our drives. We are often told as children that certain parts of ourselves are "dirty," along with any behaviors and pleasures that we may experience with them. This eventually brings us to a place where we are at odds with our own physical bodies, which has led to many problems including the patriarchal oppression of women and sexual minorities.

---

62. Anderson, *Fifty Years in the Feri Tradition*, 29.

63. Anderson, *Heart of the Initiate*, 27.

We have been beaten and subjugated into believing that sex is wrong, and that we are somehow evil because it is something that we naturally desire. That the Abrahamic traditions that gave birth to Christianity and Islam fear sex should come as no surprise. Their near universal condemnation of physical existence in general, and sexuality specifically, has spread like a psychic contagion that keeps us stunted at best and threatens the survival of our very species, at worst. We have been crippled by the fear that what is pleasurable in life must somehow be detrimental to the soul. This is a terrible lie. While it's certainly not healthy to indulge in each and every desire without restraint, it is equally unhealthy to strictly abstain from earthly pleasures. Witches seek to live this life fully, indulging and abstaining both in balance toward a life of purpose and fulfillment. We must reconcile our ideas of what is holy with an embrace of the physical and recognize our sexual desires for what they are: a precious gift of the divine and not something "sinful."

Though innocence was lost, Faery teaches us that this innocence can again be found. Working toward this is something of a Holy Grail quest for practitioners and initiates of our tradition, and, in fact, one could argue that everything that we do in the training is to cultivate the Black Heart, to restore this primal state of human and animal authenticity.

This said, it should be understood that this is not an excuse for poor sexual behavior or lack of respectful boundaries. Our own freedom does not warrant the enslavement of another. Once we are truly free of our sexual shame, we will treat it as the sacred rite it is. We will not "cast pearls before swine" and offer our precious bodies and souls to those who would not appreciate our worth. The Black Heart is also the Crown of Sovereignty, which is to say, our own natural divine authority.

I have heard it said that the Black Heart is actually an evil state because it lacks a morality, but this is a gross misunderstanding. In BlueRose we say, "The Black Heart burns with the Blue Fire of compassion." It is said that the Black Heart emerges when the points of the Iron and Pearl pentacles are clear and in balance, and so it is to these tools that we can look for insights into the question of its cultivation. If we have been diligently working with the tools of the Iron and Pearl pentacles then we will have begun to discover certain things about ourselves that do not serve our highest ideals. We will be more aware of how we are quick to anger, or how we are in denial, or how we hold a secret shame. We will be acutely aware of that nagging little voice that says, "You are not good enough" as well as the encouraging voice that says, "Yes, you can." The points of Iron have revealed to us which areas we needed to work on internally, while the points of Pearl have shown us how our energies mesh with those around us, and offers us a means to grow in beauty and in wisdom.

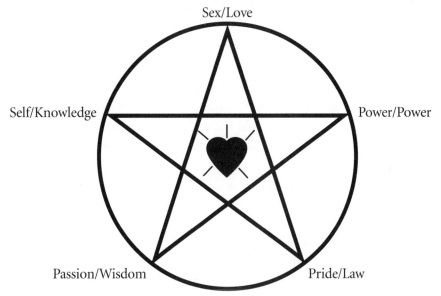

Sex/Love

Self/Knowledge

Power/Power

Passion/Wisdom

Pride/Law

*Figure 18: Iron/Pearl/Black Heart*

Achieving the Black Heart is a lifetime quest and not something that is going to happen overnight. Nor is it a static state, once achieved then always held, like a title or a possession. We catch glimpses of it, now and again. We feel it in those moments of pure freedom and of ecstatic abandon. Through sex, through song, through dance, through art, through *whatever gets you there.*

### Awakening the Black Heart Exercise

Consider an activity that you loved to do as a child. Just think of something that exhilarated you or brought you great joy. Perhaps you loved roller coasters or horseback riding. Or maybe you loved skating, or making mud pies, or catching fireflies in jars. Think of happy memories in which you were doing those things and then write about these in your journal for five minutes. (For those who may find this exercise a challenge due to a lack of happy memories, try thinking of something that either you had *wanted* to do, or that you might love doing *now.*)

Now, if appropriate, resolve to engage in this activity at some point soon. Allow yourself to let loose and get into the moment. This will empower fetch.

### Engaging the Black Heart Exercise

Through our work we have learned certain symbolic triggers along the way that can now prove useful in setting the stage for a grand invocation of power. We can channel this power toward our own betterment, here as a means to help cultivate the Black Heart. It is likely that buried energies and emotions may be brought to the surface as a result of this work. Remember the purification work we have previously learned, as this will be vital in the maintaining of our balance and energy.

Because the Black Heart is, at its core, sexual, we will now need to engage our sexuality to further explore this concept. We begin with mindful masturbation. For this you will be fully present with your body … paying close attention to every caress, every touch. You know exactly how to pleasure yourself. Take your time. Enjoy what your body has to offer you. Should you decide to climax, then enjoy the soft feelings afterward and allow this experience to nourish you and your fetch.

Open the Way. Feeling the presence of the Crossroads, invoke the Tree and feel yourself standing between the worlds.

Call to the iron in your blood and invoke the Iron Pentacle. Run the pentacle until it is humming within you.

Now, in this energized state, focus on the golden road that stretches out into the east. Feel the presence of the eagle guiding you. Call out to Star Finder … imagine him as a golden star that shines over the end of the eastern road. Feel his golden presence—the power of Knowledge—flowing into that glyph in your throat as you breathe in Resonance and Clarity.

Turn to the south and the ruby red road. Feel the lion's strength. Call out to Shining Flame, and he shines as a red star over the end of the road. Continue this method until the blue star of Water Maker and the green and black star of Black Mother shine in the west and north.

Feeling these lights all around yourself, breathe in and imagine streams of light flowing from them and into the glyphs within you, now being gathered up in a spiral like a whirlwind of colored lights. Open to aether above and to Heaven Shiner, as well as aether below and Fire-in-the-Earth. Feel your branches in the heavens and your roots deep in the earth.

Now, in this heightened state begin to pleasure yourself. This is not just the simple act of "getting off" but one of literally making love to yourself. You are worthy of love and pleasure. Allow fetch to be nourished by this. Take in life force with your orgasm.

## *Invoking the Black Heart Ritual*

Items needed:
Your black Star Goddess candle
Matches
Three taper candles: red, white, and black
A cup of pure, fresh water

Arrange your altar so that the red taper is on the left, the black taper is in the middle, and the white taper is on the right. Your Star Goddess candle should be positioned somewhere behind the black taper. Carve a pentacle on both the red and the white, and a heart on the black.

Open the Way, taking extra time to delve into fetch. Perform the Waters of Purity rite.

Sitting or standing, preferably naked, invoke the Iron Pentacle into your body. Take the time to feel each point individually. See and feel them pulsing with power in your forehead and in your feet and hands. Light the red taper from the Star Goddess candle with the prayer:

> *By my bones and by my blood,*
> *I invoke the Iron Pentacle!*

Feel how the candle flame feeds into the Iron Pentacle, allowing it to become stronger with every breath. Notice how each glows with the appropriate elemental color (violet for aether/Sex, red for fire/Pride, yellow for air/Self, green for earth/Power, and blue for water/Passion). Run the pentacle for at least a few breaths, feeling the power move in between each point until you can see/feel the pathways as being strong and clear and in balance. When you feel that the power is at its strongest, invoke the Pearl Pentacle with the formula:

> *By Sex and by aether, I invoke Love!*

See and feel the hot red iron light at the core of the Sex point begin to change into the soft pearlescent glow of Love. Continue with the following:

*By Pride and by fire, I invoke Law!*
*By Self and by air, I invoke Knowledge!*
*By Power and by earth, I invoke Power!*
*By Passion and by water, I invoke Wisdom!*

When you feel the last point change, light the white candle from the red taper and say:

*By the Iron and by the elements of life, I invoke the Pearl!*

Take some time to feel the points of the Pearl Pentacle as clear and strong. Feel the power move between each point, making the pathways in between them strong and clear. Maintain this for several breaths.

Now feel how the points of the Pearl are the same as those of the Iron, only turned outward. Maintain this for at least three breaths.

Now imagine that both pentacles are present at the same time, in fact that there is only one pentacle…the Iron and the Pearl are simply two different ways of looking at the same pentacle.

In each hand pick up both the red and the white tapers, and bring them together at the same time to light the wick of the black taper. Say:

*With Radiance and Awareness, and in the names of Sex and Love,*
*With Strength and Potency, and in the names of Pride and Law,*
*With Resonance and Clarity, and in the names of Self and Knowledge,*
*With Structure and Stability, and in the names of Power and Power,*
*With Fluidity and Adaptability, and in the names of Passion and Wisdom,*
*Primal, Innocent, Wild, Free, I invoke the Black Heart!*

Feeling both sets of pentacle points simultaneously, imagine strands of light in the appropriate elemental colors streaming forth from each of the points and flowing into your heart center, where they converge, emerging as an ever-exploding heart of pitch black. Feel how the light of the black taper is feeding into your own heart center. Breathe the Blue Fire into your heart and allow it to shine and burn with the electric blue flame. Feel it throb and thrum with every heartbeat. Hear it like a primal drum. Let the sound of it wash over you ... drowning out everything that does not serve you. Allow yourself to rock and sway to the beat ... let your body move in whatever ways you are inspired. Say the following (or better yet, whatever you are inspired to):

> *Black Heart*
> *Primal drum*
> *Child's song*
> *Feral thrum*
> *Passion's kiss*
> *Shining light*
> *Wild bliss*
> *Starlit night*
> *Serpent's skin*
> *Second sight*
> *Dark abyss*
> *Shining bright*
> *Black Heart*
> *Pulsing free*
> *Innocent!*
> *Ecstasy!*

Now begin to vibrate the *aum* as you draw even more power into your heart. Feel the elemental and pentacle powers filling every bit of you, becoming one with your essence. See your Black Heart shining now with fire in all the colors of the rainbow. See and feel this rainbow fire spilling outward and filling your physical body ... and finally your aura. Notice how this energy feels within you and on your skin; notice where you feel it in your body. Allow your body to become inspired by these sensations. If you feel like dancing, then go ahead and dance ... if you feel like singing or laughing, then sing or laugh ... If you feel like crying, jumping, masturbating, or whatever you are inspired to do, allow yourself the space to do it, feeling the radiant Black Heart pulsing within you. Maintain this for at least several minutes.

When you are finished, extinguish the tapers, feeling gratitude in your heart for the experience. End as normal and record your experiences.

## Art Project

Create an art project to express your experiences with the Pentacle as it has transformed from Iron and into Pearl. Ask yourself: What has it softened in you? What things used to irritate you that now don't seem to bother you quite as much? Where are you better able to accept criticism? Or accept help? Or love? What has the Pearl healed in your life?

# PART THREE:
# JOURNEYING BETWEEN THE WORLDS

A Witch or a Warlock gathers power by learning to move between the worlds of the everyday and those adjacent worlds that intersect our own. As the saying goes, "What is between the worlds is the focus for all the worlds."

### Invocation of the Crossroads

*By east and west, by south and north,*
*The Watchers here do we call forth.*
*By wind! By river! By flame! By stone!*
*Four stars made one with flesh and bone.*
*Where the stang does mark the spot*
*So the Crossroads here are wrought.*
*By the starry light above,*
*Behold the soaring Azure Dove.*
*By the darkness far beneath,*
*The Scarlet Serpent bears his teeth.*
*As each do turn to spy the other*
*Brother, enemy, and lover*
*And each to arms now leap and soar*
*To meet on earth in bitter war.*
*By talon, fang, and shed of blood*
*By burning fire and raging flood*
*Their battle turns to deep desire*
*Two flames into a single fire.*
*As Holy Lust meets Sacred Love*
*So joins the serpent to the dove.*

*And in their place as two form one*
*The Peacock Angel thus is born.*
*Hallowed be this convocation*
*Open be our inner sight!*
*Bear witness to the consecration*
*And bless us with your shining might.*

# CHAPTER 13
# THE MIDDLEWORLD

*Don't ask what the world needs. Ask yourself what makes you come alive*
*and then go do that. Because what the world needs is people who have come alive.*
—HOWARD THURMAN, CIVIL RIGHTS LEADER

D rawing from folkloric sources, we find many references to other worlds that intersect our own. While some tales speak only vaguely of the otherworld, further study reveals multiple intersecting realms in which the practicing Witch can interact and gain power. An effective Witch will have formed allies with the inhabitants of these realms in order to extend her magical reach further than she would otherwise be capable alone.

We engage these realms and their denizens by way of directed imagination and the conscious use of symbolism that follows a particular pattern, what Faery author R. J. Stewart refers to as "Empowered Visualization."[64] In this we are engaging fetch and allowing that soul to be the vehicle for our consciousness as we traverse the realms in shamanic fashion.

Talker knows that the underworld is not literally beneath our feet. Our minds know that it is a level of reality that we might think of as *underlying* our own: just a different vibration. We use the adoption of the external directions to describe these worlds purely as meditative tools: as tricks to help create specific geometries of sensation and consciousness, which will then better facilitate the projection of our consciousness into these adjacent realms.

---

64. R. J. Stewart, *Earth Light: The Ancient Path to Transformation Rediscovering the Wisdom of Celtic & Faery Lore* (Rockport, MA: Element, 1992), 61.

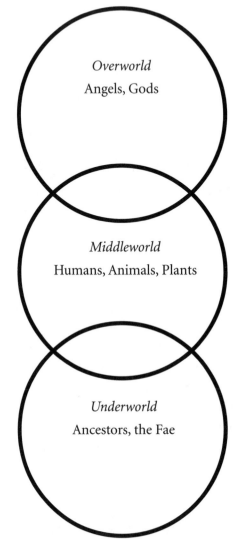

*Figure 19: The Three Worlds*

Just as each of us possesses Three Souls, so too is the "soul of the world" tripartite in nature. Celtic folklore teaches of three interconnected worlds, which they called Land, Sea, and Sky, poetic metaphors for the middleworld, the underworld, and the overworld, respectively. Each of these realms exists in the same space-time as the world of form of which we are the most familiar. We must attune our consciousness toward their particular vibratory rate in order to perceive them properly.

On one level there is just one world and these different realms are merely modes of perception not normally accessible in our normal waking state of consciousness. This is the same way that there is only one "you" and only one "me" but that we each also possess a triple nature. The world is not divided against itself any more than we are as individuals possessing three souls, or five vital organs. These layers of reality each function in much the same way as our Three Souls, each with their own laws and natures, but each working in tandem with the others toward a greater holism. As above, so below.

## The Middleworld

What has been called the middleworld is this realm here and now with which we are the most familiar. It is the realm of multiplicity and form. It has a unique vantage in that it is nestled between the other two, making it strategically important in terms of interworldly communications. It is related to the talker and is the realm that we experience as *consensual reality*. Each and every one of us takes part in its constant creation and re-creation and the majority of our life force and attention is spent navigating and maintaining the workings of this realm, leaving little else left over for other activities.

These "other activities" include magic and the expansion of our own awareness. We must learn to better gather our power and to conserve where possible. We have already been doing much of this work when we have engaged the Iron and Pearl pentacles, and especially with the Points of Flame and the Points of Flow, where we transform and reabsorb "lost" splinters of our power that have been tied up in forms that do not serve us. Little by little we have been reclaiming this power, fragments of our selves, and putting them back into place. The practice of Faery is one of integration as we collect every last scrap of power that we can find, and call it back that we may better do the heavier work of working with spirits and allies and of working our magical will into the world.

This is where a regular, disciplined practice makes its usefulness most obvious. By having something of a routine, we are better able to develop our own skills at gathering and directing this power. Often the effects of our practice will not make themselves known until we have established a good *momentum*. This effect occurs after we have "caught our stride" within the practice, which then will begin to open up in new ways, previously unknown to us.

We already know that a magical practice that contains both formal and informal elements is preferred, and if we have not yet been able to establish a robust and regular magical practice, then now is the time to make some necessary adjustments.

One simple method might be to have a list of "daily chores" of which your practice can be one of them, or even scheduling your day or week using a calendar service. There are apps for your smartphones, tablets, and computers that not only help you keep track of daily routines and larger to-do lists, but can also make the experience fun! (One app that I recently tried will even turn your real-life routine into "quests" for an RPG-style game that you can play with your friends. Welcome to the future.)

Just the same as taking a shower or brushing your teeth, your magical practice should be fully integrated into your normal routine. We are not Witches just on the weekends or whenever it suits us. Witches and Warlocks are forever, and we owe it to ourselves and to the Craft at large to be as skilled and effective as possible.

## Another Word on Formal vs. Informal Practice

In chapter 2, I mentioned the importance of establishing an *in*formal practice in addition to your regular magical workings. I am of the mind that it is *just as important* to establish an informal practice as it is its formal counterpart. Being able to translate the power of our formal practices into the "rest of our lives" is a vital skill that we must cultivate if we are to grow on our personal path. Otherwise we will have moments of clarity and power as we sit or stand in front of our altars, candles ablaze and incense smoke drifting around our heads … and then we will return to our "normal" lives of television and Internet and those few moments of connection and power we felt will be as but a memory. Wouldn't it be even better if we had some method of expanding our magical successes from within their confines of ritual and spread it outward to enchant the rest of our lives? By creating casual forms of the previous work that are better suited for everyday performance, we can better cast said enchantment upon ourselves, and truly start living a magical life.

One example might be to quickly run the Iron Pentacle while performing some other mundane activity, such as doing the dishes, vacuuming, or taking a shower. This needn't take the same form as what we have done before… you can quickly Open the Way and then call up that iron presence, feeling it within you and drawing the star on our body in the span of just a few breaths, ready to run the points of the pentacle as you clean your house or iron your clothes.

One of my early students had the idea of purchasing soap crayons used by children at bath time. She then proceeded to draw the Iron Pentacle in her shower enclosure each morning so she would have a visual reference while doing this work as she was doing her normal routine of personal hygiene. It was easy to do, and just as easy to rinse away when she was done.

The point of the informal work is to make easy versions that can be done in an instant while performing other tasks. The Iron Pentacle in the shower, Soul Alignment while walking to work, Blue Fire while waiting for the bus. You can call on Star Finder while waiting in line at the grocery store, or to Ana while making tea. We are working toward enchanting our lives, so the more contact we have with the magical the more magical our lives become. Doing your regular chores becomes golden opportunities for grand invocations of the gods involving little more than your broom and a dustpan. (Come now, did you think we were going to use it to fly?) Cleaning your house becomes *cleansing* your house. Add florida water to your mop bucket. Light a candle while you do the dishes; each dish you scrub clean represents an obstacle overcome, an impurity transformed. Each load of laundry is a little cleansing of your own soul. Even scrubbing a toilet can be magical work, if you have the power and imagination to make it so.

Through the informal practice, we will enchant our *full* lives, but only if we are able to maintain a momentum from our formal practices. It is the formal that acts as a magical generator, creating the energy that we will distribute via the informal work. This is why I stressed a four times per week *minimum* of the formal work. The *informal* work should be done *each and every day*. Certainly there will be times in which we forget or become distracted, but after a while we should be able to maintain the informal daily work, even if our formal practice stumbles, at times. Once we have achieved a strong momentum in our practice, the frequency of the formal work becomes less important, though still should be maintained to avoid a state of decay. Even professional musicians and dancers still rehearse their craft, so no matter how advanced we may think we are, it still behooves us to have a discipline in our practice.

## Creating Personal Triggers

Another important skill that will assist us in maintaining that informal practice is the creation of personal triggers. These are simple, everyday actions that we can reprogram to act as reminders for whatever piece of personal practice we wish. For example, when I am in my store I make myself available to customers for their magical questions. I have made it a personal habit that each and every time a customer asks me a question I immediately perform a quick and simple Soul Alignment. This takes place in a single breath and no one outside myself would notice a thing. But *I* notice, and it keeps me doing this essential piece of the foundational work repeatedly and not just once in front of my altar in the morning.

Author T. Thorn Coyle writes about this, which she calls Creating Keys of Remembrance.[65] This doesn't necessarily need to be a trigger to perform a certain task, but perhaps just to calm and "tune in" to your inner voice, an opportunity to simply wake up in the moment and be aware of your surroundings. These triggers can be anything at all: turning on or off a light switch, walking through a doorway, brushing your teeth, checking your rearview mirror, anything and nearly everything can be transformed into a trigger simply by using it as such.

It may be difficult in the beginning, as often we will remember after the fact and perhaps lament our missed opportunities that we unconsciously had throughout the day. But even this is a positive step, as we are closer than we had been otherwise. Continue with your efforts and you will soon find that you *are* remembering to use your triggers, more and more. And eventually you will find that your informal practice is doing its job and you are more often able to find yourself in that magical state of enchantment from which we will do the deeper work.

Though we will soon begin traveling into the worlds above and below, we begin our journeying by first going "sideways" in *this* one.

## The Thirteen Planes of Progression

At the heart of our tradition is the practice of astral flight. Competent Witches must be able to project their consciousness into other realms at will to learn the deeper secrets of our Craft. Equally important is the skill to safely return as well as to retain whatever knowledge was uncovered. All too often knowledge gained in this way is fleeting, but a memory, and then gone. We must begin to shape our consciousness into a worthy vessel for the power and knowledge we seek to gain. The Thirteen Planes of Progression, also called the "Side Planes," collectively form a map of "worlds within worlds." It describes those various bands of vibrational energy that form the material world in which the full spectrum of human consciousness interacts. Each of the thirteen planes can be understood as being stacked one upon another, from bottom to top.

---

65. T. Thorn Coyle, *Evolutionary Witchcraft* (New York: Tarcher/Penguin, 2004), 22–23.

Each world has their own set of planes, the highest and lowest of these planes marking their inverse in the immediately adjacent worlds. In other words, our lowest plane is the highest for the world below us, and our highest plane is the lowest for the world above. Our "above" is their "below." This pattern continues on and on, in an ongoing chain beyond the reach of our comprehension.

According to tradition, the planes from highest to lowest are characterized by the following colors:

| Chart of Thirteen Planes of Progression |
|:---:|
| WHITE |
| VIOLET |
| INDIGO |
| BLUE |
| BLUE-GREEN |
| GREEN |
| YELLOW-GREEN |
| YELLOW |
| ORANGE-YELLOW |
| ORANGE |
| MOONLIGHT |
| RED |
| BLACK |

The lower first three levels—black, red, and moonlight—are collectively called the sleep or dream levels. These are the varying levels of our awareness while dreaming, while asleep, or in deep trance. The lowest vibration, black, is the Abyss, the area in which nightmares occur. It is the primal, chthonic power that houses most of what we fear and therefore much power. Out of the Abyss we rise up into the place of primal, sexual power. The red level is where most sexual dreams appear. This plane is primal, ruled by fetch and pulsing with life force. Moonlight is next, considered to be a color in its own right and is the level from which most dreams arise.

Orange is the first dawning of our waking consciousness ascending from the depths of unconsciousness, where fetch moves into talker. The light of our awareness gradually increases, moving into orange-yellow, and then, as the dawn turns into full day, we bask in the yellow light. When we are experiencing a heightened sense of openness and intuition, we can even vibrate at the yellow-green level.

While these previous four levels collectively represent the area in which most people normally operate, our job as Witches is to continue our evolution toward godhood. Toward this end we work to ascend into the green level, thus beginning our true journey upward toward our higher consciousness. Here we experience a true opening of the heart and experience the emotional connections that we share with others in the world. Rising up into blue-green, we begin to experience these connections not just to people, but also to everything in our environment.

At the blue level we begin to deepen our psychic sight, and at indigo this deepens even further. Violet is that level just below our daemon and is where that soul sends blessings down to us. The white level (also referred to by the Celtic word *Gwynved*) is the level at which our holy daemon operates and interacts with the gods. It is this level, especially, with which we must attune in order to increase our power and ability to commune with gods, spirits, and powers beyond ourselves.

Our lore stipulates that we should begin this work at the level of yellow, a good midrange for normal human waking consciousness, and work our way down one by one to black, ascending the same way up to white, and then again descending and ending in yellow once more where we began. This serves to ground us first in talker, which assists us in avoiding getting stuck if we were to otherwise begin in the Nightmare Realm. From personal experience, I can attest that even following the above procedure there are times when visiting that realm in which the energy feels "sticky," as if it is resisting my attempts to leave, and can make the transition upward sluggish and difficult. (And trust me, this is not a place you want to hang out for any significant length of time without definite purpose or protection.)

## *Progressing Through the Planes Exercise*

The technique itself is a simple one, but it is not advised that it be performed while tired or emotionally upset.

Items needed:
Your black Star Goddess candle
Matches

Open the Way. Close your eyes and visualize your immediate environment. Imagine yourself and your environment as being bathed in a bright yellow light. Feel your full, waking, alert consciousness and notice how your body feels as well as your emotional state. Take time to examine every detail of your environment though the lens of this radiant color. You may find it helpful to softly repeat to yourself "yel-low…yellow…yellow" as a means to further anchor your consciousness in that band of energy.

After about one to two minutes begin to imagine the color shifting, becoming more golden until it is a radiant yellow-orange. Do the same as above, now chanting "yellow-orange" if desired, before imagining the light shifting into orange, chanting "orange," etc. After some time here, we shift into the ghostly, silver moonlight. Again examine what you see here. Then shift to red, and then finally to black, following the same procedures. Spend only a few moments in black at first, and then rise up the way you came, one by one, spending time in each, passing yellow and moving up through yellow-green, green, blue-green, blue, indigo, violet, and finally up into white. Spend extra time focusing on the vibration of this color realm and listen for whatever your daemon may have for you. Then move back down each color to end where you began, in yellow.

Once you have performed this exercise several times and feel comfortable with it, you may spend more time in each level, noticing if there are spirits that you are able to interact with. Always remember to begin by Opening the Way, which includes a strong alignment of your souls. When we are aligned with our daemon, we are free to interact with other spirits as naturally as we would with any other person. But if we are not aligned with our daemon, spirits could do terrible things to us. Attuning ourselves to the white plane will feed and strengthen our connection to daemon and prevent anything malefic from attaching itself to our energy bodies. Vibrating at this level for just a couple minutes for a few times per week should be sufficient in creating this effect.

Repeated journeying through all the levels of the Side Planes will, over time, attune us to their vibrational frequencies, allowing our consciousness to continue its evolutionary journey toward godhood. Once we have mastered this technique, we can invoke the color spectrum of the planes in order to bring about our own full spectrum of consciousness, bringing our full selves into our work. "We would know ourselves in all our parts."

### Returning to the Body Spell

To bring someone back from possession or astral travel.

Items needed:
Your black Star Goddess candle
Matches
A bowl or glass of cold water

Open the Way. Look the person in the eyes and say:

> *Elvar rides over the sea*
> *On the magic steed of black.*
> *Atho here shall now retrieve*
> *The traveling soul and bring it back.*
> *From in between the worlds unseen*
> *From the castle in the sky*
> *Return to where we now convene*
> *Horse of the witch. Blink of the eye!* [66]

On the last line, splash some of the cold water in the person's face.

While this incantation is original to BlueRose, it is based on oral lore from Old Faery, where it is explained that Atho is another name for the Blue God. This

---

66. An adaptation of Faery oral tradition.

is a petition to the Blue God/holy daemon to assist in guiding back that part of the soul, which is out traveling, namely the fetch. *Atho* is a name of the Witches' Horned God and is thought to be an English corruption of the old Welsh *Arddhu*. With this in mind, the lore connecting it to our Blue God certainly brings up some interesting questions. My interpretation is that this is really a reference to the daemon (Blue God) working with the Arddhu (the horned figure of Death and Necromancy). The Arddhu and the Blue God/holy daemon together are the powers that we are invoking in order to bring back an errant fetch. It is their *union* that helps facilitate a safe return from in between the realms of life and death.

The name *Elvar* is Icelandic and is a variant of the Old Norse *Alfarr*, which translates to "elf warrior." As a reference to the individual's fetch, this might refer to our own "Faery nature," our fetch being that part of our soul structure that is magical: it fares forth into the other worlds in various forms.

## The Faery Tree

The Faery Tree (or Faery Rose Tree) is an *axis mundi* that we may use as a sort of "psychic anchor" for when we begin traversing the various worlds beyond our own. This simple addition to the Faery/Feri tradition was inspired by the work of R. J. Stewart and entered into the Bloodrosian lineages through Sacred Wheel, a loose confederation of Faery initiates, teachers, and their students in the San Francisco Bay Area in the early to late 1990s.

During this period, many Faery initiates were avidly working with Stewart's folkloric Faery material and finding deep resonances between the two traditions. These resonances were so deep, in fact, that Victor Anderson himself spoke of whatever differences the two traditions had as being "very little," referencing Stewart's Scottish heritage and his own Irish. He then went further to say that their Faery Traditions were, in one sense, one and the same:

> *We found in talking together that we have the same tradition! It's just a difference in language, a difference in climate, a difference in race. And it brings home to me over and over again that racism should have no part in our study, because this religion that we are interested in is the religion of the human race, which originated in Mother Africa.*[67]

---

67. Victor Anderson, PantheaCon, 1996.

While there are certainly discernible differences in ritual custom between these two manifestations of Faery, this shared human heritage is at the heart of our tradition and is symbolically reflected in the image of the Faery Tree, which stands between the worlds, allowing access between them all. Faery is everywhere, in all times and places and cultures. While each branch may bear a different color rose, they are each part of the same tree, as are we all.

*Figure 20: Faery Tree*

### *Summoning the Tree Exercise*

Items needed:
Your black Star Goddess candle
Matches

Open the Way. Summon the Crossroads. As you stand in the magical space where the roads cross, reaffirm your Grounding exercise... see and feel your fetch forming into roots, which then flow down into the land and into the center of the earth. Anchored to the planet, breathe the pulsing life force of the earth upward, feeling it flood your body to flow upward filling your body and your talker. Breathing deep, feel this power flow from fetch and into your daemon, which flows out through your shoulders and crown as branches that reach up and into the stars above. Feel how this tree—*your* tree—anchors and centers you, between above and below, but also between north and south and east and west. Feel this tree as an ancient guardian that stands at the center of all the worlds. Notice the quality of the roots... gnarled and earthen. See the trunk, its bark and its textures. See the branches, now filled with a myriad of many colored roses in various stages of bloom, catching the starlight with each petal. Take some time to really feel this form using all of your senses.

When you are ready, take a deep breath and imagine stepping *backward* and out from this form, which remains before you. Behold the Faery Tree between the worlds! State an affirmation of the tree and how it exists between all the worlds. You may use the following incantation, or some inspired words of your own choosing.

> *Between the worlds there grows a tree*
> *At the crossing of the roads.*
> *Deep of root and branches free*
> *Adorned with starlit faery rose*
> *Twixt north and south*
> *And east and west*
> *Tween earth and fire*
> *Wind and sea*
> *The stars above*

*The stars below*
*The flame within*
*So must it be!*

Take in every detail of this tree before you. Notice how the gnarled roots flow down into the underworld and how its branches stretch up and out into the over-world, connecting to the aetheric realms below and above while its trunk anchors them both to the middleworld. From each of the cardinal directions a colored road runs directly to the tree, connecting it to the elemental powers.

Take some time communing with the Faery Tree. You may find that there are attendant beings associated with the tree. Often a serpent can be found in its branches or roots; openings often appear in various places in and around the tree, which serve as portals to other worlds and powers. Take as much time as you need to really examine the tree and your feelings about it, and then return to normal consciousness, ending as normal. Remember to record your experiences in your journal.

—————————————————————

The Faery Tree is our spiritual anchor when traversing the shamanic realms. This tree will serve to call you back from in between the worlds should your journeys there prove difficult. You would be wise to obtain a likeness or image that to you represents the Faery Tree. This will be used as a type of trigger to allow you to both anchor more securely prior to your trance journeys as well as at their conclusion to help bring all pieces of your consciousness back with you when you return.

When setting out to engage these other words we must make certain that we are beginning from a solid foundation. If you have been working diligently with the exercises in this book, then you will have developed some skill in achieving a state of aligned enchantment. This means that you are grounded, conscious, clear-minded, and able to move into a deep trance *and return with clear memories of the events that transpired*. If you are not yet to a stage in which you can clearly go into trance, gather information, and return with your memory fairly intact *on command* then you are not yet ready to move on to the next chapter. Continue working with the previous material until you feel secure in your abilities. This work will be here for you when you are ready.

CHAPTER 14

# THE UNDERWORLD

*The descent to the Underworld is easy. Night and day the gates of shadowy Death*
*stand open wide, but to retrace your steps, to climb back to the upper air—*
*there the struggle, there the labor lies.*
—VIRGIL, *THE AENEID*

The underworld is related to aether below and is the realm that vibrates just beneath our normal perception. It is a reflection of this world, and vice versa. For our purposes here, we will approach this realm as being twofold, as it is associated both with the dead as well as with the Fae. Both of these realms are associated with the *second sight*, a term that refers to the natural ability to see into the other worlds and commune with the inhabitants there. This could manifest as prophetic visions, seeing the Fae, or seeing the spirits of the dead.

We see this duality reflected in the Wheel of the Year in which we experience the energies of the earth as both waxing and waning. These natural currents of seasonal power shift the natural course of our underworld contacts. These shifts are marked with the highest holy days on the Faery Tradition: Samhain and Beltane, the "gates of the year." These celebrations mark the shifting of the tides of psychic power in the earth and ourselves. Because these are natural observances and not able to be accurately tied to a fixed calendar in our lineage, we observe these celebrations using their astrological dates, which vary from year to year. In the Northern Hemisphere these are Beltane at 15 degrees Taurus and Samhain at 15 degrees Scorpio. Check an ephemeris to see the exact date (and time!) that these shifts will occur, and plan your rites accordingly.

Life and death are two sides of the same coin, a passing through the veil from one form to another. In Faery, we work to become intimately familiar with this veil. Like with a lover, we strive to learn every curve, every nuance. We learn where to apply our power and consciousness to get the results that we desire. We work to be able to first perceive it, and then to draw it back and peer through.

## The Underworld Journey

When journeying to the underworld we will follow these basic steps, elaborating on them for the purposes of traveling to specific locations within the underworld or to seek audience with specific beings. This process draws from the work of R. J. Stewart and found its way into our tradition during the 1980s and 90s.

1. Open the Way.

2. Summon the Faery Tree.

3. Conjure an opening in the ground or in the roots or trunk of the tree. This could be a door, a cave, a well, a cavern, or even a rabbit hole. The form doesn't matter; we just need a symbolic opening into the world below.

4. Imagine climbing down into the opening with the definite intention to seek the underworld. (If you are seeking an audience with a particular underworld being, then you will make that intention here and may wish to speak it aloud as a spoken spell.) For your first journey, I would recommend your intention be to visit the Hag and the Dark One.

5. Find some mechanism to descend in a clockwise spiral. Sometimes this is a staircase made of stone while other times it is the roots from the tree.

6. Descend into a cavernous place. Here you may experience contacts with spirits, gods, guides, etc. Pay attention to whatever transpires here. You may be shown entrances to other places within the underworld or may be greeted by different attending spirits. If you had an intention to seek a particular being you may wish to call to them here. Make whatever offerings or observances you feel appropriate.

7. When complete, reverse your steps and ascend the spiral stairway (winding up and counterclockwise) until you reach the top.

8. Emerge through the same opening you entered, closing it behind you.

9. Once more, affirm the presence of the Faery Tree and your place in the center of the crossroads.

10. End as normal.

## Samhain: The Feast of the Dead

A common practice in many tribal traditions—of which Faery can most certainly be classified—is the spiritual communication and reverence of one's ancestors. It is understood in systems that observe these practices that ancestral spirits are closer to us than other spirits with whom we may also work, already being "attuned" to our particular genetic and/or spiritual consciousness. They are thus more immediate and accessible than spirits of other classifications, such as angels, demons, faery, totemic, and discarnate humans who are not directly connected to us.

Working with spirits is a staple in Traditional Witchcraft, so much so that it is the one area of magic that all traditions of Witchcraft follow, regardless of era, culture, or location. Being able to invoke, summon, consult, and give charge to spirits is a primal and powerful form of magic that all true practitioners of the Craft should command.

While in primitive societies the direct influence of one's ancestral heritage was more apparent, in modern times many of us have drifted away from our genetic and cultural connections, either because of negative experiences, such as abuse or trauma, or just lack of knowledge, such as might be experienced in cases of adoption. One's ancestral lineage is important in that it connects us backward through time to the great beginning; there is an individual conduit of power that stretches to us back from the beginning of time, and in Witchcraft part of this power is drawn in one's spiritual lineage. In initiatory Witchcraft traditions, this is the lineage that maps the succession of initiations stretching back to Gerald Gardner (as is the case with Wicca) or Victor Anderson (as with Faery Witchcraft).

Samhain is the time of remembering the ancestors, both our *Beloved Dead* who are our personal ancestors, and the *Mighty Dead*, great and powerful Witches who have passed on and now act as spirit guides from beyond the veil in order to help better the Craft. This celebration is astrologically marked when the Sun is at 15 degrees Scorpio (generally around November 5 to 7) and is traditionally held well after dark. It is often said that the veil is at its thinnest at this time, making it much easier to get in contact with spirits of the dead. In truth, the veil has been in the process of thinning for some time, and this celebration marks the height of that phenomena. The natural tides of power are flowing heavily from the land of the dead and into our realm at this time, and so we take advantage of this opportunity to invite our ancestors to join with us and to partake of the offerings that we lay out for them, and in exchange we might partake of some of their wisdom.

It is here that we perform the Opening of the Western Gate, which is the literal opening of a portal into the realm of the dead. While we can open this gate at any time throughout the year, the connection to the dead is most strong and clear during this particular time, intensifying the experience. For those who are naturally attuned to the dead this will be a relatively simple process, the ritual providing a container for their natural talents. For others, this will first require establishing regular practice of contact with the dead, and the best way to do this is to begin with one's own ancestors.

## Ancestor Reverence

Faery Tradition is deeply rooted in ancestral reverence. When initiated in our tradition, one is ritually and spiritually adopted into a family and it is believed that our very essence is forever altered, marking us as Fae. We are (of course) still human. But now we are something *more*. Because of this familial connection, the tradition makes little distinction between biological or spiritual ancestors as both are of our Beloved Dead. You are close to your grandmother because of bloodlines, and for those of us who have undergone the initiation we are close to those in our initiatic lineages in much the same way. We work to maintain connections with our Beloved Dead in order to continue growing in knowledge and power. These spirits are "closest" to us, and they usually will have our best interests at heart. This makes them powerful allies when beginning our explorations into the land of the dead.

### Spirits of the Dead Oil Recipe [68]

8 parts jasmine
4 parts wormwood
1 part patchouli

These may be essential oils or dried herbs or any combination of the two that results in a fragrance that is both pleasing and evokes the sense of the dead. They may all be placed into a carrier oil (such as sweet almond or jojoba) and stored in

---

68. This recipe comes from my husband, Faery initiate, and Conjure worker, Chas Bogan.

an airtight container in a dark, cool, dry place. An oil stored properly should last one to two years before spoiling. A drop or two can be dripped onto a lit charcoal to act as an incense, or it may be worn when engaging ancestral work.

---

## The Ancestral Altar

In the west, prepare an altar with a black cloth. Upon it, place the image of a skull along with a white candle. If possible, above the altar place a mirror. Adorn the altar with images of your ancestors or items that they owned or that represents them to you. Photographs in little frames… an old pair of eyeglasses… ashes in an urn. On my ancestor altar I have an unopened pack of cigarettes that belonged to my grandmother. It is in a small wooden box, atop which I have placed a small plastic dove that was a remembrance token given out at her funeral after releasing doves in a rite to honor her transition. When I connect with this token, I am transported back into that grief-wrought and powerful time, and it enables me to better open up to the realm of the dead.

Choose a particular ancestor with whom you wish to work. Closer ancestors are better in the beginning, unless you are already feeling a strong pull to another. Once chosen make sure that their image or an item representing them is prominently displayed on the altar before you. Once adorned we begin our work.

Items needed:
Your black Star Goddess candle
Matches
A glass of water
A white candle
A piece of parchment paper
A pen
Some incense
Spirits of the Dead oil
A bottle of florida water
A plate of food and/or cup of beverage for an offering to your ancestor

Open the Way. Once enchanted, sprinkle some florida water around yourself and the altar as a means to help draw in positive spiritual forces. Light the incense. Dress the white candle with the oil and place it in the center of the altar. Focus upon your particular ancestor, and call out their name three times. Tell them why you wish to work with them and what you would like to get out of the exchange. Let them know that you are interested in helping them continue their journey of empowerment and evolution and that you will work in tandem with them toward your mutual betterment. Make a sigil of their name and draw this on the parchment paper. Fold it toward yourself and place it underneath the candle. Light the candle and again call out their name three times.

Now, in the space of enchantment, open up through your daemon and out into the mythical west. To the ancient Irish, the "western lands" were the land of the dead. Gaze through the smoke, seeing it as a means to carry your prayers into the aether worlds. Place the food and/or beverage offering upon the altar and let your ancestor know that this is for them. This is a gift of life force and it strengthens the connecting link that we share. Take some time to be in a silent, observational space. After some time has passed, end by thanking your ancestor and extinguishing the white candle. End as normal, and (as always) record your experiences in your magical journal.

Adopt this rite or similar into your regular practice. After some time you will start to find that the presence of this ancestor feels stronger and may appear even without being called or fed. Use your intuition in regards to what offerings they may wish. If your ancestor had a particular food or drink that they loved in life, then that is a pretty safe space from which to begin. But what of those ancestors whom we never met or our family histories have little or no information? This is where we must use a bit of both trial and error as well as our own psychic sensitivities. Traditionally, offerings of whiskey are given to the dead, so you may wish to do this. This can become problematic for those spirits who had addictions to alcohol in life, and so you may wish to use something like coffee or tea instead, or even offerings of juice or milk. Over time you will start to get definite ideas as to what they want for an offering. These messages will likely come in the form of a little voice or inner knowing. Do not expect them to be huge, earth-shattering events or you are likely to miss these messages when they arrive. Once you have formed a strong bond of communication with an ancestor spirit, you may begin working in more specific directions, such as asking them to assist you in certain magical workings or areas of your life.

## The Mighty Dead

These are spirits of powerful Witches and Warlocks who stand on the other side of the veil, ready to assist us in our deeper workings toward the evolution of Witchcraft. These spirits have gained power over several lifetimes in the Craft and may be reborn at certain times in order to drive the Craft where it needs to go. In death, they assist as spirit guides. In life they are *ta'veren*,[69] powerful beings who act as luminaries and great teachers for the age.

While it is true that we call upon the Mighty Dead at Samhain, we also call to them throughout the year as well. To them we are connected by the mythical Black Thread, the spiritual line of transmission by which we can interact with their consciousness. Being initiated into a tradition that has energetic access to this line of transmission will greatly assist the practitioner in contacting and working with these powerful beings, but this is by no means the only way to achieve this connection. Certain individuals have left their marks on Craft history and may be contacted as easily as we would any other spirit, as long as we are aligned and enchanted.

## The Grandmaster's Chair

One curious piece of Faery lore involves the Grandmaster's Chair. This is a special altar that is placed in the northwest area of the circle. It consists of a chair draped with a black cloth, upon which a red silk pillow is placed that holds a (preferably) human skull. (This can be a facsimile, for convenience.) Before it is placed a red candle. This is to represent the Grandmasters of the tradition, those individuals who have given their life to the Faery Tradition and who act as resources for our tribe.

My Grandmaster's Chair is my late grandmother's rocking chair. I have also added two small framed photographs of Victor and Cora Anderson, along with a sculpture of a skull that I consecrated the night of Victor's memorial, underneath a very rare and spectacular lightning display over our shared home of the San Francisco Bay area. After Opening the Western Gate and inviting in the Beloved and Mighty Dead, I will often take

---

69. This term was coined by the late author Robert Jordan for his fictional series *The Wheel of Time*. It refers to certain individuals who by their very nature affect the course of events in order to bring balance to the overall pattern. Following in the footsteps of those other Faery who also drew literary elements into their lines from the Hidden Kingdom, I have adopted this term into BlueRose and feel a strong correlation between this idea and the periodic rebirth of the Mighty Dead of the Craft.

a moment and call in the lineage of the Grandmasters to watch over and bless my various rites, thus keeping their lineages alive.

## Opening the Western Gate Ritual

In the oral tradition, there is a particular non-English incantation that is used to open this portal. If we were sitting together in my office or my home, or even together over the phone or webcam, I would recite this verse and explain its esoteric meaning. But since this book is not an oral medium, I will have to refrain and will instead offer something of my own creation that I have found to be effective in doing this work.

Items needed:
Your black Star Goddess candle
Matches
Three candles: one each of red, black, and white
A mirror (to remain veiled until needed)
A ritual blade
A cup for the Waters of Purity rite

Arrange the altar so that the white candle is in the middle, the black on the left, and the red on the right. The mirror should be just behind and above the middle of the altar area. Open the Way. Cast a circle if you feel it is appropriate to your working. Invoke the Faery Tree and journey downward into the underworld. When you feel yourself as having completed your descent, open your eyes and stand before the ancestral altar in your physical working area and attune your consciousness toward it and the dead. Imagine how you are in both places at once, you are "between the worlds." Light the white candle with a silent prayer for those who have gone before and unveil the mirror. Reach out with your awareness into the realm of the dead; feel the veil that separates the two worlds as thin, but present. Stand before the altar with you blade in your hands, pointing up at heart level. Recite the following incantation:

*I stand between the worlds of fate*
*And summon forth the Western Gate*

*By my blade I part the veil*
*Across the sea*[70] *we set our sail.*

Breathe power into yourself and, by extension, the blade. Use your tool to slice open the space before you and the mirror with a vertical slash. See it separating the veil. Breathe into it, then reach into the edges of this "crack in the worlds" and, with a quick, sweeping motion of your arms, open the gate, ending with your arms open, imagining the veil-gate open wide before you. Recite:

*By moon that hangs low in the sky,*
*By ancient sea, the earth's own womb,*
*I call the Gate to open wide,*
*That leads to life beyond the tomb.*

Take a moment to feel this power shine upon you from the gate and know that *you* are the gate; the opening and the mirror are but extensions of your spiritual power. When ready, light the red candle from the white, and invoke the Beloved Dead:

*Oh, you of the Beloved Dead,*
*The Respected Ones,*
*The Mothers and Fathers of our blood,*
*Who laughed and lived and cried and loved*
*We are your children*
*Come to us.*

Reach out through your daemon and invite the Beloved Dead to come through the portal. Give yourself a moment to feel a connection to them. When you feel their presence, continue:

---

70. The imagery of the sea is invoked here in reference both to the sea being the hidden temple of water in the west, but also in reference of the "astral waves." The ocean, its waves, and its depths were often a poetic metaphor for traveling on the astral.

*Flesh and bone now laid to rest,*
*Into the earth, our Mother's breast,*
*Now by your names we here invite,*
*Into our circle on this night.*

You may invite them each by name and make any offerings that you wish. Spend a few minutes with them and be aware of any communications that you may have. This might be a good time to perform divinations or specific work involving the spirits.

Now, light the black candle from the white and invoke the Mighty Dead:

*Oh, you of the Mighty Dead!*
*We call you from between the worlds!*
*Ancient Ones!*
*Mothers and Fathers of the Craft!*
*Who watched the stars,*
*Who read the signs,*
*Who worked the herbs,*
*Who made the magic.*
*We are your children,*
*Come to us!*

As before, you may light any special candles representing the specific Mighty Dead that you wish to work with (Victor, Cora, Gwydion, etc.) and call out their names, along with any titles or descriptions of accomplishments that are relevant to their mythology. Take some time to honor their presence.

If you are celebrating the Samhain rite, then this is the time in which you offer food to the ancestors and Mighty Dead. Traditionally, this is done in complete silence and the coven will share a meal with their dead until the bell is rung, signaling the return to the world of the living. It is traditional to allow the candles used in the ritual to burn all the way out before removing any spent offerings and disposing of them in a sacred manner.

## *Closing the Gate Ritual*

Say good-bye to each of the ancestors that you called, usually in the reverse order of their invoking. When finished, say:

> *You of the Mighty Dead,*
> *Ancient Mothers and Fathers of the Craft,*
> *You of the Beloved Dead,*
> *Respected Mothers and Fathers of our blood,*
> *May you continue to guide us from your shining realms,*
> *And may there ever be peace between us.*

Extinguish the black and red candles. Holding the blade in one hand, extend your arms out to your sides so that your chest and stance are wide open as you face the gate/mirror.

Breathing into the very edges of the energetic gate, grasp them and pull them in toward each other in one quick motion as you exhale quickly. Imagine the vertical slash of light before you and "seal" it closed with Blue Fire from the tip of your blade, slowly moving from the bottom upward until done. Trace a pentacle over the area, feeling this repair, and bless the fabric of reality. Affirm: *"The gate is closed."*

Extinguish the white candle. Perform the Waters of Purity rite. Record all of your experiences in your journal.

---

# Beltane: The Faery Rade

During the time of the dark half of the year, it is easier to contact the dead in the underworld, and during the light half it is easier to contact the Fae. Celebrated astrologically when the sun reaches 15 degrees Taurus, Beltane is a festival of sexual ecstasy, at a time in which the veil is again at its thinnest, but this time the natural tides of power in the land is that from the land of the Fae; the rising life force of ecstasy, sensuality, and enchantment.

Drawing from the mythic stories of the Faery Rade, the annual procession of the Fae to a celebratory feast, we observe the rising of the Fae power into the land as the spirit of sex, beauty, pleasure, and renewal. The rushing of the procession of the Faery through the eastern gate is observed with some trepidation: folklore warns us to place a rowan branch over one's door when watching the Faery Rade or else run risk of being snatched up by the Faery and taken into their realm to who knows what fate. This is an obvious reflection of the Wild Hunt often celebrated at Samhain. Here we summon forth the Fae and invite them to celebrate with us as we join in this natural tide of rising power. At this time, we invoke the holy lust of life and revel in the ecstatic outpouring of the spirit of enchanted nature.

The bond between Witches and Faeries is deep and inseparable. Witches have always been said to work with imps and spirits and fairies. In Leland's *Aradia* we see the Great Goddess Diana who is described as the Queen of the Witches and the Faeries.

There is no consensus, even among Faery initiates, as to what *exactly* the Fae are. We can easily speak in generalities: they are a magical and noble race … they live in the underworld … they have a history of interacting with humans, etc. But we can't get too specific, as they always wriggle out of a solid definition. They are always the color that runs outside the lines. They are never quite here, but never quite gone. They are seen out of the corner of your eye. You know you saw them, but now you just can't be sure. The old tales speak of how time runs differently in their realm; minutes from our perspective could be years when lost in Faery, while one could be gone tens of years only to return just days or even hours later. We are to understand that the governing laws that rule our world simply do not apply to them, or at least not in the same way. They are the very essence of *enchantment*, and through interaction with them a Witch can gain much power *if* able to master oneself in the process. We must be "clean" in our dealings and *especially* when dealing with the Fae. Their morality is not a human one and we will have failed the moment we forget that. Not all Fae are friendly to humans, which is why our tradition has specific beings and rules with which we work, thus lessening the possibility of a negative encounter. If we have cultivated the Warrior's Will and have been working the points of the Iron Pentacle, then we will have gone far toward ensuring safe encounters while dealing in their realm.

They are the spiritual life force within the land. It is they who comprise the "fetch of the planet." They are the living presence of the land that sustains us, and they have been pleading with us for centuries. As the modern age has moved blindly onward, we have been complicit in the destruction of the natural world. We are destroying the earth at an alarming rate, and the Fae are appealing to those of us who can hear their call to spread the word: we need to change our ways. And fast.

The main thing that we have lost can still be recovered: a spiritual awareness of the sacredness of the land itself and all that lives upon it. And this is exactly what the Fae are offering us: an opportunity to re-sacralize our relationship to the land and to creation itself, to begin to see the interconnectedness of all life. To have the knowledge that human, faery, ancestor, animal, plant, land, and the divine all form a holy septagram of interconnected consciousness. Once we form spiritual bonds with the land and its unseen inhabitants we become champions for that land.

While at Samhain we work to open the western gate and commune with the spirits of the dead, BlueRose celebrates Beltane by opening the *eastern* gate and communing with the spirits of the Fae.

### Opening the Eastern Gate Charm

*By sun that rises in the sky*
*By ancient wind, the earth's own breath,*
*I call the Gate to open wide,*
*That leads to life that defies death.*

*By flesh and bone and quickened blood*
*Aroused by touch to passions' flood*
*We here invite the Shining Fae*
*To join our revelry this day.*

In Wicca, Beltane is a fertility festival celebrating the fertility of the land, of livestock, and of humans alike. While Faery *can* certainly celebrate fertility, being a tradition centered on altered states of awareness, it is far more likely to be focused on the ecstatic elements of the sexual imagery rather than the fertility aspect. That being said, for us Beltane is a celebration of sex and all that entails. As this is something that the Fae are often quite interested in as well.

As the rising spirit of the land, they are the spirit of sexuality, as all life is sexual. And since they often present themselves as exactly what you find to be beautiful, it might be quite tempting to engage in astral sex with them in the trance state. While this isn't always a bad idea, keep in mind that sexual relations with these beings constitute a type of contract. You really had better know the fine print ahead of time. The Fae are famous for their trickster ways, but this might be unfair; they simply have a different set of morals and culture. After you have formed a deep and trusting relationship with a Fae being you *may* wish to engage in what has been called a Faery Marriage, which is a bond on the soul level with a Fae being that goes beyond lifetimes. But for now we will begin by journeying to the underworld to seek a Faery ally.

---

## Traditional Prohibitions

These prohibitions are mainly collected from folklore and represent the traditional methods in which the human race has learned to protect themselves from certain negative aspects of the Fae encounter. While these all tend to make sense for the beginner, after some time we might be more relaxed in our approach, even violating these taboos once we have trust in our allies and the path before us. But before getting ahead of ourselves, we should be grounded in a common sense approach when it comes to the Fae.

1. **Do not eat or drink anything while in Faery.** This is a long-standing rule: when in Faery anything that we eat or drink will cause us to remain in Faery, sometimes forever. This is a type of "energetic contract" and unless you are truly prepared to spend your life in service to the Fae, consider a light snack beforehand and leave the Fae food for the Fae.

2. **Do not engage in sexual activity with the Fae.** This is really an extension of rule #1. To engage in sex with a Fae being is a type of contract, and you could get much more than you bargained for. And for much, much longer.

3. **Do not engage in bloodletting.** This was not something that I think I would have thought of before, had I not had a student experience this very thing. Again, this is an extension of the previous rules. If you shed blood in their realm it is possible for them to use that blood for some purpose, in essence it is giving your power away.

4. **Do not say "thank you" to the Fae.** This one struck me as quite odd when it was first taught to me. Having been raised with what I would like to consider are good manners, the thought of not thanking someone for their services was quite abhorrent to me—that is, until it was adequately explained that the difference in morality and culture meant that from their perspective our "thank you" amounts to nothing more than empty words, based on how we use our words with each other: we often tell people we are "fine" when we don't mean it, we ask how someone is doing when

we don't really care, etc. To the Fae, actions speak louder than words. So if you want to thank a Fae, send a sense of gratitude from your heart center, make an offering, but keep the "thank-yous" to yourself.

## Journey to the Mound Trance Work

Here we intend to journey into the underworld to seek the realm of Faery to make a contact as an ally. Follow the procedure given previously for the journey into the underworld. As you move into the cavernous space below look far beneath you and you can see how the staircase spirals farther downward toward a strange blue shimmering light. As you get closer to that light you see that it is an opening, and you see what appears to be impossible: it is a wide-open sunless sky, yet bright as a twilit morning. As you move through this opening, you find yourself climbing *up* and out of an old well and into a beautiful field of silver-green grass, which is swaying in an unfelt breeze.

As you look, a path has opened in the grass that leads straight ahead of you and just almost to the edge of what appears to be a dark forest. Though other paths may open up around you, you follow *only* this main path straight ahead, which crosses the field of swaying grass and then bends abruptly to the right. It follows alongside the edge of the dark forest, which is now on your left. As you follow this path, you sense that there are many unseen beings hiding in the forest, but you stay on this path. Looking ahead you can see—off in the distance—a beautiful natural mound, just to the right of the end of the path ahead. As you get closer you see it is covered with grass, plants, flowers, and small shrubs. You get the sense that it is ancient beyond all knowing. You walk around the mound clockwise three times, looking for an opening.

When you finally find it you step through into a small chamber, which is guarded by a small nonhuman being. Focus on your purpose here: to make an ally from this realm. Make this purpose as clear as crystal in your mind. See your talker shining like a golden sun. Now, feel this intent clearly with fetch. See the red moon glowing in your belly and sex. Now, feel the daemon's shining Blue Flame above you and within you, guiding all Three Souls into a unified shining light that shines your clear intention to this small being. With open mind, with open heart, with open sex. So Must It Be.

The being will respond either by barring your path or by stepping aside to allow you entry to the small door behind them. If they block your path, just end the session and return to it again later. If you are continually blocked, then you may wish to do some more work with the Iron Pentacle and especially the Points of Flame before reattempting this work. Check in with the points of Iron and see of anything is too dark … too bright … or misaligned. How the connecting lines link the points together can be just as important as the points themselves. Do some cleansing on the connecting links.

Once you have been given access to the small door, crouch down and move through it and you find yourself in an impossibly long hallway, stretching left and right much longer than the entire width of the mound! To your right the hallway is dark, but the stone hallway is brightly lit with torches affixed to the walls on your left. Looking down this direction you see that the hallway ends in a set of grand double doors, finely worked with inlaid patterns and metalwork.

As you approach these doors they open as if by magic, and you hear the sounds of the revelry: music … drums, flutes, harps … and instruments you have never heard before. And you see the throng of people and other beings dancing, laughing. Each are dressed according to different eras of human history … and still others are wearing costumes unlike any you have ever seen. The smells of cooking food waft through the air, but you remember the prohibitions and so you dare not eat a bite. As you step into this grand ballroom you see how impossibly large it is: you cannot see the ceiling, for there are gathering clouds blocking your view! The room appears to be both indoors and outdoors … What appears to be walls around the large room seem to be formed from ghostly white trees that appear to lead into a mist-filled forest.

As you look around and take in the wondrous sight of it all you remember your purpose: to make a Faery ally. Again, with open mind, heart, and sex, *beam* this clear intention through your Three Souls aligned, and outward in the form of an invisible light that carries your message to these beings here. Maintain this sensation for a few moments and imagine one or more beings stepping forward from the crowd. If there are multiple beings coming forward, then use your intuition and choose which you think you would prefer to work with. Once chosen, ask them for their name. You may need to repeat your request several times if you are not in an optimally relaxed, receptive space. I find that repeating the question like a mantra sometimes helps me align into the moment a bit more. If they refuse to give you a name, then they are not right for this work and so *respectfully* decline their invitation and again beam you intent outward for another to step up. Once you have a being with a name you can clearly understand, ask them to give you a symbol that you can use to deepen your work with them. It can be anything at all (and it might change later)… something that you can easily visualize or draw. If you need to ask more than a couple times to get this, then you should skip to the end for the return trip back and try again another day.

Once you have your symbol firmly in your mind's eye, ask for the third and final piece: a physical gesture that you can perform to act as a trigger in order to call this being closer to you. Once you have your gesture, "activate" them here by speaking aloud your ally's name, visualizing the symbol, and performing the physical gesture. Once these have been done together in this realm they are keyed to your ally's presence. Once this has been completed, stay in their presence for a time and you may ask them whatever you'd like. Your job now is to *get to know them*; just the same as you would any new person you met and will be spending time with. When you are ready, we begin the journey back.

### The Return Journey

Now we finish our conversation with our ally and we back our way back through the throng to the double doors, which again open like magic at our approach. Walk back up the hallway toward the darkness and you see the small door to the right. Go through and you are in the small chamber with the guardian being. With open mind, heart, and sex, send a sense of sincere gratitude to this being as you exit the mound and follow the path the way you came.

Back on the path with the dark forest on your right, the path bending abruptly to the left and you follow it up through the grass to the well. Look inside and see the roots and steps and climb down into it, winding down and to the left. And you climb down counterclockwise you feel a shift and at some point you realize you are climbing *up*. Continue climbing counterclockwise up, up, up until you emerge at the crossroads and the Faery Tree. Take a moment to reaffirm the roads, the tree, and your own alignment. When you feel ready, end as normal and record your experiences.

Use the name, symbol, and gesture whenever you wish to do journey work or magic involving your ally, including when making an offering.

### *Making Offerings to the Fae Exercise*

Making offerings to the Fae is a traditional method of establishing a friendly relationship with them. European folktales give some examples of traditional offerings, such as milk, cream, and honey, as well as other foods and alcoholic beverages. We may use these as starter offerings, which will suffice until our local spirits communicate their preferences.

Sometimes these offerings are made in exchange for work done. Recall the fairy tales in which the elves fix the cobbler's shoes, and so forth. Sometimes these offerings are simply to keep the peace lest the Faeries come and work their mischief. Sometimes when we cannot find a lost object we will make an offering to them and we will usually find the object soon after: in an obvious place that we had already checked. It's happened too many times for us to be shocked anymore.

If possible, designate some space outside where you can Open the Way and sit undisturbed in contemplative silence. If this is not possible, choose a corner of your house or apartment for this task. Here you will make your offerings. If indoors, make sure to adorn the area with plants and stones and shiny objects of color. We have a little area in our living room in front of a large window. Out the window are some rose bushes and our aviary. Inside the corner is filed with plants, crystals, and other items befitting them. My husband crafted for us a beautiful Faery door, the kind you sometimes see in garden shops to add a touch of whimsy to the house or garden. Ours is adorned with crystals and stones, and it is a perfect meditative device: we place our offerings here, light a candle, and reach out to the presence of the Fae. Make this a part of your regular practice. Begin with a weekly practice of tending this space and making offerings. Remember to clean up any food offerings that have been sitting around for more than twenty-four hours.

# CHAPTER 15
## THE OVERWORLD

*Be humble for you are made of earth.*
*Be noble for you are made of stars.*
—SERBIAN PROVERB

The overworld is related to aether above and is the realm of the stars, celestial deities, and those stellar beings most often called angels. Our own Watchers are angelic beings, fallen as they are to our realm. In the language of symbolism this reveals that they are messengers from the overworld; they "fell" not in terms of any morality, but as in a descent into our realm to deliver their message, which is one of evolutionary transformation. As is true with all spirits, we receive more and more of their essence or message through our interaction with them. As we work with these beings and become familiar with their energetic signatures, we begin to take on certain qualities, traits, or powers from the spirit contact.

Our interaction with the overworld is shaped somewhat differently than with the underworld. Whereas with the underworld we can use the tree to journey below, with the overworld we can only go so far using this method, and so we must rely on spirits and alternate routes to get where we wish to go.

The Guardian eagle is an emissary not only of the realm of air, but also of the overworld, by way of the symbolism of flight. So too is the Azure Dove. In BlueRose, the overworld aspect of the Star Goddess is named *Quakoralina*, a traditional name for the Faery Goddess as named by Victor in his poetry. Call to these beings in their relation to the overworld and observe what transpires. It is important to refer to your journal entries to see if you can discern any patterns over longer periods of time. What sort of issues were you going through in life during these times? What were your strengths and weaknesses?

The main method we use for traveling to the overworld is to mimic the lines of communication of the Three Souls: namely, to descend into fetch in order to communicate with daemon. Using this model, it starts to make sense how one might be able to access the realm of the stars in the spirit world was by first traveling below.

This has a few key benefits from the more intuitive "direct method" of simply ascending the tree. One is that the experience seems to often be far more grounded; participants tend to be able to more easily recall their experiences than when using the direct method. Another advantage is that this provides access to an otherwise fairly nonintuitive natural flow of psychic power by revealing a secret door into the overworld, hidden in the underworld.

### The Overworld Journey Below Trance Work

Items needed:

Your black Star Goddess candle

Matches

Open the Way. Summon the tree. Set your intention to travel into the underworld to seek the overworld. Find the opening below and enter, climbing down the staircase, which winds clockwise. Find yourself in the cavernous place. Imagine how this large, subterranean area opens up into a vast darkness all around. As you gaze into that darkness you begin to perceive the stars emerging. Move into that space and find yourself floating among the stars.

Take some time to explore the stars. You may wish to call to one of the spirits or gods with whom you work. Calling upon Star Finder would be especially potent, as his power is already aligned to mapping the tides of stellar power and navigating those currents.

When you are ready to return, simply remember your alignment and, through your daemon, call out for the cavern. Imagine the stone floor and the sound of water dripping in the echoing chamber. Smell the cool, damp air, and then find the staircase leading back—up and counterclockwise—and follow it all the way back up, to emerge at the crossroads and the tree. Reaffirm the presence of the roads and the tree, and reaffirm the alignment of your Three Souls. End as normal.

---

## The Celestial Sphere

Much of the work that we will do with the powers of the overworld will involve us calling them down to us. We first have experienced this in the act of calling the Watchers, who come into our realm from beyond the stars. We also can work with certain stars and constellations. The signs of the zodiac, for those so inclined to follow their stellar processions, can be very potent when consciously tapped into. Many indigenous cultures celebrated the observances of certain astrological phenomena, such as the rising of the Pleiades, or the appearance of Orion. These marked certain cosmic tides of power that would manifest on earth. When rituals were enacted that coincided with these observances, they were thought to resonate with that astrological and astronomical power. Thus our rites become infused with their power, giving our workings a boost. A good Witch will find power wherever they can. And there is so much for the taking, right over our heads.

Star Finder is particularly aligned to this type of work, as one might well imagine given his title. Invoke his presence as an intermediary between yourself and the stellar angelic consciousness that you wish to connect with.

## Drawing Down the Moon

This is a Traditional Witchcraft rite that involves tapping into the mystical power of the lunar sphere. The moon represents the unconscious, hidden knowledge, and usually (though not always) the power of the Goddess.

There are many layers to this practice and manifestations of it can appear anywhere from psychologically identifying with the archetype of the moon and its associated symbolism, to (in its advanced form) full-blown possession by the Goddess in her many guises, usually during a ritual or working.

What follows are two different exercises based on those taught in the Bloodrose line that are designed to allow the practitioner to begin working with this energetic practice.

## Drawing Down the Moon Exercise

Items needed:
Your black Star Goddess candle
Matches

Open the Way. Close your eyes and imagine the details of your immediate environment. See how the entire space is now enveloped in the soft silver light of the full moon shining bright above you. Engage all of your senses to make this feel more real. Breathe in this light for the span of at least three breaths.

Focus your awareness on the moon and see it surrounded by a multitude of stars. Imagine that nine stars that are brighter than all the others begin to appear and form a ring around the moon.

While taking thirteen breaths, visualize a river of white light rising up out of your belly and into the heavens above. Imagine this light connecting with the moon.

In the span of nine breaths, draw the moon and the ring of stars down the river of light, until you are finally enveloped in an immeasurable sphere of lunar light. With each breath, the moon and stars begin to shrink down to about the size of your fist and are absorbed into your body in your chest.

See the moon shining in your heart, the ring of stars slowly revolving clockwise around it. Feel this power shining brightly from your chest, completely filling your body and spilling out into your aura. Feel how this light illuminates the entire universe. Maintain this sensation for the span of at least nine breaths.

Allow the images and sensations to slowly fade while you focus on your breathing. Return to normal awareness.

## Drawing Down the Moon Ritual

Items needed:
Your black Star Goddess candle
Matches
Silver or white altar cloth
Large white (or silver) candle
Silver or earthenware bowl, filled with water

Incense
Symbols of the moon (optional)

This rite is best performed outdoors at night underneath the full moon. If this is not possible, then you will be called to use your imagination.

Prepare your altar. Light the candle and the incense. Open the Way.

Imagine yourself floating in darkness on the waves of your breath. Allow yourself to float for the span of at least nine breaths.

Imagine that your eyes slowly adjust to the darkness and you see that you are standing in a forest clearing on a clear night, seeing the sky filled with a multitude of stars, and in the very center shines the glory that is the full silvery moon. Maintain this visualization for at least three breaths.

Reach out and take the bowl of water in both hands, holding it close to your face. Softly gaze at the water so that you can see the full moon reflected on its surface. (Or catch the light of the candle and imagine that this light is actually that of the full moon.)

Repeat the following incantation nine times:

> *Holy lantern of the night*
> *Descend to me on silver light*
> *Mouth of poesy, art, and song*
> *Within me shine now clear and strong.*

While chanting this spell, feel how the light of the moon begins to become intensified and focused, becoming like a laser that shines into the bowl of water and is then reflected into your eyes through which you drink in this silver presence, so that you become completely full of lunar light and power.

Feeling yourself and the water completely charged with the presence of the moon, drink the water, feeling yourself even more saturated with this power. Feel how this light actually transforms your body into that of the Goddess of the Moon. Maintain this visualization for the span of at least nine breaths.

When you are ready to end the rite, imagine yourself shifting back into your own form, sitting in your room or working area. Allow the image of the forest and the sky to fade. Visualize the working area in as much detail as you can muster.

Open your eyes to softly gaze at the candle. Extinguish it with a silent prayer. End as normal. Record your experiences.

---

## The Star Goddess

The Star Goddess is the primary deity in the Faery Tradition of Witchcraft. She is the whole, undifferentiated universe, both manifest and non. She is the vast infinite darkness, who divided herself and brought forth the first light from the primal dark. She is the great and cosmic womb of the universe, the stirring motion of primal chaos, which is all potential. She is the Void, and that which emerges from the Void. She is all and she is nothingness, circumference and center.

All other gods and goddesses come from and are a part of her. She has many names: Sugma'ad, Quakoralina, Dryghtyn, and others. She is also often referred to in veiled terms such as Mother Night, the Black Virgin of the Outer Dark, and perhaps most common of all: God Herself. She is the sevenfold *Infinitum;* the specific grouping of gods and goddesses with whom we have been working. All the other members of this deity collective are seen as her direct reflections.

According to Victor Anderson, she is more than simply a ruler "in charge" of the others: "[T]o think of the Star Goddess as just the chief head of the Feri Pantheon is not right … God was first worshipped as the Mother and the dual Father/Son in one. Just like you have the proton in the center of the hydrogen atom and the electron going around it. It's just as simple as that."[71]

She is most often referred to in the feminine because of her ability to give birth, but she is pre-gender, containing both male and female, yin and yang, light and dark with her. She is the "clitoro-phallic presence of God Herself." It is for this reason that I have taken to sometimes placing a "/" between the two "d's" in "Goddess," thus "the Star God/dess" includes an awareness of gender-inclusivity.

She may appear as a beautiful woman with the head of a lioness, jet-black skin, and the enormous wings of a bat. In her hair are a billion stars. She sits upon a great throne of polished onyx with the silver egg of creation on her lap, and shines with a crown of black fire. Her emblem is the oroborus: a serpent with its tail in its mouth.

When Faery Grandmaster Victor Anderson was five years old, he reportedly had a vision of Holy Mother Isis, clothed in the symbols of the American flag.

---

71. Victor Anderson, *Witch Eye* #3 (August 2000).

According to Cora Anderson, this Goddess has a "gold-tinted complexion, emerald green eyes and long blue-black hair. She wears a robe of black, bespangled with stars in all of the natural colors. There is a ribbon of light falling between her breasts to her bare feet. At the top of this ribbon is an inverted blue triangle with a five-pointed, white star in the middle. The ribbon has the same number of red and white stripes as the American flag."[72]

As we have experienced in the Waters of Purity rite, the Star Goddess shines with white starfire and into each of us by way of our holy daemon; which is our beloved Blue God, her son (as the Dian y Glas) and her consort (as Melek Ta'us). As all things were birthed from her so do we all identify as her children, and by poetic extension, with her divine child, the androgynous Dian y Glas. All Faery initiates are spiritually and ritually wed to her and so we further identify as the consort to the Goddess.

### Invoking the Star Goddess Exercise

Items needed:

Your black Star Goddess candle

Matches

Light a black candle and call out to her:

> *Holy Mother,*
> *Womb of the Universe,*
> *Creator of destiny,*
> *Eater of time,*
> *All exists within your body,*
> *Your power flows within my veins.*[73]

Take time to quietly feel her presence within you. With open heart, call out to her. Recognize the divinity within you and further recognize the divinity in everything else. Everything is connected to everything else; everything is a part of everything else. Through her presence we can make magic. What magic do you want to do?

---

72. Cora Anderson, *Witch Eye* #6 (March 2002).

73. Storm Faerywolf, "Prayer to the All Mother," *The Stars Within the Earth* (Walnut Creek, CA: Mystic Dream Press, 2003).

## Daily Divination Exercise

If you have not already begun a practice of pulling a card or a rune or some other divinatory method, then you should do so now. Divinatory tools are an excellent way to train our inherent psychic skills. By engaging with them regularly we are training our brains to speak in the symbolic language. This can only help talker in understanding fetch, which will help the focus of our spells and rites. Remember to journal your findings, as you never know what things might be inadvertently prophesized.

## Flower Prayer Exercise

There is a popular prayer attributed to Victor Anderson in the oral tradition:

> *Who is the Flower above me?*
> *And what is the work of this God?*
> *I would know myself in all my parts.*

This prayer is recited along with Soul Alignment to strengthen the connection and alignment with the holy daemon. Try reciting this every day both morning and night for two weeks and record your results in your journal.

## The Shadow Lover Ritual

The Shadow Lover is a core ritual practice within the Faery Tradition, taught in its original form by Victor to his students. It seeks to isolate, transform, and reclaim one's negative personal power (i.e., life force that has been twisted or turned against itself). The rite presented here is rooted in traditional elements while offering something more in the way of stylized ritual. While it is sexual at its core, it can be easily adapted for a non-sexually explicit observance as desired.

Items needed:
Your black Star Goddess candle
Matches
A mirror (larger is better, but needs only be large enough to see
    your face completely)
A black candle, dressed with mugwort, wormwood, and cypress

A white candle, dressed with rose, lavender, and angelica
A small towel
Your favorite personal lubricant (optional)

Open the Way and perform the Waters of Purity.

Stand naked in front of a mirror, turn out the lights, and connect with fetch. Light the black candle and notice whatever shadows are cast by it. Allow these shadows to conjure forth your own shadow, feeling it stir deep within fetch. Say:

> *Candle flame that casts a shadow;*
> *Open door and open window:*
> *Reveal the stain of soul's transgression*
> *And hold no more this dark possession.*

Recall something in your life that is causing you trouble. It can be anything at all … a bad habit, negative thought patterns, etc. Allow yourself to really feel every aspect of it, imagining this energy flowing into the shadows. Breathe life force into the shadows and will them to coalesce into a single form, which appears roughly humanoid in the mirror before you. See how it is a part of you; with roughly your features and yet slightly different: it appears darker, twisted, and filled with the negativity that you have held inside. Take as much time as you need in order to really feel its presence before you.

When you are ready, focus on the light of your daemon and light the white candle from the black saying:

> *By the might of daemon's power*
> *Word of honor, reveal thy truth,*
> *From shadow form in darkness hour*
> *Bursts forth the light that does empower.*

See the shadow form begin to change: light bursting out from within its form as its features begin to change, becoming more attractive. The gender of the being may change (or not) depending on your sexual orientation, and it begins to take on those physical characteristics that you find sexually attractive. Allow this process to take as much time as it needs to. Allow yourself to become aroused by the changing image before you.

Begin to masturbate in front of the mirror, holding on to the presence of this now shining being. Imagine yourself making love to this shining being of the shadows... Feel its presence moving inside your body as you embrace, kiss, and engage in intercourse. Feel how with every thrust of your hips you are calling this power back inside of yourself. Bring yourself almost to the point of orgasm and then hold off... backing away slowly from the edge so as to maintain this presence. Focus on the power of the pleasure of your body and know that this is your sacred gift. Allow this power to wash over and through you and be open to any messages that you may receive from the shining shadow being.

When you are ready, allow yourself to have an orgasm (if that is what you desire), imagining this light shining with each and every one of your cells; feel this power resonate through every level and hear it like a great song that reverberates through your bones, your blood, your skin, and your aura. Affirm:

> *Shadow Lover,*
> *Shining Lover,*
> *We are beauty,*
> *We are love.*

Take some time to look with loving eyes at your own reflection, noticing any flaws or impurities but being aware that they in themselves are beautiful. Give yourself a hug and a big genuine smile, feeling how this feeds and nourishes fetch. Take it all in with three deep breaths of power. Towel off, if necessary.

Extinguish the black candle and allow the white to burn completely down. It is done.

## A Formal BlueRose Faery Circle Casting Ritual

This should be performed only once you feel you have *mastered* the simple circle exercise given in chapter 10 and are able to successfully invoke (and maintain) the presences of each of the Watchers.

As I was originally taught, we Faery really only cast a circle when working in groups, as a means to more easily unify the group mind. A solitary magical practice very rarely would require such an act. Unlike some other forms of Witchcraft, our magic is not confined to any circle. The Crossroads is better suited for a solitary practice, but there are certain skills to be learned from engaging in layers of ritual complexity. Experiment with this rite and see what comes of it for you.

Very rarely do even BlueRose initiates do everything as outlined here. We will draw from this script as we feel it is appropriate for the rite of the moment and may decide to move certain sections around, omit them entirely, perform abbreviated versions of them, or even do something entirely different on the fly. There are times—most notably Samhain, Beltane, Dedications, and Initiations—in which we will perform this script in its entirety, but even then only as a suggested guideline. In Faery Tradition, spontaneity trumps scripting.

Items needed:
Your black Star Goddess candle
Matches
Blue "Goddess" candle
Red "God" candle
Your blade
Your wand
A chalice
A cube
A bell

Prepare a formal altar with all of the tools as previously described.

Open the Way and perform the Blue Fire breathing along with the Waters of Purity rite. In the dark, light the Star God/dess candle and ring the bell nine times in three groups of three. The officiating priest casts the circle clockwise with the blade, feeling the Blue Flame forming a circle while speaking the following charm:

| *Incantation* | *Stage Directions* |
|---|---|
| *By forest dark and standing stone,* | (Facing north) |
| *By rushing wind and life's first breath,* | (East) |
| *By flame that burns the flesh to bone,* | (South) |
| *By ancient sea, and land of death…* | (West) |
| | |
| *By the Mother and Her Son* | (Return to face north.) |
| *Is the circle made and done* | (The circle is now a complete ring of Blue Fire. Turn to face the south.) |
| *Descend the light of Moon and Sun* | (Imagine drawing down heavenly sphere into the circle.) |
| *Our Holy Rite has now begun.* | (Feel the space charged with celestial and divine light.) |
| | |
| *Between the worlds of flesh and Fae,* | (Contemplate being in-between the worlds.) |
| *We touch the Source and form the weave,* | (Standing in the north, facing south: Trace a seven-pointed star with the blade.) |
| *A ward to keep the worlds at bay,* | |
| *That none may enter; none may leave.* | (Stab through the star in the south and visualize the ring/circle exploding into a sphere of Blue Flame.) |
| | |
| *This holy ground now lies between* | (Return blade to the altar.) |
| *The realm of gods and mortal men,* | |
| *By human eye cannot be seen* | (Imagine that the circle and participants are now becoming invisible from the outside.) |
| | |
| *The faery sight alive within.* | (Imagine your third eye opening and becoming clear.) |

| *Incantation (Cont.)* | *Stage Directions (Cont.)* |
|---|---|
| *As above and so below,* | (Gesture above and below with the wand.) |
| *Enveloped in a cobalt flame,* | |
| *The stars that shine, the stones that know,* | (Touch the cube, feeling it anchor the circle in place.) |
| *Within we speak her sacred name.* | (Priest returns wand to altar and rings the bell three times.) |

### Invoking the Watchers

The priest stands in the north facing south. S/he takes up the wand from the altar and opens her/his arms out above the head, the wand in the left hand saying:

> *Watchers from the edge of space*
> *We call you from beyond the brink of time*
> *To enter here our sacred twilight realm*
> *And guard our rites empyrean and wild.*

The priest then goes to the east, and all celebrants face that direction. If someone else is calling the Watchers, the wand is passed after each invocation.

All participants (led by the invoking priest with the wand) then perform the Salutation to the Watcher. After the Salutation at each quarter, the priest draws a pentacle visualized in the appropriate color. Then their invocations (as given previously or using another preferred method) are repeated by all present.

After the four quarters are invoked, the priest returns to the north facing south. The priest and all celebrants take a deep breath and cross their wrists as they raise their arms above their heads then open their arms out in a funnel position toward the sky, projecting their consciousness into the heavens. Everyone recites the invocation of Heaven Shiner.

With a deep breath, everyone then lowers their arms, crossing their wrists briefly before opening their arms to the below to hold their hands out over earth, projecting their consciousness deep into the planet reciting the invocation of Fire-in-the-Earth.

Everyone crosses their hands over the center of their chests, visualizing the threads of elemental power in the appropriate colors streaming from each of the six external directions converging in their individual heart centers, where emerges the Black Heart of Innocence, shining with a wild radiant light. All repeat:

> *Between six points that flow from one*
> *Calm, the eye of tempest's winds*
> *Within the center outward shines*
> *The light of three now so aligned*
> *Awake, alive, aware, divine…*
> *The coal-black heart I claim as mine!*

The priest makes a sign of prayer. Everyone says: *"By the Center, which is the Circumference of All."*

All bow toward the center of the circle, imagining it as synonymous with their own center. All say: *"So Must it Be!"*

The priest rings the bell once.

### Invoking the Primal Gods

The invoking priest takes a taper, match, or lighter and lights it from the black Star God/dess candle, and then traces an upright pentacle over the blue candle (which is positioned to the left of the Star God/dess candle). As the blue candle is lit, all chant or sing the following seven times (or until trance is achieved):

> *Ashtaroth, Ashtoreth, Belili, Belkoreth, Lilith-Aluré, Anatha, Tiamat!*[74]

The officiating priest may then say the following:

> *Mother of all the gods and mortals,*
> *Silver chalice, moon-lit sea.*
> *To you we pray*
> *We are your children.*

---

74. These names and their order come directly from Victor Anderson and are said to correspond to the following concepts: Fertility, Beauty, Power, Darkness, Above/Below, and the Ultimate.

*To you we pray*
*We are yourself.*
*Hail and be Welcome!*

The red candle is positioned to the right of the Star God/dess candle and is lit from the blue. An upside down pentacle is traced over the red "God" candle with the lit taper or match and the following is chanted or sung (at least) five times:

*Karaillos,*[75] *Keránnos, Kernunnos, Krana, Kronos!*

After the invocation all repeat:

*Son and Lover, earthly regent*
*Golden sword and sun-peaked tower,*
*To You we pray*
*We are Your children*
*To You we pray*
*We are yourself.*
*Hail and be Welcome!*

### Invoking the Divine Twins

I wrote this as a possible "queer alternative" to the above, which is sometimes seen as overly "hetero-centric" in flavor. This may be used in place of, or alongside the Invocation of the Primal Gods.

Focusing on the presence of an inverted electric blue pentacle shining in the stars in the overworld, the priest traces this pentacle over the blue candle. Feel this pentacle being projected from the stars in the overworld. All invoke:

*Shining bright, the Azure Dove*
*Born of water and of air*
*Above the stars your law is love*
*Descend from heaven, hear my prayer!*

---

75. Pronounced: Kair-EYE- se. The double "l" is like a "y" sound, as in Spanish. This collection of names also comes to us from Victor Anderson.

The priest then traces an upright pentacle that projects from the stars in the Underworld over the red candle. All invoke:

> *Serpent born of earth and fire*
> *Awaken now with deep desire*
> *Coiled deep below in lust*
> *Aroused; arise with throbbing thrust!*

### Invoking the Peacock Lord

All participants reach out with their awareness into the Azure Dove shining above, and the Scarlet Serpent shining below, while reaching one arm upward and the other downward. With three breaths and while slowly bringing one's arms toward the heart center, these divine presences are brought to the edges of the body (crown and feet) and then are brought together into the heart where—like two flames—they merge as one in iridescent, amethystine brilliance. All say:

> *Scarlet Serpent, Azure Dove*
> *Holy Lust and Sacred Love*
> *From below and from above*
> *Now shine into the heart!*

All then open their arms in a sweeping gesture, feeling this brilliant light shining outward from the heart center in the form of a peacock spreading his tail feathers, radiating and filling the ritual area. All say:

> *Melek Ta'us, the Peacock Lover*
> *Born of Beauty and of Pride*
> *Who shakes the heavens with light and thunder*
> *Guiding us from deep inside.*

At this point, any specific working may be added, followed by the ritual blessing of the wine and cakes as detailed previously.

### *To End the Ritual*

If specific deities have been invoked, they should be acknowledged and thanked first in reverse order of when they were invoked.

The primal gods should be thanked and released next, beginning with the red "God" candle. This can be done in whatever fashion feels appropriate at the time. I often simply recite their names in a quiet voice, trace an inverted pentacle over the flame, and blow it out. The same holds true for the blue "Goddess" candle, with an upright pentacle being traced over it. For each it is spoken, while feeling a sense of release:

*Hail and Farewell.*

The priest then stands in the north facing south and moving around the circle widdershins acknowledges the Watchers each by name. (Or, if other participants had invoked them those individuals should perform this.)

When this is done, all turn to the center and open up their arms to the sky and recite:

*Watchers from the edge of space and time*
*We thank you for your Power and your Presence*
*Stay if you will, go if you must.*
*But ere you depart, we bid you:*
*Hail and Farewell!*

All the participants join hands, visualizing the circle and sphere connecting and enveloping them. The priest stands holding the blade in both hands at heart level, tip pointing up. S/he stands at the north facing south, and recites the unsealing of the circle. All visualize the sphere being absorbed back into the band of Blue Fire that forms the circle as all recite:

*Peacock Lover, Starry Mother*
*Son of the Art, Heart of the Art.*
*All from air, into air*
*Now let the misty curtain part!*

On the last word, the blade is swept from the apex to waist level to part the veil, returning the sphere back to the circle of Blue Fire from which it was made.

The priest is facing the north with the blade pointing outward and slowly walks widdershins toward the west while reciting the following incantation. All visualize that s/he is gathering up the Blue Fire at the tip of the blade, which opens the circle.

*All is over, all is done.*
*What has been must now be gone.*
*What was wrought by Witches' Art,*
*Returns unto the coal-black heart!* [76]

With the last line, the priest has returned to the north. Then they move the blade to the zenith, the flame of Blue Fire at the tip of the blade becoming like a star.

When it reaches the zenith the priest thrusts the blade upward, causing the star to explode into several pieces, one for each of the participants. They each flow down through the participants' heads, descending into their hearts, to charge them with the power of the rite. Each participant then takes a deep breath and fully absorbs this power into their body/mind/aura.

The priest places the blade on the altar, extinguishes the candles in reverse order, leaving the Star Goddess candle for last. Priest again leads the Holy Mother prayer and then rings the bell three times. It is done.

---

76. This last line is inspired by the work and liturgical poetry of the BlackHeart line of Feri tradition.

# AFTERWORD

*All is over, all is done. What has been must now be gone.*
—FAERY ORAL TRADITION

Having read and (hopefully) practiced the rites and exercises given in this book, you will have gained some idea as to what the Faery Tradition is and what its tools can offer. This is but a taste, for the real transmission of Faery occurs in that intimate space between teacher and student. Even for those of my students with whom the training is being conducted over long distance, we share a deep, intimate connection, enjoying private time to discuss how we are working the practices into our lives and what effects they are having on us. I am there when they have questions and can offer suggestions as how to better fine tune the work to better suit their individual personalities and talents. A book cannot give you the same level of guidance, but it *can* offer you a general map that you may use to navigate the terrain on your own. If you are honest with yourself, take common sense precautions, and are not using Witchcraft as a substitute for therapy, then you can certainly gain much from experimenting using the techniques given here. In this we become explorers of the realms of spirit, just as our Witch ancestors before us.

After reading this material one might be tempted to think that they know what Faery is. Faery, however, is not to be found in the study of the exercises, rituals, or even the lore, but in the *results of engaging them*. The only way to come to know Faery is to practice it, to live it. One must approach Faery not as a body of mental knowledge to be dissected and examined, but as an art, to be taken in and appreciated. It must be looked at from many angles and contemplated with much thought. It must be practiced—like any art—

for one's skill in it to be carefully honed. Faery is the obsession that keeps us up at all hours perseverating over some small detail. It is the joyous passion that keeps us striving to go just a little further. It is a fevered dream that brings us visions in the middle of the night. It is the orgasmic bliss we find in the embrace of a lover. Faery is a lens through which we approach the whole of our lives, for it gives us access to that much *more* of it. It opens doors, within ourselves, and in between the worlds.

If you are called to Faery, as I was, then you can use this book to assist you along the path until you find a teacher with whom you have rapport. But remember this is only one possible manifestation of this diverse and creative tradition. Each branch of our wild tree reaches out in a different direction. But each of them also draws their lineages ultimately from the founders, Victor and Cora Anderson, and beyond them both into the misty realms of poetic antiquity.

It is often pointed out that Victor taught a lot of different things to different people. But a close look will show that these differences were merely that which was expressed in the languages of whichever particular culture from which he chose to draw examples in that moment. His fundamental system and message remained singular: one of the universalism of an underlying system of magic, centered around an ecstatic connection to God Herself ("the Mother of God"), as well as all the other "beautiful spirits that are all around us and within us."

Faery, as a realm and as a tradition, is a pretty big place. The lore we possess is that which our ancestral astral explorers have uncovered and brought back to share with their covens and students. Some covens and lineages may favor certain types of gods, spirits, cultural trappings, and workings, while others might be exploring an entirely different aesthetic.

What I have presented here will be instantly recognizable to initiates within the tradition, and yet also, perhaps, unfamiliar. The Faery passed to me was a collection of a vast amount of material from various cultures and other traditions, a "patchwork quilt" of magical rites, spells, stories, and lore. Yet it became cohesive under the guidance of a unifying and flexible practice. Each initiate takes what they have been taught *and then applies it*, which means that they will actually use the tools that they were given in order to create something new.

Faery, like any true form of Traditional Witchcraft, ultimately eschews dogmatic forms of ritual working in favor of spontaneous creativity. Witchcraft is that which runs against the grain socially, politically, and magically. Drawing largely from the Irish idea of poetic inspiration and implementation equating to magical power, our tradition encourages direct contact with the divine, as well as the creative expression of it. What forms we do share are largely the inventions of initiate teachers whose material has gained a certain popularity in their respective circles. We honor them by using them in our rituals and in passing them in the oral tradition, but also by rewriting them, adding our own creative contributions to the mix. In doing so we embody the very essence of Faery: we tap into the creative pulse of the universe, and just as we seek to align with that pulse in every ritual, so do we connect in every poem we write, in every canvas we paint, in every song that we sing. When we find our art (and each of us has even just a little bit in us, somewhere) we will have found that Faery lives in our heart.

If you are called to Faery, then here are the tools to help you a little bit further on the path. This will not be a path for everyone. Very few, it seems, are capable of traversing the other worlds with their sanity intact. But if it is truly your calling that fear won't stop you from reaching out to grasp that impossible blue rose of mystery, poetry, and magic...

*Behold the Blue Rose above me*
*A god that is a Mystery*
*I will know myself with every breath.*

And, as always, it ends as it all began...

*Holy Mother,*
*In you we live, move, and have our being.*
*From you all things emerge.*
*And unto you all things return.*

IO EVOHE! Blessed be.

# APPENDIX

## Principles of BlueRose Faery Tradition

I. We venerate the Star Goddess, God Herself; the pre-gendered force of creation and destruction, whom we see as an active force in our lives, accessible through devotion, ritual, and prayer.

II. We identify with Her Son, Lover, and other half, the Blue God; the post-gendered force of expression, ecstasy, and free will, whom we see as the gateway by which we can better come to know the divine.

III. We recognize the tripartite nature of divinity and its reflection in the three parts of the human soul, which we strive to align and keep in good health.

IV. We recognize the divine nature in all things and petition this divinity to cause change in the world in accordance with our own will through acts of magic.

V. We honor and seek guidance from the ancestors, continuing their great work of bettering the Craft, keeping alive the lineage of the Mighty Dead.

VI. Our priesthood inherits the Old Craft by way of the *Faery Power*, a current of magical energy ritually passed through a direct and unbroken initiatory lineage tracing back through the late Victor H. Anderson and —either through history or poetry— into antiquity.

VII. In keeping with tradition, we use this Power in service to those who seek our aid, as well as to better the lives of our families, our friends, our communities, the land, and ourselves.

VIII. Because our priesthood is a Mystery tradition we do not speak of certain rites or lore as determined by the individual lineages into which we were initiated or under which we study. But neither do we stifle the voices of others who may not be bound to the same degree. Secrecy in our Craft is a personal devotion.

IX. We assert that the authenticity of our tradition is not in the forms of its rituals, but in the power and divine connection of those who may perform them.

X. We strive toward the Black Heart of Innocence, which is our sovereign, natural state of sexual purity free of shame or sin, and hold inviolate the sovereignty of others. We hold ourselves to a high standard of sexual ethics as taught by Victor and Cora Anderson, and respect sex between consenting adults as sacred.

XI. We recognize the divine self-authority of every human being and hold none above another, regardless of race, gender, sexual orientation, nationality, creed, status, titles, religion, lineage, or ability.

XII. We do not coddle weakness, nor do we condemn it in others. We strive to assist those in need, but not to our own undoing. We never submit our life-force to anyone or anything.

XIII. We hold that all deities, guardians, spirits, faeries, angels, and djinn are our equals, and we honor and work with any and all who will work with us as allies toward our mutual betterment.

# BIBLIOGRAPHY

Adler, Margot. *Drawing Down the Moon: Witches, Druids, Goddess-Worshippers, and Other Pagans in America.* New York: Penguin, 1979, 1986.

Anaar (April Niino). *The White Wand: Ruminations, Meditations, Reflections Toward a Feri Aesthetic.* Self-published, 2004.

Anderson, Cora. *Fifty Years in the Feri Tradition.* Self-published, 1995.

———. *In Mari's Bower: A Biography of Victor H. Anderson.* Portland, OR: Harpy Books, 2012.

Anderson, Victor, and Cora Anderson. *Heart of the Initiate: Feri Lessons.* Portland, OR: Harpy Books, 2010.

Anderson, Victor H. *Etheric Anatomy: The Three Selves and Astral Travel.* Albany, NY: Acorn Guild Press, 2004.

———. *Lilith's Garden: the Further Poetry of Victor H. Anderson.* Self published, 2004.

———. "Speak of the Devil." *Witch Eye #3* (2002).

———. *Thorns of the Blood Rose.* Self-published, 1970.

Coyle, T. Thorn. *Evolutionary Witchcraft.* New York: Tarcher/Penguin, 2004.

Evans-Wentz, W. Y. *The Fairy-Faith in Celtic Countries.* New York: Dover Publications, 2002.

Faerywolf, Storm. *The Stars Within the Earth.* Self published, 2003.

Foxwood, Orion. *The Faery Teachings.* Boulder, CO: R. J. Stewart Books, 2007.

———. *The Tree of Enchantment: Ancient Wisdom and Magic Practices of the Faery Tradition*. San Francisco: Weiser Books, 2008.

Hopman, Ellen Evert, and Lawrence Bond. *People of the Earth: The New Pagans Speak Out*. Rochester, NY: Destiny Books, 1996.

Huson, Paul. *Mastering Witchcraft*. New York: Perigee Books, 1970.

Leland, Charles G. *Aradia, or the Gospel of the Witches*. Translated by Mario Pazzaglini, PhD & Dina Pazzaglini. Blaine, WA: Phoenix Publishing, 1998.

Starhawk, *The Spiral Dance*. New York: Harper Books, 1979.

Stewart, R. J. *Earth Light*. Rockport: Element, 1992.

Veedub (Valerie Walker). *The Dustbunnies' Big Damn Handout Book, Vol. 1*. Self-published, 2007.

Worth, Valerie. *Crone's Book of Charms & Spells*. St. Paul, MN: Llewellyn Worldwide, 1988.

———. *The Crone's Book of Words*. St. Paul, MN: Llewellyn Worldwide, 1971.

# RESOURCES

### *Faery/Feri Witchcraft Tradition*

BlueRose Faery: www.BlueRoseFaery.org

The Temple of Faery: www.FaeryTemple.org

Feri American Traditional Witchcraft: www.FaeryTrad.org and www.FeriTrad.org

The White Wand Lore: www.whitewand.com/lore.html

Feri Tradition by Valerie Walker: www.wiggage.com/witch/fericontents.html

### *General Witchcraft*

American Folkloric Witchcraft: www.afwcraft.blogspot.com

Black Rose: www.BlackRoseWitchcraft.com

Temple of Witchcraft: www.TempleOfWitchcraft.org

The Witches Voice: www.witchvox.com

### *Folkloric Faery Traditions*

Orion Foxwood: www.orionfoxwood.com

R. J. Stewart: www.rjstewart.net

### *Podcasts*

BlackHeart Radio: www.blogtalkradio.com/the-black-heart

Elemental Castings: www.thorncoyle.com/videos-podcasts/podcasts/

Modern Witch Podcast: http://modernwitch.podbean.com/

This Week in Heresy: www.thisweekinheresy.com

### Time Management Helpers

Google Calendar: https://calendar.google.com/

Habitica Smartphone App: https://habitica.com/

### Social Action

Solar Cross Temple: www.solarcrosstemple.org

Yazda: A Global Yazidi Organization: www.yazda.org

# INDEX

## To Write to the Author

If you wish to contact the author or would like more information about this book, please write to the author in care of Llewellyn Worldwide Ltd. and we will forward your request. Both the author and publisher appreciate hearing from you and learning of your enjoyment of this book and how it has helped you. Llewellyn Worldwide Ltd. cannot guarantee that every letter written to the author can be answered, but all will be forwarded. Please write to:

Storm Faerywolf
℅ Llewellyn Worldwide
2143 Wooddale Drive
Woodbury, MN 55125-2989
Please enclose a self-addressed stamped envelope for reply,
or $1.00 to cover costs. If outside the U.S.A., enclose
an international postal reply coupon.

Many of Llewellyn's authors have websites with additional information and resources. For more information, please visit our website at http://www.llewellyn.com

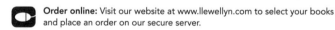

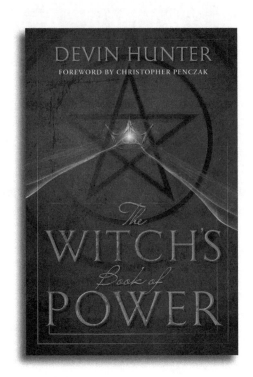

# The Witch's Book of Power
## Devin Hunter

Witchcraft isn't always about the search for enlightenment; sometimes it's about power and the path to obtaining it. *The Witch's Book of Power* shares the secrets to unlocking the Witch Power within you, offering specific techniques for working with personal, cosmic, and ally energies to realize your full magical potential.

Professional witch and psychic Devin Hunter has helped thousands of people discover their power and gain influence, and in this book he skillfully explores the concepts behind creating magic that can change your life. *The Witch's Book of Power* is the perfect resource for witches who intuitively feel that more power is available but seems to be just beyond reach.

978-0-7387-4819-1, 360 pp., 6 x 9            $19.99

---

GEDE PARMA

ecstatic
witchcraft

magick, philosophy & trance
in the shamanic craft

## Ecstatic Witchcraft
### *Magick, Philosophy & Trance in the Shamanic Craft*
### Gede Parma

Many modern Witches yearn for a deeper, more primal, and more authentic form of witchcraft. This timely book by award-winning author Gede Parma invites Witches, Wiccans, Pagans, and other seekers down a shamanic path that embraces the ecstatic, the wild, the gnostic, the transformative, and the visionary.

This unique guide presents a shamanic craft apprenticeship that readers can incorporate into their own spiritual journey. It includes techniques and rituals for fundamental shamanic practices, including drawing down the gods, working with spirit allies, moving between the worlds, ecstatic spellcraft, healing, and divination. It is designed to deepen and enhance the path already being followed by the reader.

**978-0-7387-3299-2, 264 pp., 6 x 9** **$17.95**

"I love Jane Meredith's focus on local magic . . . [She's] a true originator of approaches to magic and spirit that can inspire us in these times."—STARHAWK

# CIRCLE
## of EIGHT

*Creating Magic for Your Place on Earth*

Jane Meredith

# Circle of Eight
## *Creating Magic for Your Place on Earth*
### Jane Meredith

*Circle of Eight* is an exciting new approach to magic that is based on your geography, your climate, and your experiences. *Circle of Eight* can be used to celebrate the Festivals of the Wheel of the Year; to create an on-going ritual group; and to explore and develop magical relationship with the land around you. Providing instructions on how to set up your own Circle of Eight and stories illustrating important magical principles, the *Circle of Eight* radically re-invents our relationship to traditional circle magic. Suitable for beginners seeking ritual and magic that are relevant to them as well as advanced practitioners, this book helps you step deeply into the powerful magic of the directions and the great Wheel of the Year.

**978-0-7387-4215-1, 312 pp., 6 x 9**                    **$17.99**

---

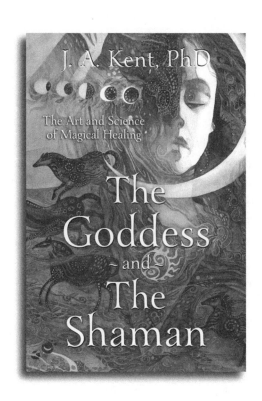

J. A. Kent, PhD

The Art and Science
of Magical Healing

# The
# Goddess
~and~
# The
# Shaman

# The Goddess and the Shaman
### *The Art & Science of Magical Healing*
### J. A. KENT, PHD

Explore the resurgence of magical and shamanic healing in the world today. Recovering from disease, pain, and mental illness often means addressing otherworldly causes such as soul loss, soul fragmentation, or invasive spirits. Interviewing modern shamanic practitioners and sharing her own experiences as a psychotherapist and healer, author J. A. Kent, PhD, shows how ritual practice and mystical experience can be used as tools to foster profound spiritual and psychological growth.

Through exploration of otherworldly phenomena, the Western mystery traditions, and the author's psychotherapy case studies, this book shows how the Goddess represents the numinous reality of the universe while the Shaman represents the archetypal figure that can access the other side to bring forth knowledge and healing.

978-0-7387-4042-3, 384 pp., 6 x 9                                   $19.99